The Sandinista Revolution

The MR/CENSA Series on the Americas is dedicated to publishing new work on the critical issues affecting the nations of the Americas, whose destinies are becoming increasingly interlinked in the late twentieth century.

The

SANDINISTA REVOLUTION

National Liberation and Social Transformation in Central America

Carlos M. Vilas

translated by Judy Butler

Monthly Review Press
Center for the Studies of the Americas

Copyright © 1986 by Carlos M. Vilas
All rights reserved

Originally published as *Perfiles de la revolución Sandinista: Liberación
nacional y transformaciones sociales en Centroamérica* by Editorial Legasa
S.R.L., Madrid / Buenos Aires / Mexico.
© Editorial Legasa S.R.L.

Library of Congress Cataloging-in-Publication Data
Vilas, Carlos María.
  The Sandinista Revolution.
  Translation of: Perfiles de la revolución Sandinista.
  Bibliography: p.
  Includes index.
  1. Nicaragua—Economic conditions—1979–
2. Nicaragua—Economic policy. 3. Education and
state—Nicaragua. I. Title.
HC146.V5513 1986   330.97285'053   86-28560
ISBN 0-85345-679-8
ISBN 0-85345-680-1 (pbk.)

Monthly Review Press
155 West 23rd Street, New York, N.Y. 10011

Center for the Study of the Americas
2288 Fulton Street, #103, Berkeley, CA 94704

Manufactured in the United States of America

10 9 8 7 6 5 4 3 2 1

Contents

Preface to the English Edition

The original manuscript of this book was completed in November 1983, a few weeks after the invasion of Grenada by the United States. This action showed once more that the most brutal and violent forms of imperialism are not something that belong to the past, but constitute a real threat for peoples who try to construct more just and fraternal forms of living. The evidence was particularly clear for Nicaragua, whose revolutionary process is being submitted to various forms of economic, propagandistic, political, and military aggression by the government of the United States.

During the year that has passed since then the signs of danger for the Sandinista Popular Revolution have increased. This, despite the reiterated proofs given by the revolutionary government of its will to develop a frank dialogue with the U.S. government, and the support it has accorded the initiatives of the Contadora Group. The elimination of the Sandinista regime seems to have been converted into a matter of principle for the Reagan administration, independently of the real threat, direct or indirect, that such a poor, backward and strife-ridden country as Nicaragua could represent for the United States.

The most relevant event following the completion of the manuscript is the calling of elections for president and vice-president, as well as representatives to a new National Assembly. In a country without previous experience in free elections, in the middle of a war of aggression openly supported by the government of the United States, the people of Nicaragua ratified the legitimacy of the revolutionary process on November 4, 1984. The opposition political parties, for their part, were able to propose their alternatives and express their dissent, in the framework of a process which, against all the adverse international publicity and the skeptical predictions of some observers, proved to be effectively pluralist.

Seventy-five percent of the registered voters participated in the voting (almost 1.1 million adults). This percentage is relatively high by any standard, but especially so when it is compared with the high margins of abstentionism in the electoral processes of neighboring countries, which are nevertheless viewed as exemplary: 34 percent abstention in the last presidential elections in Honduras (December 1981); 30 percent in those of Costa Rica (February 1982); 50 percent in those of El Salvador (1984). The FSLN obtained 62.9 percent of the vote for president and vice-president, and 63.5 percent for members of the National Assembly. The elections in Nicaragua did not show the overt military aggression that characterized the elections in El Salvador. Neither were there denunciations about irregularities during the actual voting, or with respect to the count.

The unfolding of the electoral campaign introduced a new dynamic into the political struggle in Nicaragua. The articulation of the principles of participatory democracy with those of representative democracy suggests a novel approach and defines important challenges and questions about the future configuration of the institutional process of the revolution, the type of relations that will be developed between the state and the popular organizations, and between the state and the Frente Sandinista. However, to incorporate a consideration of these elements into the original text would have implied an excessive delay in the appearance of this edition.

Regarding the economic situation, the respective information has been updated, in that figures for 1983 and, in some cases, the first semester of 1984 have been included in tables.

Finally, the author would like to express his gratitude to Judy Butler for her labor—and her patience—as translator.

Managua, December 1984.

Prologue

This study of the Sandinista Popular Revolution centers on questions fundamental to understanding any revolution: its political project, its social bases, the transformation that it generates, the strategy that orients it, and the enemies that confront it.

To write about a revolution so recently initiated runs the risk of treating as definitive what is yet being born and struggling to define itself. Another risk is that of confusing conjunctural, or secondary measures and decisions with basic tendencies, and thus losing sight of the historical project in the jumble of choices and experiments. At the same time few themes are so attractive or instructive as the initial stages of a revolution, when everything is imagination and creativity, and when the very identity of the revolution is striving to forge a new path through limitations and obstacles of every description.

This study addresses both the advances of the revolution and the difficulties that it encounters, since I believe that the lessons that a revolution offers reside in both. There are some who tend to present the processes of a triumphant revolution as an uninterrupted succession of glorious acts and connected victories; no one ever has doubts, everyone succeeds on the first try, no one is ever wrong. The result, in my opinion, has been to distance revolutionary processes from people, hiding their true evolution from public view. By contrast, I believe that no revolution offers a guarantee of infallibility, and that decisions are always the product of discussions, confrontations between different perspectives, and reflections about a reality that is frequently different from what it was thought to be, which thus fails to perform as expected.

9

This means simply that nothing is mechanical or automatic in a revolution; that the transformation of society is a difficult and complex process; that revolutions demand work, imply sacrifices and renunciation—above all for the forces that support them—and that the revolutionary triumph itself is not the final difficulty; the difficulties of the struggle for power are replaced by those of social transformation.

Each social revolution, of course, is only like itself. This specificity derives from the particular characteristics of the country's own socioeconomic structure and the way in which it is inserted into the transnational capitalist system, as well as the concrete nature of the political forces that confront one another and the dominant correlation of forces in the international system. What each revolution definitely allows us to identify and understand is its own history: the unique elements that interact in a special way in a certain matrix of contradictions impelled by the action of a political vanguard. By the same token, these specificities express the way that more general objective forces and tendencies reveal themselves in each revolutionary process. These general questions are what make possible the characterization of a revolution, the identification of its stages, and an intelligible sense of its development. To remain at the first level would be to offer a descriptive chronicle; to limit oneself to the second would imply losing sight of the specific nature and original problems of each revolution.

For this reason this study begins with a generic discussion about revolutions of national liberation, incorporating elements and experiences from various third-world formations. The goal is to demonstrate that the Sandinista Popular Revolution is neither an exception nor a deviant case, but rather takes its legitimate place in the struggle of poor, oppressed, and subjugated peoples to achieve national sovereignty, social emancipation, and more just and fraternal ways of living. What has been unique to the Sandinista revolution is the way in which this universal struggle has been triggered and organized by the Sandinista National Liberation Front over two decades of revolutionary struggle, in a society whose capitalist development was somewhat different from that of the rest of the region.

Following this scheme, Chapter 2 presents the principal features of the type of capitalism developed in Nicaragua in the last thirty years, influenced by the new forms of imperialist expansion: the economic structure, the concrete configuration of social classes, the type of foreign investment, the role played by the Somocista regime—at the same time a product and a guarantor of this system. Chapter 3 investigates the elements of the urban socioeconomic structure that formed the basis for the massive incorporation of the population—starting with its popular classes—into the insurrectional strategy that marked the culmination of the Sandinista struggle. Given that no revolution occurs in a vacuum, nor can fail to come to terms with the existing socioeconomic structure, the analysis offered in these two chapters permits a better understanding of the orientation adopted by the revolution after the July 19 triumph, the way in which it has faced many problems, the alliances and confrontations in which it has chosen to engage.

Chapter 4 studies the strategy of national unity and mixed economy that characterizes the current stage of the revolution, in particular the space permitted for the non-Somocista groups of the bourgeoisie, and for the articulation of small and medium production with the new social sector of the economy. Chapter 5 analyzes this strategy of national unity and a mixed economy as it relates to the working class, detailing the workers' movement, the debates that have arisen in this regard, and the experiences of worker participation that evolved in the first four years. Chapter 6 presents the principal transformations in the area of education—an aspect of Nicaraguan popular democracy that has as yet been little studied. This permits us to examine the progressive displacement of social contradictions into the realm of ideology. Finally, Chapter 7 again takes up the questions outlined in general terms at the beginning of the book, based on the results of the study itself and the elements that make up the current period.

This volume is the result of research carried out in Nicaragua during the first four years after the triumph of the Sandinista Revolution. Many people helped, facilitating my research, commenting on parts of the study, challenging perspectives, discussing hypotheses. I would like particularly to mention Virgilio Godoy, Miguel de Castilla, Orlando Núñez, Eduardo Baumeister, Eugenio Espinosa, Liz Maier, John Weeks, Martin Carnoy, Norma Cabrera, Andreas Scheurmeier, and Bernard Albrecht. Naturally, only I am responsible for the final content.

Managua, November 1983

1

National Liberation and Social Revolution

Revolutions in dependent capitalist societies raise four basic and interrelated questions: (1) the question of class, tied to the end of mass exploitation under the guidance of a particular class or class fraction; (2) the question of national sovereignty, referring to the liquidation of imperialist domination and the redefinition of the way in which the nation is economically and politically tied into the world system; (3) the question of development, through the expansion of the productive forces and the rationalization of the productive structure; and (4) the question of democracy, or the dismantling of the state that has guaranteed class exploitation, economic backwardness, and imperialist domination, and the building of a new kind of political power. The character of a revolution derives from the manner in which these interrelated questions are faced and resolved.

This chapter addresses some of the most relevant aspects of each of these issues within the context of Latin America (although some examples from other parts of the third world have been included where useful).

THE QUESTION OF CLASS AND THE POPULAR SUBJECT

Social and political struggles as well as class structure in Latin America reflect the mode of capitalist development—the effect of Latin America's process of insertion into the imperialist-dominated world system and the resulting international division of labor. The way in which capitalism subordinated other modes of production in the periphery determined the nature of classes, fractions, and groups in each. Between the so-called traditional peasant, integrated into a simple mercantile economy, and the agricultural or industrial proletariat "liberated" from direct appropriation of a source of consumption and from the means of production, a wide range of forms of production and circulation evolved—the result of different degrees of proletarianization coexisting with direct ties to the land, to instruments of labor, to a monetary surplus, and to a mode of reproduction. The subordination of the "previous" forms of production to capitalism does not necessarily signify the quantitative predominance of the latter (for example, in terms of the proportion of the product generated in each form of production, the labor force employed, or similar criteria).[1] The primacy of capitalism manifests itself through its capacity to determine the general conditions of production and the orientation of the productive system, and the subordination of these forms to the process of capital accumulation on a transnational scale. The development of dependent capitalism historically indicates that this process is compatible, at least during a certain period, with a capitalist presence more marked in the sphere of circulation than in that of production. This is not only an effect of the prolonged character of the transition to fully developed capitalism, but also expresses objective necessities of capitalism itself: superexploitation of the labor force fundamentally rests on the coexistence of capitalism with simple mercantile forms of production, in which capitalism is dominant (Oliveira 1972; Corten 1974).

As a result, the view of capitalism as industrialized production with a salaried workforce is not sufficient to characterize the peripheral formations in Latin America. The minimal proletarianization of the labor force no more calls into question the capitalist character of the society than capitalist domination necessarily implies a total or even extensive proletarianization of the labor force.

Furthermore, the presence of small holdings or the fact that producers still have direct ties to the means of production, and to the family as the source of reproduction, does not reflect the "survival" of "backward" forms of production which capitalism requires today but will have to do away with tomorrow. The way in which monopoly capital has developed in the region in the last three decades demonstrates that new forms of peasantry, small cottage production, and so on, have been *created* by capitalist expansion, and can hardly be branded as precapitalist or traditional (see Vilas 1981; von Werdhoff and Neuhoff 1982; Miró and Rodríguez 1982).[2]

This relative predominance of situations in which capital does not take direct control of the labor process, but subordinates the labor force by economic means outside the productive process—through commercialization, financing, supply of inputs, processing—indicates the widespread existence in many of these societies of what Marx called the *formal* subordination of labor to capital (1971: 54–58). In Marx's analysis this appeared as one form in the transition toward a fully developed capitalism, but in Latin America and other regions of the third world this subordination of the direct producer to capitalism is a product both of the concrete way in which the most modern forms of capitalism operate in these societies and of the power that commercial and financial capital acquire in them.

The proletariat in many dependent capitalist countries thus constitutes a small—sometimes tiny—fraction of the dominated classes. The working class is submerged in a mass of peasants, urban and rural poor, office workers, domestic workers, artisans, seasonal workers, people with no place under the sun, who often are not fully differentiated from the proletariat, and for whom production, circulation, and consumption are not always differentiated. In such societies therefore, the fundamental contradiction of capitalism—the bourgeoisie-proletariat contradiction—is expressed as the dominant classes-dominated classes contradiction.[3] In the same way that capitalist relations "illuminate" the whole society, so too the fundamental contradiction of capitalist relations of production overshadows the dominant classes-dominated classes contradiction. But this process is neither automatic, nor necessarily rapid. It develops through intense struggles, the formulation and reformulation of alliances and antagonisms in which the fundamental contradiction is not always obvious.

Nor is the process confined to the material sphere of the productive structure. Classes are constituted as collective subjects of social action in the political-ideological terrain, and this occurs through a process that includes not only the acquisition of awareness and the rejection of economic exploitation, but also the experience and repudiation of political oppression (Marx 1847: 173–74; Marx 1852: 99–100). The relations of production express themselves as class power, which is dynamically tied to political relations and practices. These relations therefore are not tacked on *from outside,* but are already present in the very relations of production themselves.

The dominated classes become conscious of their exploitation in the framework of the political domination that obscures it, and they do not separate the two dimensions of the struggle. As Miguel Mármol, Salvadoran revolutionary, commented:

> The important thing to highlight here is that the moment these organizations are founded, their members demonstrate that their awakened interest in unionizing and economic demands are accompanied by a political interest. Often we begin to timidly outline the future struggle of a union in pursuit of better salaries or better treatment and food, when the peasants say that it would be best to begin thinking how to defend the union given the persecutions and outrages of the judges, mayors and armed groups, and still better to plan how the organization could get the workers' and peasants' own authorities into public offices in the zone and, if possible, the Department, and, if it could be done, in the whole country (Dalton 1972:130–31).[4]

The contradiction between the dominant and dominated classes is expressed in political struggle as a state-nation/*pueblo*-nation contradiction. The state apparatus—whether functionally differentiated from the ruling class or submerged in different ways into it—constitutes the arena in which the dominated classes confront the dominant power—economic, political-military, cultural. If political power hides, legitimates, and defends economic exploitation, it is through confrontation with the former that the elimination of the latter is advanced.

Nonetheless the elevation of the "economic" struggle of classes to the level of *political* class struggle—what Marx called the move from class *in itself* to class *for itself*—does not arise automatically. It involves the development of a political organization of the working classes and other popular forces, the development of the class conflict into a struggle for the popular conquest of political power, and the taking over of these processes by the working classes. Because this complex process is specifically shaped within each society at a given time, it makes no sense to try to elaborate a general model. Just as there is no automatic conversion of the peasant or artisan into a proletarian except by a complex and contradictory process of proletarianization that could last for generations, so the awakening of consciousness regarding the common condition of oppression and exploitation by a dominant class power—the process by which subordinated groups and fractions are constituted within classes—is no less complex and contradictory.

This is a historical process, not in the trivial sense of temporality (any process is, from this viewpoint, historical), but in the sense that it is subject to the very activity of the popular classes themselves and to the way in which they perceive it. Thus structural factors are no more important than the perceptions, experiences, and organizations, the way in which the structure is lived in the consciousness of the people.

The small size of the working class and its marginal differentiation from the artisans and peasantry helps to explain how what is frequently called the *proletariat* in these first stages of capitalist development in many cases has more points of contact with the urban and rural poor than with the industrial or even agricultural workers—what have been called in previous epochs the lower classes. In these formations the characterization of the proletariat usually rests on features that are not properly proletarian from the perspective of the sphere of production, although they are from the general context of their condition as classes oppressed and exploited by the dominant classes—in the traditional and permanent sense of dispossessed classes.

The predominant role of artisans in the initial stages of labor struggles is well known (Spalding 1977). Here I will only highlight the way in which this heterogeneous social grouping can be considered proletarian—unified more through its political subordination and poverty than through its common relationship to the production process.

For example, in El Salvador, in the second decade of this century, according to Miguel Mármol:

> a group of carpenters, tailors, hand weavers, shoemakers and activists from the Tenants' League (which had developed parallel to the union movement) began to concur around communist positions. . . . With great difficulties principally due to the backwardness of the ideological level of the whole movement, we began to conceive a struggle to be led by the organized Salvadoran proletariat. From the point of view of its real influence among the masses, the Regional was successful from the beginning and rapidly joined to it unions of mechanics, drivers, textile workers, shoemakers, bakers, street vendors, carpenters, tailors, bricklayers, barbers, tinsmiths, *saloneros,* railroad workers and, what was most important, farmworker unions, which were formed by the proletarians . . . and the poorest of peasants, and what were called Unions of Mixed Trades, urban and suburban . . . that is to say, unions

as mixed by the diverse branches of production from which the members came as because into them came urban workers, artisans and agricultural proletarians without distinction (Dalton 1972: 134–35).

Later, Mármol, a leader of the Communist Party of El Salvador, noted the original leaders included two carpenters, three shoemakers, two bricklayers, two typographers, and two professors, a situation that did not prevent him from noting that "our Communist Party is the child of the Salvadoran working class . . . ; it came from the very guts of our working class" (Dalton 1972: 155, 157). Proletariat as used here means *working poor*, subordinated in a more formal than real way to capital.

This is not a peculiarity of Latin American capitalism, but rather a fundamental element of these first stages in the development of capitalism in general, and of the working class in particular. In the revolutionary climate of Germany in the 1840s, for example, the use of the word "proletariat" was still sufficiently vague and elastic to serve a wide variety of situations. According to Barrington Moore (1978: 134):

> proletarians could be dwellers in the countryside as well as in towns or cities. Almost certainly the bottom layer of the rural population was much larger than that in the towns. In the second place, proletarians were uprooted and lacked any recognized, or at least any fully recognized, place in the existing status system. Occasionally they were referred to as the Fourth Estate. That is perhaps one reason why an acute contemporary observer of Berlin included in his definition of the "pure proletariat" those who had given themselves over to scholarship, art, or education in an effort to realize some modest hopes. Others whom he included were day laborers, journeymen, marginal independent craftsmen, and small tradesmen. Marginality was another important trait. They were marginal in the sense of somehow appearing to be extruded from the traditional status order and also in the sense of being very poor. In another sense of the word, a narrow margin also separated them from very severe economic distress. But they were *not* marginal in the sense of playing no significant role in the economy. The upper classes depended on them to perform a whole variety of tasks essential to the workings of the economy. These tasks were at the same time poorly paid and required little or no skill. Finally, proletarians were obviously poor. They had little or no property—in most cases in the towns very likely none at all. They did have to live from poorly paid labor. In all likelihood their employment was highly irregular and depended on the ups and downs of a very unpredictable business cycle.

In the rest of Europe the situation was no different. According to Eric Hobsbawm, the expression "working class" appeared in England around 1810 and in France after 1830, referring to a labor movement which was "neither in composition nor in its ideology and programme a strictly 'proletarian' movement" in the sense of factory workers or even wage workers. Rather, he noted, it was a "common front of all forces and tendencies representing the (mainly urban) labouring poor."

The leadership of the new movement reflected a similar state of affairs. The most active, militant and politically conscious of the labouring poor were not the new factory proletarians but the skilled craftsmen, independent artisans, small-scale domestic workers and others who lived and worked substantially as they had done before the Industrial Revolution, but under far greater pressure. The earliest trade unions were almost invariably those of printers, hatters, tailors and the like. The nucleus of leadership of Chartism in a city like Leeds—and this was typical—consisted of a joiner turned handloom weaver, a couple of journeymen printers, a bookseller, a woolcomber. The men who adopted Mr Owen's co-operative doctrines were in their majority such 'artisans', 'mechanics' and handworkers. The earliest German working-class communists were travelling journeymen craftsmen—tailors, joiners, printers. The men who rose against the bourgeoisie in the Paris of 1848 were still the inhabitants of the old artisan Faubourg Saint-Antoine, and not yet (as in the Commune of 1871) those of proletarian Belleville (1962: 212–13).[5]

Finally, more than two-fifths of the outstanding members and founders of the International Workingmen's Association (the *First International*, created in 1864) were artisans and tradespeople, and only 20 percent were workers or nonartisan laborers (Table 1.1).

I have spent time on these references because they help put the question of the formation of the working class in Latin American capitalism into proper perspective: the specificity of the Latin American capitalist formations does not consist in the heterogeneity of what is called the *proletariat,* or in the small size of the working class as such, but rather in the central fact that this situation takes place *in the full stage of monopoly capitalist domination and of the transnationalization of the movement of capital.* The incipient workers' movement, thus constituted, comes face to face not with the capital of a new national bourgeoisie, flourishing and even democratic in its way, but with a power bloc dominated by imperialism, which in-

Table 1.1

Occupational Profile of Founders, Directors, and Outstanding Members of
the Workers' International Association (c. 1870)

Occupation	Number	Percentage
Craftspeople and tradespeople	55	43
(10 shoemakers, 7 tailors, 6 carpenters, 5 painters, 5 engravers, 5 mechanics, 3 watchmakers, 3 typographers, 3 bookbinders, 2 bakers, 1 furnituremaker, 1 maker of musical instruments, 1 hairdresser, 1 locksmith, 1 goldsmith, 1 plasterer)		
Journalists, writers, politicians	27	21
Workers and unionists	26	20
Professionals	14	11
(2 engineers, 2 historians, 2 teachers, 2 philosophers, 2 doctors, 2 jurists, 2 architects)	6	5
Others		
(2 former military men, 2 merchants, 1 judge, 1 artist)*		
Total	128	100
No information given	61	
Grand total	189	

Source: Based on biographical information contained in Padover (1973: 589–603).
*Does not include two infiltrators/spies in the membership of the AIT for the police forces of England and France.

cludes some elements of the local dominant classes, as well as with some form of authoritarian state.

Two common assumptions must therefore be rejected. The first is the tendency to imbue the proletariat of much of Latin America with the same attributes as those of Europe and other developed areas. As one Central American organization points out:

> In appearance, the repetition of postulates that emanate from this error have a classist, "worker" character, but in fact it obscures the tasks that still must be carried out to promote our proletariat as it concretely exists to its mission as vanguard; it attributes to it revolutionary characteristics already achieved, which in truth must still be forged in our country (PCS 1980: 42).

The second tendency which must be discarded is the sociological one of making formal equivalencies between various stages of capitalism—for example, to consider Latin American capitalism as a sort of "functional equivalent" of European capitalism of the eighteenth century. The development of monopoly capitalism and the transnationalization of capital have created problems in the peripheral formations that have not been experienced before. The articulation of heterogeneous forms of production into a single economic structure makes its class profile more complex. If the classic analysis holds that the proletariat surges forth as the vanguard of the revolution in developed capitalist formations, Lenin pointed to the role of the peasantry and the need for an alliance between the peasantry and the working class in a backward capitalist country such as Russia. And in the dependent colonial and neocolonial formations, the question arises of the "intermediate fractions": the nonsalaried workers, small merchants, and professional, technical, and intellectual petty bourgeoisie, and their incorporation into the struggle for national liberation and social transformation.

If the classes and groups that constitute the popular terrain cover such broad ground in the area of production/circulation relations, the way they are interrelated as "the people" *(pueblo)* is the result of the way in which the political struggle evolved, the nature of confrontation, and the concrete alignment which they adopt to deal with the contradiction that drives the struggle forward. The evolution of the people as a historic reality and as a theoretical concept is the product of the thousand forms of protests, mobilizations, and riots that the dominated classes have used to resist their economic exploitation and political oppression, to combat poverty, to break down the colonial or imperialist subjugation they experience, and all in a process of constituting themselves as a political subject that does not stand outside the system of domination but within it, and within which they express their identity as a people and their will to emancipate themselves.

When we speak of struggle, we understand by *pueblo* the great irredentist mass, that to which everything is offered and all is tricked away and betrayed, that which longs for a better, more dignified and more just homeland, that which is moved by ancestral yearnings for justice for having endured injustice and mockery generation after generation, which longed for great and wise transformations in all spheres and is ready, when it believes in something or someone, above all when it believes sufficiently in itself, to give every last drop of blood to achieve them.

What we call *pueblo,* when we refer to struggle, are the 600,000 Cubans who are without work . . . the 500,000 farmworkers . . . the 400,000 industrial workers and day-laborers . . . the 100,000 small farmers . . . the 30,000 teachers and professors . . . the 20,000 small merchants weary of their indebtedness . . . the 10,000 young professionals. . . . This is the *pueblo,* which suffers all the adversities and is therefore capable of fighting with complete courage! (Castro 1981: 36–37)

This famous summing-up presents clearly the elements noted above: (1) the recognition that the popular subject is constituted in political struggle; (2) the importance of the ideological question—the development of popular consciousness regarding exploitation and oppression, recognizing that this exploitation and oppression *unifies* the people over and above their working, educational, income, and other differences; and (3) the call to the working masses, small propertied classes, intellectuals, and professionals (see Fernández 1981).

By regarding the *popular* subject as a political-ideological process which has a class base but is not reducible to it, we can look at how the non-proletarianized—or not fully proletarianized—working masses are subordinated to the dominant classes and how they get incorporated into the popular camp. Their relative distance from the dominant relations of production means that ideological considerations figure strongly in defining their political position (Laclau 1977: 117). If, as Gramsci suggests, people become conscious of structural conflicts on the ideological plane, democratic, patriotic, and religious considerations become greatly important in the nature and alignments of these popular masses in their constitution as subjects of political action.[6]

At the same time, however, this marked diversity of dominated groups and fractions impinges on the manner in which the struggle against the prevailing social order is shaped—allowing room for various projects. This leads to contradictions and eventually to confrontations for the effective orientation, the real characteristics, and the political leadership of the social struggles. A good part of the failure and isolation of the Latin American left originates in the elaboration of social paradigms which begin with the interests of fractions and classes which, not to belittle their participation in the national-popular camp, are lumped together by virtue of their participation. The proletariat as such, the peasantry, and the urban petty bourgeoisie are all elements of the national-popular camp, around which are projected alternative forms of social organization which imply different strategies, though they may be popularly framed as unified (see Lenin 1905).

In the same way, socialism often appears more as a question of international relations than of relations of production. Elements that are frequently regarded by third-world movements as *socialist* include the project of national liberation, the anti-imperialism that they practice, the general democratization of economic life that they promote, the emphasis on social equality and justice, the conviction that the international capitalist system is opposed to national autonomy and economic development. Much less attention is given to the transformation of the relations of production and the socialization of the economy, which is seen as a long and complicated process. A large part of the academic discussion about *transition* starts from this misunderstanding.

THE QUESTION OF NATIONAL SOVEREIGNTY

The question of national sovereignty in third-world countries is posed in the context of dependent capitalist development. Here the state both institutionalizes political domination by an antipopular class, and reflects its own subordination to the exterior. Thus the national project becomes one of anti-imperialist struggle by the popular classes: national sovereignty becomes an attribute of social emancipation.

Not every third-world social revolution is necessarily one of national liberation, but all at least have a component of national liberation. The experience of Latin America in particular shows that formal political independence does not necessarily imply a real emancipation from outside domination, in that this can continue through channels that are no less decisive. The existence of direct colonial domination—and hence the absence of a national power structure—is not the essential element in a revolution of national liberation, but rather the experience of imperialist domination, which can be expressed via colonialism as well as through formally autonomous power structures. When socioeconomic transformation requires removing political-military, economic, financial, and other forms of subjection to developed capitalism and its states, the tasks of national liberation are unavoidable. But their weight in the social revolution, particularly in postcolonial situations, varies according to how deeply the political and economic power structure has taken root internally. In this sense, there is a sharp contrast between Central America, where local power structures show a strong subordination—political and military as well as economic—to the United States, and the situation in South America, where the dominant classes display a greater relative autonomy, and where the elements of *association* are usually stronger than those of *subordination*. While in the first case, the popular struggle takes on an anti-imperialist character, in the second it is defined more in class terms.[7]

Imperialist domination cannot be characterized simply as a relation *between nation-states*. An international relation *by its form* is *by its content* one of class, and in a double sense: (1) it expresses the extent of class domination of the central bourgeoisies on an international scale; and (2) it reflects the contradictory relation of subordination and privileged association between the central bourgeoisies and the peripheral dominant classes. By virtue of this link, the latter consolidate their international domination at the same time that they are directly or indirectly reaching some form of insertion into the international market.

In general, this second aspect of imperialist domination is easier to discern in some Central American and Caribbean countries (Nicaragua, Honduras, Dominican Republic, Haiti), due to the low level of development of the productive forces at the point at which imperialism burst into them, and because of the impact of this low level on the political arena and on the state: hence the weakness of the dominant classes and the fragility (or absence) of a national system of political domination. U.S. invasions in the Caribbean at the beginning of the century are illustrative in this sense. The Marines displaced the local dominant groups and developed political-military, economic, and cultural projects that conditioned these countries for the new stage of U.S. imperialist expansion (Vilas 1979a).

But the link was no less profound in those countries where the dominant classes controlled the export sector at the time of integration into the international market, and where an internal political order was relatively advanced. Imperialist expansion strengthened international integration through the introduction of profound modifications in the export sector—in international commerce, financing, transport, and warehousing. Furthermore, imperialist capital and states appear even more clearly here than in the first group of countries as the allies of the local dominant groups, expanding the scale of their accumulation and consolidating their political power. Thanks to the European railroads, refrigeration, ports, and financing, the agrarian bourgeoisies of Uruguay and Argentina, for example, effectively participated in the transnational process of capitalist accumulation as early as the end of the last century.

In each case the dominant *national* class was that local fraction or group which managed to generate a stable relationship with *international* capitalist expansion. The national character of political domination is a function of the efficiency with which a particular fraction of the local dominant classes can articulate its own subordination to foreign expansion (Vilas 1980a).

The existence of a national state and a power structure that answers to local decisions about the class struggle, and the way the state and dominant classes mediate imperialist domination, open up space for contradictions between those local groups with privileged associations with imperialism, and other fractions of the dominant classes which for various reasons remain relegated to secondary positions.

The privileged association of the dominant Latin American classes to imperialism is expressed in terms of the international division of labor that allocates the role of producers of primary commodities to the periphery. While the superstructural expression of this system of international specialization in general is the state, its expansion, together with wars and other international crises, created some differences. In some cases the expansion of the export sector created the possibility of growth of manufacturing activities, while at the same time imposing limitations generated by the reproduction of the primary export scheme. Furthermore, the weakness of the groups that were pushing these new facets of the accumulation process, due to their recent origin and lack of a developed ideological expression of their class interests—the lack of *organic intellectuals*—additionally assured their subordination to the export groups. The same process that created the space for these new bourgeois fractions also outlines their limitations. Confrontations around tariff policies, taxation, bank financing, and exchange rates are some of the areas in which the contradiction between various fractions of the peripheral bourgeoisie is expressed. To the extent that the international division of labor is manifested in primary export specialization and supports the domination of those fractions of the bourgeoisie, it is less the result of a "natural" endowment of factors than a product of imperialist domination. In the eyes of these bourgeois fractions the hindrance to their development is due in large measure to concrete aspects of imperialist penetration: the design of the productive structure through the system of transport and communications, the control of financing and commercialization mechanisms, and so on.

It would be senseless to deny the relevance of these contradictions; significant aspects of class struggle have revolved around them in the region for several decades. The passage from a mode of exploitation of the labor force based on the extraction of absolute surplus value to one based on the exploitation of relative surplus value—with all the material and political transformations that this carries with it—took place in the heat of the development of such contradictions. Modifications in the relations with the world market, and in particular with the new hegemonic centers of capitalism (the displacement of England by the United States, integration into local productive activity and spheres of circulation of transnational industrial and agribusiness firms, etc.), are some of the expressions of these contradictions.

The expression of these contradictions in dependent capitalist societies does not address the question of eliminating social exploitation, however, but rather of modernizing its terms; not breaking with imperialist domination, but only putting an end to subordination of certain groups of the dominant class. As Mariategui (1929) pointed out, anti-imperialism is attractive to elements of the bourgeoisie "for reasons of expansion and capitalist growth and not for reasons of socal justice and socialist doctrine." And in all cases, the project of these subordinated fractions of the dominant class, limited as it was, could exist to the degree that there also existed a mass mobilization which contributed a political force that the bearers of the project generally did not have, and a state which provided it with a coherence its beneficiaries generally also lacked.

Despite their subordinate character, the lesser fractions of the local bourgeoisie participated in the capitalist process of exploitation of profits generated by the working class, peasantry, and artisans, and benefited as well—in a lesser manner in some cases, perhaps, but always benefited—from the general conditions of accumulation guaranteed by the peripheral state. For these fractions the national contradiction usually revolved around the participation of different dominant groups in the distribution of the product of the world system of exploitation. In particular, it focused on their subordinated position in this distribution, a consequence of the primacy of the fractions directly allied with imperialism. Overcoming the national contradiction thus appears as the necessary condition for a fuller development of the process of accumulation on which it is based.

Populism presents one of the clearest expressions of the contradictions and limitations of the processes of anti-imperialist confrontations dominated by fractions of the Latin American bourgeoisie. The economic nationalism that originally characterized this populist bourgeoisie was always selective, focusing on foreign activity that restricted internal market expansion while ignoring imperialist expansion in the industrial sector. Moreover, at the same time as the railroads and mineral deposits were being nationalized, foreign investment was encouraged in the new dynamic sectors—above all in the intermediate and capital goods industries. The goal of the populist bourgeoisie thus basically consisted of a certain diversification of external sources of investment and financing, and therefore a new kind of relationship among the new sectors prompted jointly by foreign capital, the industrial, commercial, and financial fractions of the local bourgeoisie tied to the growth of the internal market, and the peripheral state (Vilas 1979b).

For the workers, on the other hand, the national contradiction is, objectively, a dimension of the fundamental contradiction, since imperialist exploitation is not distinct from capitalist exploitation, but rather a higher stage of it (Lenin 1916b). Furthermore, when private ownership of the means of production is largely imperialist ownership, the anti-imperialist struggle led by the popular classes produces profound alterations in the relations of production, once these means of production are nationalized, thanks to the creation of an area of social property which can become the dynamic nucleus of a new economic reality.

Given that in the final analysis imperialist domination is a form of capitalist exploitation, the elimination of all forms of subordination to imperialism is a task that can be successful only through the hegemonic project of the popular classes and, within the popular camp, of the working class. The structural class identity between the nationalist and pro-imperialist fractions of the bourgeoisie fills the former with doubts. They are caught between their reliance on the mobilization of the popular forces to compensate for their own weakness vis à vis the groups that control the state and which have a privileged relationship with imperialism, and their fear of popular organization. Their demands on foreign monopoly capital incorporate them into the national camp, but the limited character of these demands blocks them from assuming a leadership role.

For this reason national liberation movements in both colonial and postcolonial situations stress the necessity of worker and popular leadership:

> The vacillators, the timid ones, due to the character that the struggle takes, will abandon us. . . . Only the workers and peasants will go to the end; only their organized force will achieve the triumph (Sandino 1979, 8).

> The struggle against imperialism, which is the enemy of the people, will only have full political and economic significance if the problem of the oppression of one weak class by another powerful one is correctly resolved (Hou Yuon 1964).

> In order that the national revolution may triumph, passing all the phases of development of the national democratic state, the working class and its Party must assume the leadership of the revolution (Ho Chi Minh 1979, 127).

> Whether it is called "national liberation," Black Power, or simply "democracy," the struggle for liberation from imperialist domination is inseparably linked by thousands of threads to the struggle to make the working class the one that decides its own future (Percy 1982).

Worker and popular leadership of the process of national liberation expresses the process of progressive social emancipation of the dominated classes, and therefore of withdrawal from the old dominant forces—including the national fractions of the bourgeoisie. The level and continuity of the struggle, the capacity to draw together the forces of the national-popular bloc, as well as subordinated elements of the dominant bloc, and so force a political-ideological shift of such elements, all depend on the effective political leadership of the process by the working class organized as vanguard.

Around the axis of imperialist domination, then, are at least two contradictory camps. On one side are the classes and fractions incorporated as lesser partners but beneficiaries of imperialist expansion; the antinational camp—what in ordinary political language are called oligarchs, sell-outs, and traitors *(vendepatrias* and *cipayos)*. On the other side is the complex of classes and fractions exploited or oppressed by imperialist domination: the national camp.

The contradiction between the two, that is to say the national contradiction, is not in itself a class contradiction, since the national camp can be constituted by opposed classes or class fractions, unified only by their subjugation to imperialism. The fundamental contradiction—the bourgeoisie/proletariat contradiction—remains a part of the national camp, until this camp is also a popular camp. Until this point, the fundamental contradiction develops among the forces that constitute the national camp just as much as between them and the antinational camp.

The national contradiction interacts with the class contradiction in the degree to which the first is an aspect of the way in which the second evolved. This does not exhaust the class contradiction; on the contrary, it is subordinated to it: the dialectic of the national contradiction (the terms of the anti-imperialist opposition, the level and modalities of the struggle, etc.) is, in Althusser's usage, "overdetermined" by the class struggle. And since the class positions of the forces that in principle constitute the national camp are distinct— given that the fundamental contradiction puts them in opposed camps—the depth and breadth of the national contradictions are also different.

For these reasons the appeal to the anti-imperialist struggle is always broader than the appeal to socialism. Vietnam offers a clear example. The *Call to Found the Communist Party of Indochina* (February 13, 1930) was directed to the "Workers, peasants, soldiers, youth and students! Oppressed and exploited compatriots!" (Ho Chi Minh 1973: 99), in explicit class terms, while the call for the *League for the Independence of Viet-Nam* (the famous Viet-Minh created in 1941) appealed to the "respected elders, patriotic personalities," and the "notable wealthy, soldiers, workers, peasants, merchants, young functionaries, and women that love their country! Currently the most important problem is national liberation. Unite!" (Ho Chi Minh 1973: 104). While the former has class exploitation and oppression as its central focus, the latter is constituted on the basis of national oppression (see Mariategui 1929).

The "notable wealthy," the worker, the merchant, the peasant, all have something to gain in the struggle against imperialism. But contradictions exist among these classes. The class-nation contradiction therefore poses the question of how to resolve the *class conflict* in practice without losing *national unity* in the anti-imperialist struggle.[8]

THE DEVELOPMENT QUESTION

The material base of the peripheral states reflects the effects of imperialist domination. The *backwardness,* that is to say, the poor development of the productive forces, the forms of production, the primitive technical levels, and so on, is articulated with acute sector imbalance, both products of the subordination of the local productive structure to the necessities of the process of world capital accumulation. It is not only a problem of the kind of productive specialization imposed by this process, but also the way in which such specialization was historically organized; it is not a problem of *use values* (what is produced) but of *exchange values;* how and for whom it is produced. Even in the more advanced economies of Latin America, where the structural disarticulation and productive backwardness are less marked, the original design of the productive apparatus by the metropolitan capitalist economies and the consequent social structure continue to limit possibilities for development.

Development and underdevelopment are two faces of a single historical process of capitalist expansion; underdevelopment manifests the international division of labor generated by capitalism. To the degree to which the backwardness of the productive forces and the disarticulation of the economic structure are simultaneously product and base for sustaining the kind of capitalism dominated by imperialism, the question of economic development appears as one of the central points of revolutionary process. Furthermore, it is a question tightly linked to the anti-imperialist struggle—overdetermined, as is that struggle itself, by the fundamental capitalist contradiction.

This determination of the development question by the national question and, through it, by the class perspective, is not always evident, though that makes it no less real. The problems of development are problems of economic and therefore of political and cultural domination, in that here too the international dimension is a way of expressing the transnational presence of classes and groups. Development of the productive forces does not exist outside of the class struggle or of particular forms of social organization of production. To the contrary, only superior relations of production assure its continuity. Therefore, the tasks of development, of the stage of "national reconstruction," neither exist apart from nor can they be confronted except from a resolute class perspective. The basic issues of development—what to produce, how, for whom—have no answer outside of class projects; the *social cost* of development has a class character as well.

Issues conventionally considered as *natural* are also the product of the action of sociopolitical factors, as for example, the question of the viability of small third world countries (Jaguaribe 1964). From a revolutionary perspective, their small size is only an insurmountable obstacle to the development of the productive forces when the objective is to develop some type of national capitalism (Thomas 1974: 16). As Maurice Bishop, former Prime Minister of Grenada, explained:

> the real problem is not the question of size per se, but the question of imperialism.
>
> How can we plan? How can we develop ourselves? How can we grow economically and satisfy the necessities of our people when we are suffering various kinds of war directed by the largest and most powerful country, which is right on our doorstep, and when we ourselves are one of the smallest and poorest countries in the world?
>
> The key obstacle to the progressive development of our countries is not the physical fact of size. The key obstacle is imperialism (Bishop 1982: 198, 205, 206).

Within the national camp contradictions are generated around the project of revolutionary development. Often greater technical experience permits local bourgeois groups in contradiction with imperialism to gain control of the policies and economic apparatus of the new state; the scarcity of revolutionary technical cadres at this first stage is proverbial. On the other hand, the crisis of traditional—*class*—criteria of labor discipline, efficiency, and productivity are not immediately followed by new criteria, superior in that they do not support, or support less, the exploitation of the labor forces. This generally produces a hiatus characterized by trial and error; comings and goings, confusions, and failures occur, denounced by bourgeois groups as *chaos*. These groups try to take advantage of this situation, proposing formulas for *order* that reiterate the subordination of the worker and popular organizations in the process of production.

Since from the viewpoint of these bourgeois fractions what is desirable is to eliminate the obstacles to their own process of accumulation, *development* can be nothing other than the strengthening of their own material bases, a redefinition of foreign economic, commercial, and financial links, and a ratification of the principle of private entrepreneurial authority. Improvement of the living conditions of the masses is characterized as a necessary price of capital accumulation and therefore something that should be submitted to their dominion.

From a revolutionary perspective on the other hand, development is part of the profound transformations that the revolution seeks to introduce into all aspects of society. The creation of new forms of production, of new kinds of social relations, is designed to free the material and human productive forces from the shackles that have bound them. Reconstruction, far from being a process of recomposing the prevailing economic structure, is rather characterized as putting a stop to the surviving activity of imperialist domination and the effects of the liberation war, in order to confront from this minimum basis the tasks of social transformation.

THE DEMOCRATIC QUESTION

The different class positions regarding the national and development questions also express the confrontation of the two class conceptions of the democratic question: a contradiction between the democratic-bourgeois forces and the popular-democratic forces.

While the democratic orientations of some fractions of the Latin American bourgeoisie cannot be reduced to their economic bases, an examination of their content, breadth, and limitations should not obscure the identification of these bases. In this sense, and simplifying in the interest of brevity, it is possible to outline two situations which in the last three decades have generated favorable conditions for the development of a democratic perspective by some fractions of the region's bourgeoisie. Both have in common the control of political power by fractions of capital which impede the growth of accumulation by bourgeois groups marginalized from the center of the political scene, obliging the latter to turn to the dominated groups and classes—the workers' movement, the petty bourgeoisie—to help realize the political modifications which their material interests claim.

The first situation is that of prolonged dictatorships or autocratic governments, such as that of Rafael Leónidas Trujillo (1930–61) or Joaquín Balaguer (1966–78) in the Dominican Republic, or the Somoza family (1937–79) in Nicaragua—to mention only the most notorious examples. The direct and absolute exercise of state power by small cliques generates a true personalization of political power and operates as a launching pad for enrichment and accumulation through the manipulation of state apparatuses. Control of the state is in itself an economic power that permits the conversion of fractions which were originally defined by political-ideological features—elements of the bureaucracy, professional groups, private armies—into fractions defined structurally by their control of means of production and exchange (see, e.g., Vilas 1980b). Contradictions of variable complexity thus appear between the fractions whose accumulation is thanks to or based on the manipulation of power and state apparatuses, and those whose sole or predominate arena of accumulation is in the market. The *modus operandi* of these holders of political power appears to the other fractions of the bourgeoisie as unlawful and systematically violating the rules of the game—that is, the rationality of the market. Their own capacity for economic expression is called into question through the use of favoritism, privileges, private appropriation of public funds, nonreproductive use of investment funds, and so on.

The second situation takes place at more advanced levels of development of the productive forces, when the fundamental lines of the accumulation process are being pushed by the most concentrated and denationalized sectors of monopoly capital. Whether through terrorist or fascistlike forms of the state, such as those in Chile and Uruguay, among others, or through more subtle or sophisticated schemes, the hegemony of transnational monopoly capital implies a reshaping of the local market. It also implies the displacement of political power to the detriment of competitive groups of the internal bourgeoisie, those with smaller production units and lesser levels of financial integration, oriented fundamentally towards markets that cater to salaried and middle-income sectors. State policy favors the most concentrated sectors of local capitalism and the transnational firms, accelerating the displacement of those fractions more tied to mass consumption, accentuating the tendencies of the economic structure itself. In these conditions, and in the midst of well-known effects generated by the "Chicago model" (productive recession, high and sustained inflation, a fall in real salaries and employment, powerful growing foreign indebtedness, etc.), local bourgeois groups call for economic reactivation programs, increasing incomes, and reopening of the democratic space. They call for elections, reestablishment of parliament, renewal of civil liberties, relative trade-union autonomy, and so on.

Structural factors are a necessary but insufficient condition for the development of democratic orientations in some fractions of capital; also needed are political-ideological conditions which are tied to those but which have their own specificity and relative autonomy. Basically these conditions refer to the level of political mobilization of the popular classes—the extent of their organization and struggle, perception of their class interests, development of their own forms of political demands and confrontation, among others. Taken together, these elements constitute the *political conjuncture* on the basis of which can emerge some kind of democratic formula. This is not always inevitable, however: democratic orientations are not inherent in certain fractions of capital, nor is bourgeois democracy the typical or natural political regime of a particular stage of capitalist development in either center or periphery (see Therborn 1977, 1979).

In general, bourgeois-democratic orientations have grown fastest where the working class and other popular sectors are politically weak, while in the periods of growth of popular struggles the subordinated fractions of capital have tended to tag behind; in these cases the fundamental contradiction obscures the secondary contradictions within the class. This is also because while the democratization of political power in practice may be necessary for capital accumulation by these lesser bourgeois fractions, this does not extend to questioning capitalist domination. The democratic project of these sectors is also fundamentally, though not exclusively, *superstructural:* it is an attempt to democratize the apparatus and political-institutional practices, rather than the material base from which these have evolved. In the final analysis, democratization for these fractions is practically synonymous with a change in government through some kind of electoral practice—independent of the material conditions that effectively frame, and eventually restrict, this electoral practice. This does not rule out the possibility that in certain circumstances the bourgeois democratic project might permit elements of material democratization, but generally only as a result of pressure by the popular classes.

The instability and limitations of these democratic initiatives of sectors of the Latin American bourgeoisie are well known. Their economic and political marginalization limits possible action: they lack a sufficient foothold in the repressive apparatus of the state to attempt a military coup, while their political weakness and fear of a popular overflow inhibits any thought of a call to popular insurrection. The appeal to electoral practices, then, permits them to aspire to mass support. Their class content is hidden behind the facade of citizenry, within well-defined institutional channels by which they can hope to guarantee the dominant fractions that the popular unleashing either will not occur or could be institutionally managed.

While this scheme still relies on a repressive apparatus, the space it opens can rapidly become the arena of expression for popular demands and claims. If not always planned as an assault on power, popular militancy can produce obstacles to the overall process of capital accumulation, not just to the segment controlled by the fractions most closely tied to monopoly capital. Popular incorporation into the political system at this point ceases to be seen as a condition for the furthering of accumulation, and becomes instead a synonym for chaos. The difference between *participations* and *subversion* is usually no greater than a few points of difference in the rate of earnings. The elimination—political and if necessary physical—of popular mobilization then appears as the condition for the advancement of the process of accumulation.

For the popular classes on the other hand, political movements tend to see democratization as a more complex and prolonged aspect of a movement designed to eliminate all forms of exploitation and oppression. Although less strongly than in developed capitalist countries, the workers' movement in Latin America was from its origins one of the most decisive participants, together with the petty bourgeoisie, in the democratic camp, though rarely its directing force (see, e.g., Godio 1980). Nevertheless, popular focus on the democratic question was until recently centered in the urban arena and democratic demands were articulated more in terms of incorporation into a state and an existing economy—thus with a given class character—than in terms of imposing a worker-popular design on either. The democratic question tended to be characterized implicitly as the attribute of a given class or class fraction, an inconclusive project that could be realized only with worker and popular support. Democratic tasks were consequently seen as a part of a process of laying the conditions through which the popular classes could finally pose the question of power (development of the productive forces, bourgeois-democratic revolution, etc.), but in which the political leadership of the process was beyond the working classes and their political organizations.

For the revolutionary organizations, however, the characterization of the democratic tasks as *reformist,* if not *bourgeois,* led to their repudiation as outside the *revolutionary* project. This contributed to the political isolation of the revolutionary organizations not only with respect to the democratic fractions of the local entrepreneurs—when they existed—but, even more serious, with respect to the peasantry and petty bourgeoisie.

In both cases class reductionism led to a refusal to constitute the democratic terrain as a popular arena of struggle, with the result that given projects and regimes were prejudged through a set of rigid equations that flattened the richness of the conjuncture: proletariat equaled socialism; petty bourgeoisie or bourgeoisie equaled democracy; and monopoly bourgeoisie equaled fascism.

The Caribbean offers two opposing examples of the importance that the ability of a revolutionary organization to lead the democratic question from a popular class perspective can have in the subsequent development of the revolutionary process. In Cuba, placing the struggle against the Batista dictatorship and imperialist domination as a dimension of the worker and popular struggle for its social emancipation guaranteed the class autonomy of the proletariat and other popular sectors in the democratic-national opening, obliging the antidictatorial fractions of the Cuban bourgeoisie to resign themselves to the political leadership of the 26th of July Revolutionary Movement.[9] In the Dominican Republic, the early military defeat of the Dominican Liberation Movement—which united socialist goals to an immediate democratic-revolutionary program of confrontation with the Trujillo dictatorship—and the elimination of Trujillo in May 1961 through the machinations of the U.S. government and anti-Trujillo fractions of the Dominican bourgeoisie, allowed the issue of democracy to remain in the hands of the bourgeoisie.[10] The revolutionary movement, meanwhile, outlined as an immediate task—in one of the most backward Caribbean societies—the proletarian revolution, deepening its isolation from the peasant masses, the petty bourgeoisie, and even the level of real consciousness of the small

proletariat—in sum, from the vast majority of the country's population.

The advent of fascist dictatorships and state terrorism in various
countries of the region, the limitations of democratic and reformist
perspectives of the subordinated bourgeois groups, the necessity of
broadening the social bases of the revolutionary movements, and the
triumph of the Sandinista revolution all created the possibility that
the issue of democracy might be incorporated as an integral dimension of popular struggles. As such, democracy implied the creation
of a political system which, together with effecting socioeconomic
transformations, would open all arenas of society—political, economic, defense, and cultural—to the full participation of the people.
As Salvadoran Communist Party leader Shafik Handal put it:

> the socialist revolution cannot be realized except with the anti-imperi-
> alist, democratic banners unfurled . . . nor can the democratic anti-
> imperialist revolution be realized to its core or its conquests defended if
> it does not move to socialism. Said in another way, it is not possible to
> move to socialism except through democratic, anti-imperialist revolu-
> tion, but it is equally not possible to consummate the democratic, anti-
> imperialist revolution without going towards socialism. Between the
> two there is an essential and insoluble nexus; they are facets of one
> single revolution and not two revolutions (1982).[11]

THE CHARACTER OF THE REVOLUTION

Third-world revolutions thus articulate four kinds of issues: the
national question, the *development question,* the *democratic question,* and the *class question,* the last of which, with its fundamental
contradiction, crosscuts the other three. The character of each process is a result of the way in which these four issues are articulated
within the overall framework of revolutionary struggle.

The discussion about the class character of revolutions of national
liberation arises from the fact that they are, *to a certain degree and
during a certain period,* multiclass processes, when the national-
democratic and development tasks bring together classes that are
located in different camps with regard to the fundamental contradiction, and involve them in demands and objectives of unequal breadth
and depth.

The mode by which these questions are interwoven explains the *primacy of the political* in liberation movements and in the constitution of the national-popular camp. This does not deny the final framing of the political issue within a matrix of objective possibilities generated by the material forces, but rather accentuates its relative autonomy.

In the first place, if the national-popular camp is crosscut by the class contradiction, only political leadership of the whole process can maintain the unity of opposites as long as necessary, or possible, for the revolutionary movement. Second, the construction of the national-popular camp around the leadership of the working class cannot take place except through a *political organization* of the popular classes that expresses this leadership in its structure, strategy, and forms of struggle. Above all this is true where the importance of the working class in the social structure appears relatively diluted compared to the peasant masses, urban and rural semi-proletariat, artisans, unemployed, and so on.

Hasty or sectarian analyses of Latin American liberation movements have often dismissed them (especially when their chances of triumph seem small or distant) in the name of theoretical purity which is compatible only with political isolation and operational inertia. Organizations that push liberation struggles are accused of being petty bourgeois and thus reformist, due to the presence within them of elements belonging to these *intermediate* sectors, and to the fact that such organizations raise and advance the claims of broad sectors of the population together with the demands of the proletariat.

Such a narrow view obscures the fact that this type of revolutionary liberation movement not only politically expresses the concrete nature of social contradictions, but also represents the element that pushes the progressive political-ideological make-up of the working class, its growing subjective differentiation from the other components of the national-popular camp, and therefore accelerates the convergence between its material position in the productive structure—class "in itself"—and its position in the political struggle—class "for itself." Liberation movements do this by starting from effective demands, concrete problems, and the dialectical understanding of worker and popular interests, and from a comprehension of the worker and popular struggles in the international camp.

The issue comes down to the complex problem of *representation*. Often a social class identity measure is used: if the class position of the members (or directors) of the organization is similar to this or that sector of the population, there is representation; if the position is different, there is none. Consequently, if the majority of the members of a party are workers, we are in the presence of a workers' party; if they are a minority, we are not. If a good part of the members of an organization's leadership is recruited from the petty bourgeoisie, we have a petty-bourgeois organization. If the officers of the armed forces belong to *middle-class* families, the coups that they champion will be middle-class military coups, and so on (see Nun 1967; Miliband 1970; and a critique by Poulantzas 1977).

This is of course a profoundly erroneous conception. The massive presence of workers and artisans at the barricades in Paris in 1789 did not affect the bourgeois character of the French Revolution, nor did the active role played by the petty-bourgeois masses alter the class character of European fascism. Nor can these and many other similar realities be salvaged by referring to the "false consciousness" of the masses or the "demagoguery" of certain leaders.

Representation is a *political relation,* not a *sociological* one. The class character of an organization does not derive from the social situation of its leadership, but from its involvement in the class struggle and, therefore, from the class project that they assume, express, and promote. Their members "can be a world apart" from that class, "by their culture and individual position"; what makes them class representatives "is the fact that their minds are restricted by the same barriers" which the class itself "fails to overcome in real life, and that they are therefore driven in theory to the same problems and solutions to which material interest and social situation drive the latter in practice" (Marx 1852: 176–77).

What characterizes representation is the *function* developed in relation to the given class: consequently the representation of a class, alliance, or project can be in the hands of organizations or state apparatuses whose management corresponds to class or fractions distinct from those whose interests are pushed in a given project. The *political* relation can be out of phase *sociologically* without that necessarily detracting from its content. Gramsci (1977b) called attention to this point when he noted the formation of intellectual sectors that concretely went through complex historic processes, constituting groups or fractions that "produced" intellectuals for the fundamental classes of capitalist society: the petty and medium urban bourgeoisie, the petty agrarian bourgeoisie.

The issue is particularly important in national liberation movements. In them, "the historic subject that carries the struggle often does not coincide with the content of the struggle nor the methods used, thus mixing various subjects, different aspirations, and combining diverse methods of struggle" (López et al. 1979: 13). In other words, the direction of the liberation movement by the national democratic contradiction, in the struggle to seize political power, can and in fact does involve forces and groups distinct from those that push the popular camp and the project of social transformation from the workers' perspective.

This theme is directly related to the question of the character of the revolution in backward societies. The possibility of a socialist revolution in formations with strong precapitalist components and a pattern of development different from that of Western Europe—especially England—was first addressed by some Russian populists, motivated by the translation of the first volume of *Capital.* They upheld the specificity of the way in which the revolution developed in their country and the possibility of passing directly from a semifeudal society to socialism based on the rural commune, without passing through the contradictions of capitalism. In that period the question was fundamentally theoretical: the *narodniki* were not an alternative for power and their principal concern was to know Marx's opinion about the validity of his analysis of capitalism for Russia—particularly regarding whether the expropriation of the direct producer had a necessary or historically contingent character. As we now know, Marx supported with some shadings the populist thesis, while Engels was more reticent (Marx and Engels 1980).[12]

The discussion around the populists' thesis, and in particular Marx's reflections, served among other things to demonstrate the specificity of capitalist development in backward societies, and the possibility and necessity of socialism in order to put an end to it. That the answers offered by the *narodniki* have not always been on the mark should not obscure the fact that in general the questions they formulated were correct. Now that many of these questions have been reopened by the revolutionary movements of Latin America and the third world, it is not enough to brand them as *populist, utopian,* or *romanticist.*[13] Their experiences suggest that a socialist revolution is possible in backward formations and that, in the words of Fidel Castro, "excellent perspectives exist to be able to pass practically from tribalism to socialism, without having to go through certain stages that other regions of the world did" (1977).

Nevertheless the tendency to characterize capitalism as a universal mix of industrialization, salarization, and urbanization led first to a frequent denial of the capitalist character of social formations with different characteristics, and a consequent denial of the viability of socialist revolution. Instead of seeing socialism as a road to overcome backwardness, backwardness was looked at as an obstacle to socialism.

If "no social order is ever destroyed before all the productive forces that are implicit in it have been destroyed, and new and superior relations of production never replace the old ones before the material conditions of their existence have matured, in the heart of the old society," if consequently, "humanity inevitably only takes on the tasks it is capable of resolving" and these "only emerge as a problem when the material conditions for their solution are already present or are being created" (Marx 1859), socialism could only be viable starting from a capitalist—that is, industrialized, salarized, urbanized—society. Marx's text was thus interpreted, not as a challenge to creative praxis, intellectual courage, and a weapon in the search for elements that would advance the social struggles and revolutionary project, but as a call to push the development of the productive forces so that once the peasants and artisans were salaried, the society urbanized, and the economy industrialized, socialism would become possible.

With some variations, this interpretation constituted the theoretical foundation of the strategy of some political organizations of the continent, and persists in the writings of some academics. Its proposition was the encouragement of a *bourgeois democratic revolution*. Apart from the erroneous characterization of Latin American capitalism and the unhappy way the bourgeois-democratic revolution is conceptualized, it seems clear that there is no bourgeois-democratic revolution without a bourgeoisie interested in it. There was an effort to remedy the suspicions of the bourgeoisie toward popular mobilization by reducing the latter to the level of the bourgeois design and to their contradictions with "feudalism." The historic necessity of *certain tasks* was confused with the historic necessity of *certain agents* in the framework of European bourgeois revolutions and justified the abdication of political leadership of the process for the sake of some fraction of the bourgeoisie. Fearing that the popular forces would do "more" and chase away their allies, it was seen as a better risk that they do "less," and so they did. Without a doubt there was a bourgeoisie, but there was neither revolution, nor, generally speaking, democracy. Objectivism was substituted for materialism as a method of analysis, and any political proposal that went beyond this and opted for different strategies and methods of struggle was dismissed as *adventurist, provocateurist, divisionist,* and, above all, *petty-bourgeois.*

Now it is clear that if capitalism manifests itself differently in Latin America and Europe, the mode of development of the revolutionary process will also have to be distinct even if its class content is the same. The productive backwardness, the less marked capitalist differentiation of the class structure, and imperialist domination all impose different methods and alliances. But it is precisely for this reason that revolutionary practice enriches theory. And in the same way that capitalism is manifested differently in Sweden and in Honduras, thus too the construction of socialism is different in Czechoslovakia or the German Democratic Republic than in Mozambique or Vietnam. The objective possibility of a passage "from tribalism to socialism" surrounds the transition with characteristics that necessarily differentiate it from other revolutionary roads, however much the goal may be the same.

One of these differential aspects—already noted above—consists in the quantitatively reduced character of the proletariat compared to the peasantry and the petty-bourgeois masses; while without doubt this makes the question of the class predominance of the former more complex, it does not discard it as an issue in principle. Here the role of the political vanguard of the revolutionary process is key, not only to direct the socioeconomic transformations that follow the taking of political power, but to do so from a class perspective that expresses, within the heart of the people, the hegemony of the working class. And hegemony is *leadership,* a political question that, in principle, has little to do with the statistical weight of a class in the population. But if the dominant numerical weight of the proletariat is not by itself synonymous with proletarian political leadership, it is also true that the issue of worker hegemony, when the proletariat is numerically small, poorly organized, and not totally differentiated from forms of family property or self-employment, is one of tremendous complexity.

The development of a capitalist pole at the level of the productive structure suggests the objective possibility of negating and overcoming it more completely and radically by means of workers' struggles. But the articulation of the proletariat with other exploited classes suggests the necessity of integrating a broader project of social liberation with the demands and contradictions protagonized by the peasantry, artisans, petty merchants, youth, the urban and rural poor, and the broad sectors of the population identified more by their placement in the arena of reproduction than in that of production (housewives, squatters, tenant movements, etc.) or by their insertion in ideological practice (students, religious groups, teachers, and the like).

Abandoned to their own dynamic, the demands of these classes and fractions tend to be diluted within a sea of sectorial and segmented pressures. The subordinated character of their material bases with respect to the capitalist pole of the social formation, and their consequent distance from the determinant nucleus of its productive structure, conditions and limits the depth and breadth of their own projects. The experiences of third-world liberation struggles suggest that even the broadest forms of rebellion by these fractions have tended to exhaust themselves when their dynamics could not be framed within national political processes that expressed, at least tendentially, worker hegemony in the popular camp.

The Mexican revolution between 1910 and 1915 testifies dramatically to these limitations. Referring to the peasants, Arnaldo Córdova points out:

> Hatred of the landowners did not translate into coherent programmatic action against capitalism (in reality they were antilandlord, not anticapitalist) and their localism impeded their ability to confront the reformist program of the constitutionalists and struggle for the conquest of political power, an objective which, at bottom, they neither proposed nor, when it was within their reach, did they know what to do with it.
>
> The successors of Madero . . . adopted popular demands in order to gain the masses to their causes and manipulate them. This they finally did, as the events of 1915 demonstrate, but exactly as manipulated masses, integrated into a new political system to which they allied themselves, but the direction of which would not be in their hands. The reason is that those masses could not go beyond their immediate interests . . . nor create an ideology that would organize them indepen-

dently. Their ideology and even their leaders, despite having had a legitimation and recognition at a national level, did not express projects of national development or organization. The projection of their positions at that level either was accidental or limited itself to immediate demands. A clear idea of a new State was absent: they lacked a full-fledged conception of economic or social organization, in a word they lacked a clear vision of the future, rather looking backward, as if to a lost world that must be reconquered. . . . Anguished to the point of desperation by their real and present situation, they created caudillos of whom they demanded nothing more, or who were nothing more, than the incarnation of their immediate and limited needs (1979: 25, 143, 144).

The final subordination of the rebellions to the political project of one or another of the fundamental classes of capitalism does not imply, however, the futility of these experiences. After them, things do not return to their former state, however much the final result is different from that aspired to by the peasantry, petty-bourgeoisie, and other such groups.

During the period that culminates with the taking of political power, and while the new correlation of forces is being consolidated, the process tends to be led by the national-democratic contradiction. In this stage the revolution assumes an *anti-imperialist, democratic,* and *popular* character, in which the political-ideological category of "the people" focuses and synthesizes the totality of social forces that have taken up the struggle on the national-democratic side, together with the exploited and oppressed classes. During this period unity at the heart of the popular camp does not halt the development of the class struggle around the fundamental contradiction, although it subordinates its development to that of the struggle against imperialist domination, economic backwardness, and the counter-revolution.

In this period the consolidation of popular power implies the realization of tasks that are not *in themselves* proletarian, but which are only possible under proletarian leadership. The class content of one or another such task depends less on the task itself than on the character of the process that is pushing it: it is not the tasks that qualify the process, but the process that qualifies the tasks. It is erroneous to think in terms of a predetermined correlation of classes and tasks, by virtue of which there will be tasks that by definition are bourgeois, or petty-bourgeois, or proletarian. The class character of a policy does not depend on its formal features or its technical aspects but on the political project to which it belongs, and on the level of popular organization that its promotion involves. As a consequence, measures that in another context could be branded reformist, petty-bourgeois, or whatever, change as a function of the level reached by the popular struggles and by their articulation into a revolutionary project. It is this project that gives a revolutionary character to the measures and, in this way, a class nature. What in other experiences may have been decisions adopted "from above," in a revolutionary context are measures of a project that arises "from below." Cmdte. Humberto Ortega stated in 1981:

> We are expressing the power that we have conquered through a popular democracy, which means that here in this country we are trying to and will carry out tasks that historically were the lot of others to resolve, because an Agrarian Reform is not a demand, it is a requirement, a necessity for the development of capitalism itself, and here there isn't even industrialization and it also falls to us to confront a series of problems that historically the bourgeoisie was incapable of working through, because they dedicated themselves singlemindedly to robbing, exploiting together with somocismo the labor force of our people in the most brutal way without worrying about their own development as a national bourgeoisie. . . .
>
> . . . the fact that we have to meet demands that these sectors did not address, and which it fell to them to address historically, does not signify that this revolution is framed within a bourgeois democracy, as some pseudomarxists, some radicalists, have at times proposed. Here in Nicaragua there is a popular democracy, in which power is exercised by Sandinismo, which means the people, through a higher form of organization and their own form of mass organization; here other sectors that are not Sandinistas subsist, but they subsist inasmuch as this power permits them to and inasmuch as they really do not affect the revolutionary project (H. Ortega 1981: 89, 90).

On the other hand, the relation between the political-democratic stage of the revolution (the struggle against the state as the privileged arena of class domination) and transformations in the socioeconomic structure in bourgeois revolutions is different from that in popular revolutions. The bourgeoisie was the socially dominant class before it was the politically dominant class; it first revolutionized society in order to then take the state by assault (in England and France) or to participate in its direction (Germany and Central Europe). In the popular revolutions the relation is the reverse. It is necessary to first overthrow political power, politically expropriate the dominant classes, to begin from the constitution of the popular state to impel transformations in the material structure of the old society. They are not two distinct processes, but two dimensions that involve distinct methods and strategies and, eventually, different alliances.

The *social subject* of the struggle against the state is not necessarily the same as the *historic subject* of the revolutionary transformations of the material structure of the society. The first speaks of a relation with the empirical *sociological profile* of the revolutionary troops; the second refers to the *political project* of the class that leads the war, and that therefore determines the nature of the revolutionary transformations. The articulation between the two highlights the transition from the popular to the proletarian, the passage within the revolution from the hegemony of the popular forces in the anti-imperialist struggle, in the tasks of development, and in the construction of a political power of a new kind, to worker hegemony in the popular camp. Popular-revolutionary leadership of the process assesses the necessary conditions for this transformation and again highlights the strategic relevance that in this sense the vanguard has.[14]

This is nothing novel.[15] But it is clear that, in its concrete steps, this transformation obeys particular conditions with which each revolutionary process inscribes itself in the general framework of struggles of national and social liberation. It also refers to a process open to the development of its internal forces and to the tensions and contradictions that emanate from the international setting. The transformation is not, therefore, mechanical, easy, quick, or inevitable.

THE SANDINISTA POPULAR REVOLUTION

Within these general considerations, Nicaragua developed its own features.

Although formally independent from the early nineteenth century, Nicaragua achieved effective control of all its territory only at the end of that century. Nicaragua endured successive invasions by the United States, inaugurated by the adventure of William Walker in the 1850s and continuing until the 1930s, when U.S. troops were forced out by the Army in Defense of National Sovereignty led by Augusto

Sandino. But by then the United States had created the National Guard and put at its head Anastasio Somoza García, supporting him when he took over the government by force and (after assassinating Sandino and savagely repressing his followers) initiated a family dictatorship that would last until 1979 (see Diederich 1981).

Throughout this period, the Somoza family could always count on the political and diplomatic support of the White House, the Department of State, and sectors of Congress, and on sufficient economic and financial assistance from U.S. development agencies and international financial bodies. Imperialism had more political-military than economic presence in Nicaragua, and within the economic sphere, more in circulation than in production. Nicaragua never wore the face of an enclave society so common in the region. Its principal importance for the United States was always its geographic position—the eventual site of a new interoceanic canal—and the political fidelity of the dictatorship.[16]

The general backwardness of the country occurred within this context. The capitalist development of Nicaragua was particularly late and was basically circumscribed to certain sectors of agroexport and to the western region of the country. In general, capitalism was more advanced in the area of commercialization and finance than in production. In the absence of an enclave sector, the greater part of production was in the hands of local producers, though subordinated to commercial and financial capital, and to processing controlled by foreign capital and the large local bourgeoisie. The process of proletarianization of the labor force was slow, and subject to a strong seasonality. Spatial and intersectoral inequalities, the lack of physical integration of important parts of the territory due to the absence of access roads, communications, and so on, accentuated the general disarticulation of the Nicaraguan economy. The fragility and backwardness of the productive apparatus was aggravated by a very broad opening of the whole economy with respect to the international capitalist system.

The decisive role of imperialism in installing and maintaining the dictatorship gave a strong anti-imperialist content to the popular struggles, without parallel in other Latin American countries. At the same time the complicity of the dominant local groups with foreign domination and with the dictatorship, and the good relations that the latter maintained with them until the 1970s, lent a class component to the struggles against the dictatorship.

The Sandinista National Liberation Front thus had a fertile terrain for its revolutionary practice. For broad sectors of the people, the FSLN was the continuation, with new strategies and focus, of a war against imperialist aggression and dictatorial opppression that dated at least from the beginning of the century.[17] The national consciousness of the Nicaraguan people was always nourished by anti-imperialist and antidictatorial components, which grew out of their own history and were articulated by their intellectuals and leaders.[18] The anti-imperialist spirit of the poetry and prose of Rubén Darío was continued in the heroism of Zeledón; popular nationalism was interwoven into the anti-imperialist struggle of Augusto Sandino. And, at every moment, the necessity and legitimacy of armed struggle: "The sovereignty of a people is not to be discussed; it is to be defended with weapons in hand" (Sandino, cited in Ramírez 1981).

The FSLN collected these elements of popular consciousness and built a revolutionary strategy around them (see Fonseca 1981: 315). While breaking with traditional political practices—including those of the existing leftist organizations—the FSLN nonetheless presented itself as the continuation of an anti-imperialist and democratic armed struggle profoundly rooted within Nicaraguan popular culture.

2

The Economic and Social Structure of Peripheral Capitalism

N icaragua, like other Central American countries, was incorporated into the international division of labor as a primary export economy. But these exports were of little relevance until the coffee period began in the last third of the nineteenth century. During the colonial period the production of indigo was the principal source of external income; this was combined with extensive livestock breeding and subsistence farming in an extremely backward productive structure. Low population density and abundant fertile land generated a pattern of direct ties between worker and land. But these were subordinated to tenant farming methods of surplus extraction, with payment either in labor or in kind.

Coffee production began later than in other countries of the isthmus and reached its peak between 1920 and 1940. The formation of an agrarian bourgeoisie is tightly linked to this coffee expansion, although coffee did not introduce great changes in the economic structure: the latifundist patterns of extensive stockraising easily adapted to the new export crop. The search for lands appropriate to coffee affected not the landowning oligarchy but the tenant farmers, indigenous communities, squatters, and others, who were dispossessed and pushed into marginal zones. For many landowners and merchants, on the other hand, coffee signified the opportunity to expand their activity to a new and very lucrative field.

Coffee thus implied a reorientation and diversification of the old productive structure rather than a break with it. It also implied tensions and contradictions between new and old groups for control of the state and society.

The innovative orientations of the emerging groups—with all their limitations—were quickly truncated by the U.S. invasion of 1912. The Marines decisively contributed to the defeat of the Liberal government of José Santos Zelaya and consolidated the return to power of the most retrograde landowning and commercial groups.

Cattle and coffee interests thereafter formed the basis of the Nicaraguan economy until the middle of this century. In the 1920s and 1930s coffee came to represent between one-half and two-thirds of the country's exports. But by World War II its dynamism had declined appreciably, without being compensated for by other agricultural goods (bananas, hides, wood, sugar) or by a short-lived gold boom in the early 1940s.

Cotton ultimately filled the vacuum. Impelled by the rise in international prices, within a few years production soared, changing the profile of agricultural production and the composition of exports. Between 1950 and 1965 cotton production leaped from 3,300 to more than 125,000 tons; its share of total Nicaraguan exports went from 5 percent to 45 percent in the same years.

The best cotton lands were found in the northeastern zone (the departments of Chinandega and León). Expansion forcibly displaced the farmers occupying these lands and producing foodstuffs, principally basic grains. Insofar as the growth in production was done by cultivating new lands rather than increasing yields, cotton cultivation generated a massive population push toward the agricultural frontier (the departments of Nueva Segovia in the north and Zelaya and Río San Juan in the Atlantic Coast region), as well as to urban centers. This migration process, which continued into the 1970s, was reinforced by the development of beef exports and the introduction of irrigated rice production (CSUCA 1978a, 1978b). The land planted in cotton went from 23,900 manzanas in 1950–51 to 123,600 in 1953–54, 164,700 in 1963–64, and 259,300 in 1973–74.* The ruthless expropriation of peasant lands drastically changed the structure of rural land tenure; between 1950 and 1963 the Gini index of tenant concentration grew from G = .74 (the lowest in Central America) to G = .81 (Seligson 1980: 35; Censo Nacional Agropecuario 1973).

Cotton expansion also gave a strong impulse to capitalist relations of production and introduced a new dynamism to the whole econ-

---

*A manzana is equal to 0.7 hectares.

omy, although its fruits were obviously distributed quite unequally. The growth of cotton accelerated the proletarianization of the work force, although at the beginning the seasonal character of employment meant that this was manifest more in terms of peasant displacement than in the creation of wage laborers. The greater need for machinery and equipment (tractors, crop-dusting planes, harvesting machines, cotton gins, etc.), industrial inputs (fertilizers, pesticides, herbicides), modern technology, and financing generated a greater demand for capital. Indeed, the development of commercial and financial capital for the local and foreign bourgeoisie was closely tied to the development of cotton production on a grand scale. Finally, cotton produced two additional economic consequences: (1) since it is not limited to the tropical zones of the third world, but is also produced in the advanced capitalist countries, it obliged local producers to emphasize efficiency and general modernization criteria; and (2) it defined important internal ties to a broad spectrum of new industrial activities (oil, agrochemicals, textiles, etc.).[1]

The gross domestic product (GDP), which in 1945–49 had grown at an annual average rate of 3.6 percent, went to 8.5 percent in 1950–54 and 6.3 percent for the rest of the 1950s—the highest in all Central America. The diversification of production and of exports generated a diversification of foreign markets. If in the second half of the 1940s between 70 percent and 90 percent of exports went to the United States, in the last five years of the 1950s this had diminished to 35 percent. Nonetheless, imports continued to be strongly dependent on the U.S. market: 56 percent at the end of the 1950s. In the 1960s the introduction of beef for export would lead to an even greater diversification of agroexports. The land dedicated to beef doubled between 1960 and 1975, provoking a new displacement of small producers in the central region, many of whom had settled there after having been expelled by cotton. Between 1960 and 1970 the relative share of beef in total exports tripled, so that by the middle of the 1970s the value of beef production represented 25 percent of the value of all food production; 90 percent of the beef exports were absorbed by the United States and virtually all the rest by Puerto Rico.

By the end of the 1950s capitalism, dominated by agroexports, had developed in the countryside. In the 1960s the creation of the Central American Common Market opened the Nicaraguan economy to industrial investment in assembly plants as well as processing of agroexports. The industrial share of GDP rose from 16 percent in 1960 to 22 percent in 1970, all carried out under the control of foreign capital (direct investments, licensing, financing). Although Nicaragua has received less foreign investment than any other Central American country, this was concentrated more in the manufacturing industry than was true in the rest of the isthmus. Foreign investment in the manufacturing industry went from 27.8 percent of total foreign investments in 1959 to 54.4 percent in 1969, while in the region as a whole in that year it was 30.8 percent, 43.6 percent in Guatemala, 38.1 percent in El Salvador, 21.1 percent in Costa Rica, and 11.2 percent in Honduras.

A number of indicators illustrate the strong foreign dependency of Nicaragua's manufacturing industry. Table 2.2 shows the coefficients of imports and of the consumption of imported inputs for all the branches of industrial production in the middle of the 1970s. Apart from the predictable case of oil refining—Nicaragua does not produce hydrocarbons—the paper industry, printing and publishing companies, chemical substances and products, fabrication of rubber products, basic metals, and machinery construction are notable for their high dependency. Together these branches account for almost 40 percent of the gross production value (GPV) and 30 percent of the value added in the manufacturing sector in that period.

Table 2.3 shows the commercial balance of the industrial sector. Between 1960 and 1977 it showed a deficit of almost $700 million, and

Table 2.1
Nicaragua: Composition of Exports, FOB
(in percentages)

Categories	1930	1935	1940	1945	1950	1955	1960	1965	1970	1977
Coffee beans	45	55	22	26	50	35	31	18	18	31
Cotton	1	1	2	—	5	39	24	45	19	24
Gold	5	10	61	51	23	10	11	4	2	1
Beef	—	—	—	—	—	—	5	5	15	6
Sugar	4	2	—	—	—	—	6	4	6	5
Bananas	27	21	5	—	—	—	—	1	—	1
Sesame	—	—	—	—	4	2	4	1	1	—
Others	18	11	10	23	18	14	19	22	39	32
Total	100	100	100	100	100	100	100	100	100	100

Sources: 1930–55: Belli (1975); 1960–77: Banco Central de Nicaragua.

this negative balance continued to grow. As a net importer, the industrial sector contrasts clearly with the net export character of the agricultural sector, despite the fact that throughout the period the industrial share of total exports grew, and that of the agricultural sector shrank (Table 2.4). Throughout the period under consideration the negative commercial balance in the industrial sector was equivalent to almost 40 percent of the favorable commercial balance of the agricultural sector in the same period.

The effect of import substitution was also minimal. In 1960 industrial production represented 60 percent of the value of the country's industrial imports, and in 1970 it was still at the same level, but by 1977 it had dropped to 54 percent. Furthermore, since the industrial

Table 2.2
Nicaragua: Coefficients of Direct Imports
in the Manufacturing Industry, 1976

Sector	Import coefficients	Imported inputs / Total inputs
Food	.087	.133
Drinks	.177	.471
Tobacco	.055	.297
Textiles	.277	.618
Clothing and shoes	.199	.392
Leather industry	.120	.204
Wood	.045	.100
Furniture and accessories	.189	.536
Paper and paper products	.646	.992
Printing and publishing	.330	.876
Chemical products and substances	.494	.653
Oil refining	.928	.980
Rubber products	.412	.961
Nonmetallic mineral products	.081	.372
Basic metal industries[a]	.470	.851
Construction of machinery[b]	.435	.957
Construction of transport materials	.385	.953
Others	.040	.045
All sectors	.228	.411

Source: Weeks (1981).
[a] Includes fabrication of metal products.
[b] Includes electrical machinery and equipment.

Table 2.3

Nicaragua: Commercial Balance of Industrial and Agricultural Sectors
(in millions of current dollars)

Period	(1) Exports of industrial origin	(2) Imports for industry	(3) 1-2	(4) Exports of agricultural origin	(5) Imports for agricultural sector*	(6) 4-5
1960–64	97.5	209.3	− 111.8	301.3	34.4	266.9
1965–69	243.2	403.4	− 160.2	471.7	94.6	377.1
1970–74	633.6	749.9	− 116.3	624.5	122.9	501.6
1975–77	701.1	988.3	−287.2	825.0	139.0	686.0
1960–77	1,675.4	2,350.9	− 675.5	2,222.5	390.9	1,831.6

Source: Figures compiled from the Banco Central de Nicaragua.
*Does not include fuels.

Table 2.4

Nicaragua: Value of Exports by Sector of Origin
(in percentages)

Period	Agriculture	Industrial	Others	Total
1960–64	66.2	21.2	12.6	100.0
1965–69	62.0	31.4	6.6	100.0
1970–74	48.0	50.5	1.5	100.0
1975–77	52.0	46.2	1.8	100.0

Source: Figures compiled from the Banco Central de Nicaragua.

structure was designed on the regional integration scheme, when the latter fell into crisis at the end of the 1960s, this scheme had to operate with higher margins of idle capacity.[2]

Without dismissing a certain specialization in agrochemicals, agroindustry (milk products, sugar), and metal-mechanics, the diversification of industrial production has been minimal in the last two decades. In 1979 the processing of foodstuffs, drinks, and tobacco provided 60 percent of total industrial value added, practically the same as in 1969 (63 percent).

The capacity for generating employment was also small. The economically active population (EAP) in industry went from 11.6 percent of the total in 1963 to 12.3 percent in 1971 and 9.6 percent in 1975; in absolute figures it grew from 55,631 workers the first year to 62,864 the last (a growth of only 7,233 in 12 years). As the agrarian sector expelled the work force toward the cities, where industry generated little employment, it was the tertiary sector that had to give refuge to the migrant workers and the new urban labor supply. The EAP in the service sector doubled between 1963 and 1975, growing from 65,546 people to 131,945 (from 33 percent to 39 percent of the total EAP). In that latter year 70 percent of the EAP could be found in nonproductive sectors, against 61 percent in 1963 (Table 2.5).

Capitalism grew with profound intersectorial, spatial, and, obviously, social inequalities, reinforcing the disarticulation in the economy (between agriculture and industry) and aggravating its sub-

Table 2.5
Nicaragua: EAP by Branch of Activity, 1963 and 1975

Activity	1963			1975		
	Thousands	*Percent*		*Thousands*	*Percent*	
Total	*479.9*	*100.0*		*654.6*	*100.0*	
Agricultural	283.1	59.0		313.5	48.0	
Nonagricultural	196.8	41.0	*100.0*	341.1	52.0	*100.0*
Mining			2.0			1.4
Manufacturing industry			28.2			18.4
Construction			8.0			8.1
Electricity, gas and water			0.6			1.4
Total productive			*38.8*			*29.3*
Commerce, hotels, and restaurants			17.5			21.9
Transport, warehousing, and communications			6.1			6.5
Financial establishments			4.0			3.4
Personal services			33.2			38.6
Total nonproductive			*60.8*			*70.4*
Others, nonspecified			0.4			0.3

Source: Censo Nacional de Población, 1963; and Oficina de Ejecución de Estadísticas.

Table 2.6
Income Distribution in Central America and Other Countries

Recipient (%)	Nicar.[a]	Costa R.[b]	El Sal.[b]	Hond.[b]	Guat.[b]	D.R.[c]	Arg.[d]
Top 5	28	22.8	15.4	21.8	35.0	38	21.4
Next 15	32	27.9	49.4	29.5	23.9	15	26.0
Middle 30	25	28.5	22.8	25.2	23.8	27.	29.4
Bottom 50	15	20.8	12.4	23.5	17.3	20	23.2
Total	100	100.0	100.0	100.0	100.0	100	100.0
Polarization index	18.6	11.2	15.0	9.2	20.0	19.0	10.7

[a] 1977. Source: CEPAL (1979).

[b] Source: Rosenthal (1982), table 8. Costa Rica: 1971; El Salvador: 1974; Honduras: 1976–79; Guatemala 1976.

[c] 1969. Source: Vilas (1973), table 12. The information corresponds only to the city of Santo Domingo.

[d] 1970. Source: Vilas (1974), table XX. The information corresponds to the metropolitan area.

Polarization index: $(Y_5/P_5):(Y_{50}/P_{50})$, where Y_5, Y_{50} represent the percentage of income received by the top 5 percent and the bottom 50 percent of the population, P (respectively, P_5 and P_{50}).

ordination to the exterior. Growth was limited fundamentally to the Pacific region (the departments of Managua, León, Chinandega, Carazo, Masaya, and Granada) and to a few social groups. Toward the end of the Somoza period the "heart" of the agroexports absorbed a maximum of some 500,000 manzanas—130,000 in coffee, 250,000 in cotton, 60,000 in sugarcane and others—of a total of almost 7,000,000 manzanas: less than 10 percent of the farmed land. But, given its intensive labor character, it controlled almost 54 percent of the rural work force (Baumeister 1982). Per capita GDP grew in real terms (1978 prices) from U.S. $451 in 1950 to U.S. $595 in 1960, U.S. $898 in 1965 and U.S. $955 in 1975, reaching U.S. $966 in 1977, but its distribution was markedly unequal. That of the bottom 50 percent of the population in this last year was less than $300 per year and represented 15 percent of the total GDP, while the top 20 percent concentrated 60 percent of the product with an average of almost U.S. $3,000 per year (CEPAL 1979)

Income distribution followed the same pattern. In Table 2.6 Nicaraguan income distribution shortly before the triumph is compared to that of the other Central American countries and of two other countries outside the region: one with a similar pattern of economic and political development—the Dominican Republic—and the other which offered a very different type of development—Argentina. From it we can see that income polarization in Nicaragua is the greatest in Central America, with the exception of Guatemala, and almost equal to that in the Dominican Republic.

This type of agroindustrial capitalism created a marked difference between production for export and production of basic grains for the internal market. The best lands, technological improvements, and techniques of capitalist exploitation were concentrated in the export sector, with the result that production of basic grains, on which the reproduction of the work force rests, was left in profound backwardness. At the beginning of the 1970s only 3 percent of the farms used fertilizers, and only 14 percent used insecticides. At the beginning of the current decade the technical level of this sector remained extremely primitive: according to recent estimates, 75 percent of the production of basic grains is carried out with the use of a handspike.[3] Production for the internal market declined during the 1950s and per capita production of corn and beans stagnated after 1960 despite an increase in the amount of land cultivated. Local food supply depended in large measure on imports, but even then did not reach the entire population.[4]

Thanks to their capacity to generate foreign exchange, agroexports have been the source of finance for imports of industrial inputs, final consumption goods, and for payment on the foreign debt inherited from the Somoza period. For this reason the Nicaraguan agroexport sector has been viewed as the equivalent of "department I" in Marx's *Capital,* at times even playing the role of "heavy industry" (Fitzgerald 1982a).

This analogy is the unhappy product of a focus on appearances, and confuses the issue. In the first place, while it is theoretically true that primary materials are means of production, it is one thing to view petroleum, iron, or bauxite in this way, and entirely another to so regard coffee, beef, sugar, shrimp, or hides, products that make up two-thirds of Nicaragua's agroexports. In the second place, the supply of means of production is spatially located outside the Nicaraguan economy and thus mediated by an international market controlled by imperialism and subject to the laws of unequal exchange. This means that the role of Nicaraguan exports as the "means of production of foreign exchange" has always been prob-

Table 2.7
Nicaragua: Effect of the Relation of Prices of Foreign Trade
(in millions of 1980 U.S. dollars, cumulative 5-year periods)

Period	Effect
1960–64	+ 132.8
1965–69	− 1,268.7
1970–74	− 3,408.1
1975–77	− 3,687.3
1960–77	− 8,231.3

Source: Banco Central de Nicaragua.

lematic. Between 1960 and 1978, due to the deterioration of the terms of exchange, Nicaragua accumulated a negative balance of more than U.S. $8 billion (Table 2.7), a circumstance that, peculiarly, is never mentioned. Finally, a large share of imports consisted of consumer goods—food, to be sure, but also nonbasic consumer goods for the high-income groups. Industrial inputs, except those for agrochemical production, were also destined for the production of industrial merchandise for middle- and high-income group consumption—fundamentally in the cities and for the other countries of the isthmus, thanks to the regional integration scheme. As with many other countries of the third world, Nicaraguan capitalism specialized in the production of means of consumption, leaving "department I" located within the dominant economy.

Agroindustrial disarticulation was reinforced by the extremely low level of agricultural processing: 50 percent of production went to local consumption or was exported without any industrial processing whatever, and the rest consisted of beef, sugarcane, milk products, or other such products, with very little value added in processing.

The agroindustrial system worked to fuel the consumption patterns of the dominant groups and reinforced the general vulnerability of the economy. The negative balances in commercial exchange combined with payments for services, utilities, and so on translated into systematic drops in the balance of payments current account and a growing external indebtedness (Table 2.8). In 1975 almost 55 percent of total investment was financed with foreign resources, while in 1970 it was only 26 percent. The total foreign debt, which in 1950 was no more than U.S. $2 million, and by 1960 had reached $22 million, was $145 million in 1970, $466 million in 1974, and had reached $900 million in 1977. Only political loyalty to the United States and, especially, the virulent anticommunism of Somoza's foreign policy guaranteed the financial assistance necessary to relieve the most visible effects of this external vulnerability.

In reality, foreign exchange income facilitated the accumulation of some local financial groups as well as "Somocismo" itself. In 1963 the Central Bank eliminated foreign exchange controls and established free-money convertibility. This mechanism, plus the existence of cheap dollars due to the overvaluation of the cordoba, facilitated the flight of surplus generated in agroexports and industry, naturally at the price of a growing external debt.

The entire system was based on intense exploitation of the work force. Efficiency and international competitiveness of the agroexport system as well as capacity for foreign indebtedness ultimately depended on *appropriate treatment* of the labor question. The miserable living and working conditions for the agricultural and industrial proletariat, the peasantry, the working masses in general (men, women, and children), were combined with high levels of unemployment and underemployment, low and irregular incomes, begging, overcrowding, and premature death. The backwardness in the basic grain sector necessitated greater labor time in production than was

Table 2.8
Nicaragua: External Vulnerability of the Economy, 1970–78

Years	External Opening (percentage)[a]	Import Coefficient[b]	Commercial Balance millions US$)[c]	Current Account Balance (millions US$)[d]	Indebtedness Coefficient[e]
1970	48.6	.256	− 20.1	− 38.1	.225
1971	48.1	.254	− 23.2	− 42.8	.258
1972	53.1	.248	− 30.9	− 21.7	.290
1973	55.3	.299	− 49.0	− 65.1	.317
1974	61.9	.369	− 180.7	− 256.7	.331
1975	56.1	.325	− 141.7	− 184.1	.405
1976	58.1	.288	+ 9.8	− 38.7	.368
1977	66.3	.361	− 125.1	− 182.0	.315
1978	61.6	.295	+ 52.0	− 25.0	.373

Sources: [a](X + M)/GDP × 100: Elaboration of INEC figures.
[b] M/GDP: INEC and CEPAL.
[c] INEC and BCN (Banco Central de Nicaragua).
[d] CEPAL.
[e] Debt balance/GDP: INEC.

remunerated to workers, thus in Marxist terms created more value, via superexploitation of the work force.

The disarticulation and foreign dependency that shaped the economy were in turn reproduced by it. The surplus extracted brutally from the working masses throughout the society, but above all in agroexports, was incorporated into the worldwide process of capital accumulation controlled by imperialism by means of unequal exchange, remittances on foreign investment capital, and foreign indebtedness, all mediated through local dominant groups. It will be useful to detail some specific aspects of this dependent capitalism, in order to better understand Nicaragua's economic and class structure as well as to illuminate the postrevolutionary period and the debates that took place in the first four years: What to do with industry? How to face the urban question? What kind of agrarian reform? What are the conditions for a worker-peasant alliance? What treatment to give small landholdings?

AN UNEQUALLY DEVELOPED PROLETARIAT

The kind of agroindustrial capitalism that developed in Nicaragua generated an unequally developed proletariat, with a tremendous occupational instability and an unfinished process of separation from the means of production and a family source of subsistence. This has led to frequent comments regarding the small size of the Nicaraguan proletariat, especially compared to simple petty mercantile production. The lack of updated statistics—the last population census was in 1971—has meant working with estimates, which point up the scanty size of the permanent agricultural proletariat compared to the huge labor force which does salaried work for no more than two or three months a year—in the agroexport harvests—and then returns to nonsalaried forms of labor.

Possibly the best-known work of this sort is that of Deere and Marchetti (1981). The authors estimate that toward the end of the 1970s the agricultural proletariat consisted of only some 33,000 people, or 7.5 percent of the agricultural EAP. This figure refers to landless laborers who sell their labor power in a permanent fashion and who have stable work in some agricultural enterprise. Apart from this miniscule rural working class, there exists what the authors call the agricultural *subproletariat*, consisting of workers who sell their labor power seasonally, for lack of stable employment. This comprises some 138,000 people, or 32 percent of the agricultural EAP; the short span of salaried work is spent in coffee and cotton harvests, and the rest in nonsalaried occupations. Deere and Marchetti thus established a marked differentiation between the rural workers with stable employment and those who lack it, changing jobs based on fluctuations in demand for labor power. This situation has raised doubts about the truly proletarian character of these workers. Finally, there is a *semiproletariat* of poor peasants, *minifundistas* whose families cannot live from the product of their tiny farms and are obliged to sell their labor power to other producers. They encompass some 165,000 people, or 38 percent of the agricultural EAP.

I think that these estimates undervalue the real magnitude of the *permanent* rural proletariat and give a distorted image of the class structure of the country. In particular, the notion of *subproletariat* is confusing. Since the weakness is conceptual as well as empirical, I will formulate an alternative concept before contrasting their data with more adequate information.

The concept of *proletarianization of the labor force* refers to the way in which direct producers are related to the means of production and confront capital: a relation of dispossession and of opposition. Their salaried situation derives from this relation, but it is not a mechanical derivation, since it is mediated by the effective possibility each worker has to find a salaried job. Whether or not it is found, the worker's condition as a proletarian is not altered.

Consequently the seasonality of this or that activity—in this case the harvest of exportable agricultural products—determines the seasonality of work, but does not in turn make the class situation of the labor force seasonal. *What is seasonal is employment, not the class or fraction that fills this employment.* The labor force does not cease being proletarianized by the fact that its labor relation with a given capitalist ends; it continues being proletarian with respect to capital in general. Workers affected by this cyclical movement of demand for labor power and by the general level of agricultural activity have been forced to seek other occupations or to endure longer or shorter periods of unemployment, but none of this detracts from their proletarian character.

Although the available information is incomplete, it tends to confirm this view. The survey of cotton pickers carried out in January 1981 by the Ministry of Labor-CSUCA cooperative research project points up the contrast between the seasonality of work in agroexport and the permanency of the workers' proletarian condition throughout the year. An average of 71 percent of the cotton pickers maintained their position as salaried workers during the entire year (Table 2.9). The average is higher in the department of Chinandega than in León, and suggests the existence of greater proletarianization there. As a complement, the average for nonsalaried workers (self-employed, or nonremunerated family workers) is noticeably higher in León.

Taking a base of 100 as the average number of salaried workers in the months of the cotton harvest (December, January, and February), an average of 84.5 percent stayed in this condition throughout the year—here again in more pronounced fashion in Chinandega than in León (Table 2.10).

During the months when there is no harvest, the "freed" salaried cotton workers basically move to the service sector (57 percent), agriculture for the domestic market (18.4 percent), construction (15 percent), cattle ranches (8 percent), or whatever, but *always as salaried workers*. The greatest change, from salaried workers to self-employment, is registered among those who move to production of basic grains, but even here the figure is barely significant (7 percent).

These results are consistent with those obtained for cotton and coffee pickers by the Agrarian Reform Research Center (CIERA) in 1981. Sixty-seven percent of the cotton pickers and 61 percent of the coffee pickers were landless before the revolutionary triumph.[5] Coincidentally, 62 percent of the labor time of the work force of families of cotton pickers, and almost 48 percent of that of families of coffee pickers, was absorbed by some kind of salaried activity—in agroexport, in agricultural production for the domestic market, or in nonagricultural activities; the latter accounted for 17 percent of the labor time for families of cotton pickers and 15 percent of that of coffee pickers.

In synthesis, the extent of proletarianization of the agricultural work force appears considerably higher than generally recognized. The *seasonal character of employment* in agroexport harvests does not seem to be an obstacle for the *permanent character of proletarianization* of an important part of the work force. Both by its lack of means of production (fundamentally land) and by the predominant type of labor (salaried), this mass of workers clearly constitutes a *proletarian* work force. The designation of *seasonal* proletariat is deceptive because it projects the adjective about the activity (harvest) onto the class situation of the subject that occupies the position and carries out the activity. The notion of *subproletariat* further confuses the issue. If one must find a qualifier for this fraction of the agricultural proletariat, I think that the most appropriate one is *itinerant proletariat,* in that its proletarian condition is expressed in this mobility between occupations and sectors of the economy.

The 1971 population census allows us to see that the proletarianization process of the rural labor force was much more advanced than later estimates would have suggested. According to this source, agricultural salaried workers amounted to almost 109,000 workers and represented 41 percent of the EAP of the sector; as the census was carried out in April, these results were not affected by the seasonal increase in agricultural employment between December and February. This census is the last that has been carried out to date, so current figures can only be estimated. Projecting the results of that census, combined with results of recent studies by the agrarian reform research center, CIERA, and the Ministry of Labor, we can estimate that toward the end of the 1970s the agricultural proletariat averaged between 120,000 and 130,000 (approximately one-third of the agricultural EAP). Only some 50,000 would have had permanent salaried employment throughout the year, while the rest had fixed employment for only two or three months at a maximum.[6] The rest of the year they functioned as an *itinerant proletariat* that, once the cotton and coffee harvest season had passed, moved to urban services, construction, or whatever, generally maintaining their salaried conditions.[7]

Apart from this permanent proletariat there exists a vast *semi-proletariat* of poor peasants, *minifundists,* who cannot live from the product of their farm (owned or rented), and who are obliged to sell their labor force to other producers. According to some estimates (Deere and Marchetti 1981) this fraction represents two-thirds of the peasantry and amounts to almost 165,000 people, or more than a third of the agricultural EAP. Clearly this is a segment of the labor force whose movement toward proletarianization is already in process. The impoverishment of the small peasantry and the seasonality of employment in agroexports forces these workers to suffer a process of *proletarianization-deproletarianization;* said another way, this is one of the peculiar forms of the proletarianization process of the agroexport capitalist model (Núñez 1980a: 39).

This process has no predictable end, not only because the revolu-

Table 2.9
Work Schedule of Salaried Cotton Pickers, 1980

Department	Months of the year												
	Jan	Feb	Mar	Apr	May	June	July	Aug	Sept	Oct	Nov	Dec	Average
Chinandega and León													
Salaried (%)	82	78	75	73	64	66	65	68	67	69	68	70	71
Nonsalaried (%)	18	22	25	27	36	34	35	22	33	31	32	30	29
Total	100	100	100	100	100	100	100	100	100	100	100	100	100
n	480	459	457	449	448	432	453	431	458	463	472	475	456
Chinandega													
Salaried (%)	85	83	79	74	69	70	71	72	71	75	75	76	75
Nonsalaried (%)	15	17	21	26	31	30	29	28	29	25	25	24	25
Total	100	100	100	100	100	100	100	100	100	100	100	100	100
n	297	280	281	274	275	277	280	270	281	287	296	299	283
León													
Salaried (%)	76	70	69	70	56	59	55	61	59	53	60	64	63
Nonsalaried (%)	24	30	31	30	44	41	45	39	41	47	40	36	37
Total	100	100	100	100	100	100	100	100	100	100	100	100	100
n	183	179	176	175	173	155	173	161	177	176	176	176	173

Source: Compiled from the Ministry of Labor/CSUCA cotton pickers survey, 1981.
Those interviewed were asked what kind of work they had carried out during each of the 12 months prior to the survey (January 1981).

Table 2.10

Level of Salaried Employment Among Cotton Pickers

Department	Months of the year										Average
	March	April	May	June	July	August	Sept.	Oct.	Nov.		
Chinandega and León	95	90	79	78	82	81	84	88	90		84.5
Chinandega	94	86	80	81	84	83	85	91	94		86
León	98	98	78	73	77	78	84	82	84		83

Source: Compiled from results of the Ministry of Labor/CSUCA survey of cotton pickers, 1981.
Average for December, January, and February equals 100.

Table 2.11
Nicaragua: Estimation of the Rural Class Structure at
the End of the 1970s

Fraction	EAP	
	Percentage	*× 1,000*
Proletariat	29.3	125.0
Semiproletariat (poor peasants)	38.4	164.5
Middle peasants	22.3	95.5
Wealthy peasants	8.0	34.5
Bourgeoisie	2.0	9.0
Total	100.0	485.5

Source: Based on figures of INEC, MIPLAN, MITRAB, CIERA, and MIDINRA.

tion has introduced profound cuts in it, but also because of the tight and contradictory relationship between the plot of land and the salary. On the one hand, the lack of adequate land and other resources forces the peasant to take up salaried work during a certain period of the year—or, in the case of daughters who work in domestic service, all year long; on the other, the salary thus viewed contributes decisively to the re-creation of the peasant economy and reinforces the attachment of the producer to his land.

Be that as it may, it is evident that the dependence of the economy on a few export crops has repercussions within the working population, forcing workers into migratory movements in response to the harvest calendar and the spatial location of the activities. If the semiproletariat of peasant origin is added to the *itinerant* fraction of the agricultural workers, we end up with between 230,000 and 240,000 workers in these conditions of occupational/spatial displacement.

By the end of the 1970s the Nicaraguan class structure could be broken down as indicated in Table 2.11.

Contrary to the usual picture, *the process of proletarianization of the labor force is broader in the rural than the urban sector.* At the end of the 1970s the urban working class was about 113,000 workers (in industry, construction, transport, energy production, and assimilated industries), or 20 percent of the nonagricultural EAP. The limited capacity of the kind of industrialization developed since the 1960s to generate employment, together with the pre-existing urban economy, tended to create self-employment, petty commerce, artisanal production, and personal services among a large proportion of the already existing active population, as well as among the new urban and urbanized labor force.

Nevertheless, to the degree to which proletarianization signifies *dispossession* of workers with respect to their means of production and subsistence, and not necessarily industrial *salarization,* it is clear that proletarianization was far-reaching, notwithstanding its slow development. It is also clear that a large proportion of the working masses was subordinated to capital in a formal manner—that is to say from outside the process of work itself—more than in a real one.

Table 2.12 shows the progressive displacement of artisan production during the 1960s in the industrial sector, and the corollary growth of an increasingly proletarianized labor force. It is worth noting that along with this increase in industrial proletarianization there was also a growth of petty-bourgeois technicians and professionals, and a burgeoning stratum of administrative and managerial employees.

If on the one hand the proletarianization process was more advanced in the countryside than in the city in both absolute and relative terms, on the other the proletariat concentrations were greater in the city than in the countryside. Taking as an approximate indicator the salaried worker/employer relation, in 1971 this relation was 13.9 salaried workers per employer in the rural sector, 28.8 in the manufacturing and construction industries, and 35.6 in the totality of nonagricultural economic activities. At the end of the decade, 75

Table 2.12
Nicaragua: Composition of the EAP in Industry
(in percentages)

Occupational category	1963	1971
Artisans and laborers	91.5	72.8
Workers and apprentices	0.8	5.7
Office employees	3.5	6.7
Professionals, technicians, etc.	0.6	3.7
Managers, administrators, and directors	0.8	2.5
Others	2.8	8.6
Total	100.0	100.0

Source: De Franco and Hurtado de Vijil (1978).

percent of the industrial workers were concentrated in factories that averaged more than 170 labor posts (INEC 1981b).

In more or less the same period, laborers received the lowest income of all urban workers, even including workers in the informal sector. According to data collected by a mid-1976 survey of the urban employment situation, with an average value of 100 corresponding to total urban economic activities, the monthly income of workers equaled 35.9, compared to 55.2 for artisans, 44.6 for service workers, 196.3 for professionals, and 274.5 for managers (OEDEC 1976).

Nothing is farther from reality, then, than the image of an industrial proletariat in a *privileged* working and income situation relative to the rest of the urban working masses. As will be seen in the next chapter, the low income levels were joined by serious labor instability and wretched working conditions, all within the framework of bosses' arbitrariness and a repressive institutional climate.

At the same time this small industrial working class was highly dispersed in the urban socioeconomic landscape, living together with a mass of nonsalaried, or salaried but nonproductive, workers, which easily surpassed them in both relative and absolute terms. Approximately one-third of the nonagricultural EAP (some 150,000 people) consisted of nonproductive workers—administrative employees in the private and public sectors, salaried informal sector workers, and so on—and almost 40 percent consisted of artisans, petty merchants, tradespeople, and in general self-employed or non-remunerated family workers in the petty production and petty property sector.

These marked imbalances, added to the skimpy salaries and in many cases a relatively brief proletarian, or urban, experience, somewhat obscure the separation between the laboring class and the nonproletarianized workers. This is true above all in terms of the reproduction of the work force, where in a large number of cases the salary was combined with a thousand forms of petty commerce, simple mercantile production, informal sector services (or pseudo-services), and so on. Available studies indicate that the proletarian family—given the relativity that this concept implies in an economy such as that of Nicaragua—does not reproduce itself exclusively, and at times not even *principally,* on the basis of a salary. The income contributed by the work of minors (as street vendors, shoeshiners, car watchers, etc.) and of women (through preparation and sale of food, petty commerce, sale of fruit and vegetables, taking in washing and ironing, etc.) frequently surpasses the amount of the laborer's salary.[8]

The unequal pace of proletarianization in the countryside and the city, the complex forms of articulation of the urban working class with simple mercantile production and petty commerce, and the strong weight that the nonproductive population acquires in the cities frame the question of how a worker-peasant alliance should be developed. If this alliance has traditionally been thought of as an urban-rural process (workers in the city, peasants in the countryside), in Nicaragua it is in an important sense a rural-rural issue, in that the agricultural proletariat constitutes the majority of the working class. This is made more complicated by the differences between rural and industrial workers, and by the framework of an urban pole in which the majority of nonproletarianized working masses demand their share of the benefits of such an alliance.

SMALL AND MEDIUM PRODUCTION

The unequal character of capitalist development has determined not only different levels of proletarianization, but also distinct levels of concentration of property and production in one or another sector of the society. The early appearance of oligopolistic forms of industrial and financial capital contrasts with an agrarian structure in which the middle-sized producers were able to hold their own.

Table 2.13 shows the distribution of land in the 1960s in each of the Central American countries and in the region as a whole. Nicaragua and Costa Rica are the countries where large, multifamily farms (the large agrarian bourgeoisie) had the greatest concentration of land. But Nicaragua is also the country where the medium-sized family and multifamily units (the small and middle rural bourgeoisie) had greater weight in the tenure structure: almost half the total units with more than half the land.[9] In Costa Rica these same strata had a similar share of land, but their participation in the total number of farms was a third less than in Nicaragua. The difference is observed in the proportionally much higher number of subfamily farms (minifundist peasants) in Costa Rica and other countries in the region than in Nicaragua.

In Nicaragua the medium-sized multifamily farms not only represent a greater proportion, but their absolute weight is stronger than in the other countries of the isthmus. In El Salvador there are a few

Table 2.13
Central America: Land Distribution by Farm Size, 1960s (in percentages)

Size of Groups	Central America		Costa Rica		El Salvador		Guatemala		Honduras		Nicaragua	
	No.	Land	No.	Land	No.	Land	No.	Land	No.	Land	No.	Land
Subfamily	78.9	9.8	68.0	3.2	91.4	21.9	88.4	14.3	67.5	12.4	50.8	3.5
Family	15.0	16.2	19.8	14.2	6.7	20.6	9.5	13.5	26.4	27.4	27.4	11.2
Medium-sized multifamily	5.6	35.6	11.3	41.2	1.5	19.8	2.0	31.4	5.7	32.7	20.3	44.1
Large multi-family	0.5	38.4	0.9	41.4	0.4	37.7	0.1	40.8	0.4	27.5	1.5	41.2
Total	100	100	100	100	100	100	100	100	100	100	100	100

Sources: CEPAL, FAO, OIT, IICA, SIECA, OCT, and OEA (1972).

more than 3,000 farms of this sort, in Costa Rica some 13,000, and in Guatemala around 7,000, compared to more than 20,000 in Nicaragua. At the same time the agricultural family income generated by these farms was much less in Nicaragua (U.S. $2,248 annually) than in most of the region: $8,000 in Guatemala, something more than $7,100 in El Salvador, and much farther from the average annual family income generated in the large multifamily farms of those respective countries: 88 percent less in Nicaragua, compared to 80 percent less in Guatemala, 73 percent less in El Salvador (CEPAL/FAO/OIT/IICA/SIECA/OCT/OEA 1972).

All of this suggests that for the second half of this century the great hacienda was no longer predominant in Nicaragua—unlike in Guatemala and El Salvador. In this sense the figures about land tenure, number of farms, and levels of income are consistent with my view of the proletarianization of the agricultural labor force. Together with this advanced proletarianization of the rural workers, the marked weight of the rural medium bourgeoisie is one of the central features of the Nicaraguan agrarian structure and shows a clear difference with regard to its neighbors.

The tenure pattern is repeated with regard to production. Table 2.14 shows the distribution of agricultural production by size of farm. The peasantry contributes one-quarter of the total product, and the medium-sized bourgeoisie almost half. Small producers account for more production in basic grains than in exportables. In cattle raising, half of the total production is in the hands of small producers, although their herds are oriented mainly to the internal market. It is similar in coffee: four-fifths of production was in the hands of small and medium-sized producers, although 70 percent of the production for the world market was controlled by the large owners (Wheelock 1976: 143). But even in cotton, almost 60 percent of the production was carried out by small and medium growers.

The large agrarian bourgeoisie represented in all only a third of rural production, with a decisive participation in just two categories: sugarcane and rice—both of them capital intensive and linked to agroindustry.

In the nonagricultural sector the picture is much less defined, but equally appreciable. Fifty-four percent of the industrial establishments employ less than five people each and can be characterized as artisanal. Excluding these, we can approximate the situation in the manufacturing sector (Table 2.15). The small establishments (those

Table 2.14
Nicaragua: Distribution of Agricultural Production
by Size of Producer, 1971

Producers	Cotton	Coffee	Beef[a]	Sugarcane	Rice	Sorghum	Corn	Beans	Total
Small[b]	6	22	52	4	9	34	32	59	25
Medium[c]	52	58	29	18	18	28	57	38	45
Large[d]	42	20	19	78	73	38	11	3	30
Total	100	100	100	100	100	100	100	100	100

Source: E. Baumeister (1982).
[a] Small: up to 200 manzanas; medium: 201 to 1,000 manzanas; large: more than 1,000 manzanas.
[b] Up to 50 manzanas.
[c] From 51 to 500 manzanas.
[d] More than 500 manzanas.

with less than 30 workers per establishment) constitute 83 percent of the total and generate only 24 percent of employment and 10 percent of the value added. Medium industry, for its part (from 30 to 99 work posts per establishment), with 10 percent of the establishments and 18 percent of the personnel, generate 28 percent of the value added.

However, the differences in size—in terms of average employment and value added per establishment—do not reflect equivalent differences in terms of productivity or efficiency; the large firms are not necessarily more productive or efficient than the smaller ones.[10]

Small industry includes nearly 8,000 establishments, with 37 percent of industrial employment (almost 28,000 workers) and around 18 percent of gross production value (GPV).[11] As shown in Table 2.16, 85 percent of the establishments and 83 percent of employment is concentrated in only four branches. Ninety-six percent of the GPV goes to the internal market, although in 1980 this sector generated exports at a value of almost U.S. $9 million—the majority (97 percent) directed to the Central American market. The largest export category is shoes and leather products (55 percent), followed by clothing (31 percent). In general, small industry exports are effected by numerous individual merchants who go with the merchandise to the neighboring countries, in an international version of the old figure of the tradesperson. Almost 40 percent of employment generated by small industry corresponds to nonremunerated family workers, but in establishments with less than three workers this figure rises to 57 percent. Seventy-seven percent of the establishments are

Table 2.15
Nicaragua: Structure of the Industrial Sector,
by Size of Employment, 1980 (in percentages)

Personnel	Establishments	Employment	Remunerations	Value added
5 to 9	59.3	13.0	7.4	3.9
10 to 29	24.2	11.6	10.0	5.8
30 to 49	4.7	5.7	5.7	3.6
50 to 99	5.6	12.5	13.1	24.2
100 and above	6.2	57.2	63.6	62.5
Total	100.0	100.0	100.0	100.0
	1,412	45,040	1,256.8*	3,941.8*

Source: Elaboration of INEC figures (1981b).
*Millions of cordobas

Table 2.16
Nicaragua: Small Industry, 1980

Branches	Establishments (%)	Employment (%)
Food	28.4	28.3
Shoes and leather	22.3	22.2
Clothing	20.0	20.0
Wood and furniture	13.6	12.7
Others	15.7	16.8
Total	100.0	100.0

Source: Ministry of Industry (1980).

located at the home of the proprietor—83 percent in food, 80 percent in clothing, 81 percent in shoes, and 74 percent in wood products and furniture.

Due to its magnitude and its articulation within the economy as a whole, this petty industry cannot be thought of as *marginal*. Its production satisfies the demand of broad sectors of the market—including medium- and high-income groups. The notion of a kind of parallel industrial market for lesser income groups, filled by this small industrial production, is thus also invalid in the Nicaraguan case. This petty industry competes for the same market with medium and large industry, and in some categories manages to control significant portions of it: shoes, clothing, bakery products, and printed matter are examples. Nor is it a *traditional* sector; it participates actively in exports and is an important input importer. In the clothing industry, 87 percent of the inputs utilized in 1980 were imported (cloth, dyes, thread), in printing 83 percent, and in chemicals 66 percent.

By contrast, the large bourgeoisie is involved very little in direct productive activity, though this differs markedly between the agricultural and the industrial sectors. In the former, the large bourgeoisie effectively represents a small proportion of production, while in the latter it generates more than 80 percent of the value added and two-thirds of employment, representing an oligopolistic concentration of capital. The small size of the country, its small population, the concentration of income in minority groups, all favored the tendencies toward concentration of the industrial-urban economy and allowed it to reach high levels of concentration earlier than in larger capitalist economies.

Where the large local bourgeoisie participates most strongly is in commercial and financial capital. Especially since the 1950s, financial capital has been the core of their economic power and the arena of their interaction with imperialism and with the state. Thus it was the control of financial and commercial capital in the broadest sense—banks and financial companies, real estate operations, securities and exchange, financing of productive activities, imports and exports—rather than control of means of production that gave this fraction control of the economy.

Contrary to what has been observed in other Latin American countries, the absence of ties to the international market through a foreign enclave in Nicaragua did not mean that that tie was made by a large local bourgeoisie that primarily owned the means of export production. But nor did the participation in the export sector of small- and medium-sized national productive capitalists result in a parallel control of production. These fractions were subordinated through financing, commercialization, and agroindustrial processing to large local and foreign capital, and to the agencies of the dictatorial state. But the uniqueness of Nicaraguan capitalism, above all agrarian capitalism, did not consist only in the strong weight of small and medium production, but in the *mode in which they are articulated into the general cycle of capital* as well.

Without having to go farther, Costa Rica is also a country in which small property, even smaller than in Nicaragua, is a feature of the agrarian structure (Table 2.13). But the articulation of this mass of small producers with the agrarian bourgeoisie occurs in such a way that it generates the material base of a relatively stable political system and, for the last few years, one of doubtless legitimacy (see Stone 1975; Vega Carballo 1979). What in Costa Rica was interdependence and complementation between latifundio and minifundio, and between agriculture, commercialization, and processing, was in Nicaragua contradiction and exploitation. The reasons for this are several.

In the first place, a process of progressive fusion of commercial and financial capital with agroindustrial and productive capital in general developed relatively early in Nicaragua, producing a small but powerful collection of *financial groups*. These groups relatively quickly began to control a large share of activity in such sectors as construction, finances (banks, securities), commerce, agroindustry, manufactures, and real estate (see Strachan 1976; Wheelock 1976).

While the degree of control they exercised over the economy is frequently overestimated, these groups undeniably played a leading role in the direction of Nicaraguan capitalism, particularly in its most dynamic sectors, during the 1960s and 1970s, devising new and more efficient forms to subordinate other fractions of local capital and exploit the work force.

In the second place, the economic orientation of a good part of the large bourgeoisie—especially landowners—seems not to have been totally freed of elements that are not properly capitalist. Tenant farming of various types, for example, existed until the defeat of the dictatorship in 1979. Effective exploitation of vast landholdings demanded more working capital than landowners could manage, obliging them to either marginalize themselves from modernization or accept the conditions of the new groups of financial and commercial capitalists.

I have already pointed out that, unlike in Guatemala or El Salvador, the traditional hacienda is absolutely not the central element of the organization of Nicaragua's agricultural economy. But in any case the reduced participation in production of the large agrarian bourgeoisie contrasts vividly with the high concentration of land in their hands (Tables 2.13 and 2.14). This acutely polarized relation between tenure and production suggests a great deal of idleness and absenteeism; it has been estimated that 65 percent of the large landowners did not reside on their farms: half of them went to the countryside only during the harvest, and the rest only sporadically.

The political behavior of these groups affected their subordinate position. Lacking the ability, and possibly interest, to aspire to effective political power—which would have implied an open and direct confrontation with the dictatorship—they limited themselves in general to pressuring the state to concede some favorable treatment—in the form of credits, export facilities, fair competition, and the like.

Between this large landowning bourgeoisie and the minifundio was the eminently productive, self-made, medium-sized bourgeoisie, capable of organizing and directing the productive process—although its subordination to large commercial, financial and agroindustrial capital makes this relative. The employment of workers who are totally separated from the family unit is reduced—becoming seasonal in the case of agricultural products for export. These characteristics, plus the direct attention to the progress of production, and its incorporation, in the lower strata of the fraction, into productive tasks are connected with residence on the farm or in the urban nucleus of the area, and with a nonconsumer and modest lifestyle: what Baumeister (1982) called "chapiolla bourgeoisie." The surplus that finally remained in the hands of the producers was destined fundamentally for the satisfaction of their basic necessities and for productive recycling on the farm.[12]

Baumeister (1982, 1983) has analyzed the form in which the small and medium producers were subordinated to the financial, commercial, and agroindustrial capital of the Nicaraguan large bourgeoisie, imperialism, and the Somocista state. We have seen that the biggest part of agricultural and livestock production was in the hands of the sectors with a weak presence in the control of agroindustrial processing, internal and external commercialization, and banking or extra-banking finances. Reciprocally, the types of capital established outside of agricultural and livestock production (in commerce, finance, and processing) did not generate significant proportions of farm production. It is worth saying that while integration between direct production and its commercialization, financing, and industrial elaboration was weak, integration between these three spheres was tight.

In coffee, the owners of the drying enterprises were important buyers and even exporters, who at the same time financed their sellers (the direct producers). By the end of the Somocista period, one single firm commercialized more than 50 percent of the coffee production in the north-central zone (Matagalpa and Jinotega). Their dealings ranged from financing, drying, threshing, and the like, to purchase and export operations, passing through the sale of accessories, agricultural machinery, fertilizers, farm properties, and so on (Wheelock 1976: 144). In the cattle sector more than 30,000 producers were confronted with only seven export slaughterhouses, three export firms, and three banks. The large slaughterhouses—where the presence of Somocista capital was important—bought the cattle, financed the producers, and processed and exported the meat. Between 50 and 60 percent of the national slaughter was controlled by four large slaughterhouses for export, while the rest was dispersed among more than a hundred municipal ones.

In cotton, several thousand producers were connected to twenty-eight cotton gins, eleven export firms, and three banks—the most important of which was a state bank. Commercial-agroindustrial capital had a relatively smaller financial role in cotton than it did in either coffee or cattle, but it was somewhat more complex, since it included rental landlords as well as suppliers of agrochemicals and petroleum products. Between 50 and 60 percent of cotton production was carried out on rented lands, and the expansion of cultivation was effected by increasing the area rented; in the last years of Somocismo, land rent came to represent almost 25 percent of the producer's income (O. Núñez 1980a; Baumeister et al. 1983). The proportion of rented lands was greatest among medium producers; the large producers basically used their own lands and, in fact, frequently simulated rentals to members of their families. Seventy-five percent of the sales of raw cotton were controlled by the cotton gins and 90 percent of the sales of ginned cotton was in the hands of intermediaries (O. Núñez 1980a: 30). Agrochemicals were also controlled by a small number of private commercial houses, in several of which large producers had invested.

This contradiction between relatively high concentration of property in the nonagricultural sectors and the relative dispersion of farm production was reinforced by a strong dependence on credit. Toward the end of the Somocista period, banking credit in Nicaragua represented 62 percent of the value of the agricultural product, compared to 64 percent in Costa Rica, 25 percent in El Salvador, 31 percent in Honduras, and 10 percent in Guatemala (Baumeister 1982). But small producers had no access to banking credit and depended on the financing of wholesalers or agroindustrial capital, becoming thus forever indebted, trapped in a system of having to sell their harvests in advance without any ability to control prices. According to Orlando Núñez (1980a), 93 percent of ginned cotton was sold as futures, but only 13 percent of the growers knew the prices on the internal market, and hardly 11 percent knew those of the international market.[13]

The grower thus had to pay land rent, interest, and commercial rent to sectors located basically outside of production. Productive capital consequently appears subordinated to the commercial and financial capital of the large and foreign bourgeoisie. But in reality, this subordination expressed in turn the subordination of the Nicaraguan economy to the global economic system, and the articulation of the large bourgeoisie and the dictatorial state with this system.

These characteristics of the rural medium-sized producers favored the development of democratic and reformist tendencies. Since they did not base their productive activity on the exploitation of the work force, or did so in a reduced or seasonal fashion, they could see more clearly the various kinds of political oppression and of subordination to the landowners and large capital, without being able to transfer to the wage worker at least part of the cost of either. At the same time, the heterogeneity of these middle fractions with respect to their access to land and to the conditions of organizing production, generated equally heterogeneous and complex demands. Pressure for land combined with claims for better business conditions: credit, inputs, technical assistance, prices, favorable conditions for commercialization, and so on.

Contradictions with large landlord property and large commercial, financial, and agroindustrial capital became more acute in the 1970s, in a context of expansion of agricultural production and a rise in international prices. Evidence that the price bonanza was being appropriated exclusively by the large bourgeoisie, and that the Somocista state was participating actively in this unequal distribution of earnings and losses, deepened the contradictions and laid the groundwork for the FSLN policy of attracting support among these rural sectors.

But the dynamism of rural medium-sized producers and their demands on the dictatorial state and large bourgeoisie should not hide the fact of the vast peasant masses, who were unquestionably paying the bills of the existing economic system. In general terms the Nicaraguan peasantry at the end of the 1970s represented 60 percent of the rural EAP—some 260,000. It is estimated that approximately 22 percent were medium-sized peasant producers, and the rest minifundistas in the process of proletarianization, who moved into salary relations on a seasonal basis since their access to land did not generate sufficient subsistence income. Lacking sufficient or good land, with primitive production conditions, low yields, and lack of access to financing or technology, Nicaraguan peasants over the last thirty years have endured an accelerated process of expulsion from their original lands toward the frontier zones, first by cotton and later by export beef. Lack of access roads and low population density deepened the dispersion and spatial isolation of the class.

Yet as we have seen, with little more than 10 percent of the land they generated one-fourth of the agricultural product; thus their productive backwardness is not the same as *marginalization,* but rather expresses the conditions of exploitation and oppression through which the class was integrated into the economic structure.

The peasants, however, exhibit profound internal differences as a class, both in terms of endowment of economic factors and by historic origin and location. We can distinguish between the impoverished peasant of the Pacific zone, and the medium and rich peasant of the interior. In the case of the former, the development of agroexports created a large number of semiproletarian peasants, pushed onto the marginal lands of León and Chinandega by cotton, who functioned as a reserve labor force for the cotton harvest; in other departments of the same zone, on the other hand, they supply seasoned labor to the most modern cattle and coffee enterprises (Rivas, Carazo, Granada). These peasants sustain themselves through subsistence production (corn, beans, wheat) and seasonal work in agroexports; in some areas of the zone there are also very fragmented minifundia which combine the production of coffee on a very small scale, fruits, vegetables, and basic grains, with seasonal migrations to pick coffee (MIDINRA 1982c). Right up to the end of the 1970s, the monetary rent that they had to pay the landowners was combined with rent in labor and kind.

On the other hand, in the interior of the country a low level of capitalist development and the existence of a broad agricultural frontier fostered a medium and wealthy peasantry based on coffee and cattle production in the zones where the latifundia had not penetrated. The medium and wealthy peasants of Matagalpa, Jinotega, and parts of Boaco and Chontales coexist with coffee and cattle exploitation and take advantage of the existing infrastructure. If in the Pacific zone the lack of sufficient land and the burden of land rent constituted the principal problem, for the coffee peasants further inland it was centered more on lack of capital and labor, and for the cattle ranchers it was the lack of sufficient land to increase their herds (MIDINRA 1982c). For their part, the medium peasants of the agricultural frontier (Nueva Segovia, northern Jinotega, Madriz) practiced a migratory agriculture in relatively extensive productive units over which their control was precarious. The system of preparing the land (slash and burn) and the lack of a sufficient labor force only allowed them to put very small portions of land into production each year.[14] In the large majority of cases, they were peasants expelled from their lands by the development of coffee and cattle in the region; their principal problem was the lack of conditions (technology, labor force, credit) that would permit them to exploit large areas of their land and lack of infrastructure (access roads) for commercialization (G. Baez 1981; Morales 1981). This compelled some of them to sell their labor power for the coffee harvest. Finally, in the dry zone of this region (from northern Nueva Segovia, through Madriz, Estelí and the southeast of Matagalpa), one finds subsistence peasants who make up the army of coffee and tobacco harvesters. Here one also encounters the highest indices of rural poverty, and the predominance of precapitalist forms (sharecropping, labor rent, etc.) articulated to the extensive cattle ranches.

In the urban area, on the other hand, small and medium businesses both accumulated capital and reproduced themselves on the same bases as did large capital: exploitation of the labor force. Though to the extent to which large capital expropriated part of the surplus of the lesser fractions through mechanisms such as the generation of monopoly rents, differences of productivity, the type of interest on lending capital, and so on, their interests were contradictory, regarding the working class, their interests were the same. It has already been pointed out that these lesser fractions of capital are not much less efficient than the large bourgeoisie, and although the rate of surplus value that they extract from their labor force is lower than that extracted by large capital—denoting in some cases elements of management of the labor force that are not strictly capitalist—this difference is in general less than the difference in size of the respective establishments or capitals.

Thus the way in which contradictions within the urban bourgeoisie were resolved was to increase pressure on the work force: the labor policy of the Somocista state and its repressive apparatus were always at the service of the bosses' demands for a "hard hand" and worker discipline. In this the unity of the class showed itself to be very solid. As a result, the development of democratic, anti-imperialist, and revolutionary positions took place in the cities fundamentally among the artisans and in the sphere of small personal or family property.

WEAK DIRECT FOREIGN ECONOMIC PRESENCE

Foreign capital was never determinant in Nicaragua's economic structure, as the means of production were always fundamentally in the hands of local capitalists and producers. Foreign investments in such sectors as bananas, wood, and mining were relatively small. The plantation enclave on the Honduran, or even Costa Rican or Guatemalan, model was virtually nonexistent in Nicaragua, and the participation of these areas in the country's economic activity and in its articulation to the international system through exports had been receding for several decades before the revolution.

The high point of banana production by the U.S. corporations (United Fruit/Standard Brands, and Standard Fruit/Castle & Cooke) had been reached in the 1930s, but even then its role was secondary to coffee (Velázquez 1977). The latter was always in the hands of local producers, as was later true of cotton and beef exports. From this perspective, Nicaragua was a case of "national control of the productive system" of exports in all the periods of "expansion from outside" (Cardoso and Faletto 1969). However, the property of the export sector did not prepare the ground for its effective control, because foreign participation, however weak in the sphere of production, was much stronger in commercialization and financing, as well as in the determination of external prices. This permitted foreign capital to subordinate local production with very little direct investment in it.

With the cotton boom and the Central American Common Market, direct foreign, particularly U.S., investments increased, but always on a small scale. Between 1959 and 1969 they went from U.S. $18.7 million to U.S. $76.3 million, and were increasingly oriented toward manufacturing. In the middle of the 1970s Nicaragua was receiving only 9.4 percent (U.S. $90 million) of all direct investment in the isthmus by the advanced industrial countries, and by 1977–78 only 15 percent of the 614 transnational firms with operations in Central America were situated in Nicaragua; 86 percent of these firms were of U.S. origin (Castillo 1980a). Just before the fall of the dictatorship it was established that total foreign investments in the country were somewhere between $95 and $130 million.

In addition to the manufacturing sector, 71 percent of the foreign companies operated in the chemical industry and in agroindustry. Direct foreign investment tended, therefore, to specialize in areas that complemented export activity: inputs, processing, and so on, in a process that did not displace local producers from ownership of the means of production in the most strategic sectors of the economy, but which in the end subordinated them to foreign capital.

The strong external dependence of the Nicaraguan economy was consequently created with relatively little direct investment, through the circulation and realization of capital more than through the direct production of exportables or by the internal market. Export specialization, small incidence in international markets, inability to fix prices, and the wide-open nature of the economy served just as well.

Imperialism in Nicaragua was one of ambassadors and generals, more than industrialists and bankers. Since its independence from Spain, the key to Nicaragua's history has been the struggle for national survival against U.S. military aggressions. The enthroning of the Somoza dictatorship in the 1930s was the culmination of a series of efforts that really began with William Walker in the middle of the nineteenth century. The personal style that propelled his adventure should not obscure the articulation of his project with U.S. imperialist designs, which remained a constant throughout the following century. A poor, small, backward country, Nicaragua was always an easy prize for U.S. expansionist ambitions, especially given the obsequiousness of the local dominant classes. Anti-imperialism, as a consequence, today expresses the struggle for national identity and at the same time expresses the class identity of the people involved in that struggle.[15]

THE ROLE OF THE SOMOCISTA STATE

The best-known facets of the Somocista state are repression and the ability of the Somoza family to enrich itself within it. Yet the personalization of power and the obviously dynastic character of the dictatorship that made this true should not obscure the class content: repression as well as dynasty were the product and expression of the kind of half-bourgeois and half-oligarchic capitalism that evolved in the context of imperialist domination. It was a capitalism in which family lines, personal relations, and *caudillismo* were the means by which the bourgeoisie struggled to emerge from the bosom of an oligarchic society. The long period of family feuds and bloody battles among self-designated *generals* was an expression of the internal contradictions of a class in formation in this type of peripheral capitalism.

The Somocista state was itself an effect of this emergence and of the domination that U.S. imperialism exercised over it. Even more, it was a direct product of U.S. military invasions, which established the conditions for the dictatorship from the outset. With all its limitations, even with the space it left for the reproduction of not fully capitalist forms, the Somocista state was the historically determined form that the capitalist state assumed in Nicaragua. It was the state of the Somoza family for sure, but it was also, in its own fashion, the state of capital.

As such, the state contributed decisively to the advance of capitalism in the country. The expansion, diversification, and modernization of the economy that began in the 1950s was greatly assisted by the state, especially through the construction of a road and electricity infrastructure and through financing provided by the Banco Nacional.

At the beginning of the 1950s, the physical integration of Nicaragua was still problematic, even in the Pacific region. The lack of access roads impeded transport to storage and distribution centers as well as ports. While in 1951 the road network covered less than 2,500 kilometers, in 1958 it reached more than 5,500 km and by 1962 almost 6,300 km. In the same span public investment destined for economic services had grown by a factor of six in real values. Investment in energy went from an average 3.4 million cordobas annually in 1950–54 to 20.4 cordobas in 1960–63 (Belli 1975). Public credit facilitated the cotton producers' access to agrochemical inputs, new seed varieties, and the purchase of machinery and equipment.[16] Through the National Bank and the Instituto de Fomento Nacional (INFONAC) the state provided cheap loans and technical assistance for the promotion of such activities as tobacco, beef, shrimp, bananas, irrigated rice—in many of which the Somoza family had a share. But as has already been pointed out, the development policies, investments in infrastructure (roads, energy, irrigation), credit, and subsidized inputs were above all oriented toward large producers for export and activities connected to processing.

The tensions generated by the transformations in agriculture increased the misery of the rural population through this favoritism toward the large producers, combined with the loss of lands. During the 1960s more than 200 land invasions and evictions in the Pacific region were registered, and the opposition of these displaced sectors to the dictatorship was slowly growing.

In this period, one of reformist and modernizing winds blown in by the Alliance for Progress, the Somocista state faced up to some redistributive measures designed to temper rural unrest and create the modifications necessary for the kind of agroindustrial capitalism that was developing in the region. Marginal lands were distributed to peasant groups, but in small quantities from areas of inferior land quality, and without the necessary technical assistance. The inadequacy of these measures provoked more frustration than solutions and strengthened the confrontation between these disillusioned sectors and the regime (Talavera 1978; Morales 1981).

In the mid-1970s the Institute of Peasant Welfare was created, financed by the U.S. Agency for International Development (AID), oriented toward integrated rural development: credit and assistance programs, road construction, health and community development. Although more dynamic than the experiences of the previous decade, its coverage was minimal, and tended to benefit the better-off peasants rather than the most needy, serving in practice to consolidate a small fraction of the rural petty bourgeoisie. On the other hand, the bulk of foreign financing was deposited in the banking institutions of the large financial bourgeoisie and the Somoza family, who used it for their own investments, thus providing liquid resources for the activities controlled by the respective groups (O. Núñez 1980a; Mayorga 1981).

The subordination of the timid reformist policies to a project of modernization and expansion of capital hastened its failure, making it clear that repression constituted the major relationship between the state and the popular masses.[17] Reformism, just like the demagogic whims before it, was the product of a necessity for political accumulation and reproduction, not of social justice or democracy. In the same sense, the repressive measures facilitated palatial enrichment and accumulation. The imposition of a state of siege from the end of 1974—after the audacious Sandinista operation against the residence of José María Castillo—to September 1977 was designed not only to repress the FSLN but also to increase the exploitation of the labor force, via trade-union repression, cutbacks in labor gains, and the like.

The portrayal of Somocismo as a mere repressive apparatus has led some researchers to emphasize the efforts of the dictatorship to gain some popular support (e.g., Chamorro 1982). While this contributes to a more complete picture of the regime, we should not lose sight of the subordinated role of these efforts to a strategy of class power. The approaches of the dictatorship to some segments of the working class, when they took place, were really the product of a Somocista strategy in relation to the portion of the dominant classes that belonged to the Conservative party. When that relation took hold and consolidated, the utility of a hegemonic base in the popular classes vanished.

Toward the end of World War II, the first Somoza dictatorship—along with those in Guatemala, El Salvador, and Honduras—was confronted with mobilizations of groups of small and medium bourgeoisie supported by the Conservative party. Only Anastasio Somoza García emerged with flying colors—in large part due to the regime's rapprochement with the working classes. The incipient labor movement was struggling to form a trade-union central; given his need to weaken the Conservative opposition, Somoza offered a political accord: elaboration of a Labor Code, freedom of union organization and mobilization, and so on. While this no doubt permitted the young labor movement to gain force, in the first instance it benefited Somoza himself, in that it separated the labor movement from the opposition forces (Gutiérrez 1978; Booth 1982a: 65). This strategy was consolidated by the ideological primitivism of the Conservatives, who harshly criticized the Labor Code—and later the establishment of an incipient system of social security—from a typically precapitalist position.[18] By contrast, the regime appeared relatively democratic, and perhaps even progressive.

But the true character of these maneuvers became evident at the beginning of 1950. In April, the Generals' Pact between Somoza García and the Conservative *caudillo* Emiliano Chamorro assured the acceptance of Somocista primacy in exchange for minority participation by the Conservative party in the state apparatus—and therefore in the benefits that derived from it. Successive pacts assured Somocista hegemony among the Nicaraguan bourgeoisie and constituted the political framework for capitalist growth. Hegemonistic concerns were placed within the sphere of contradictions *internal* to the dominant class, and no longer as a part of the relation of the Somocista state to the labor movement. From the moment that the Liberal-Conservative political alliance was made explicit, expressing the internal unity of a class under Somocista leadership, repression became the dominant method of managing the popular question. The National Guard became the central axis of the state, permanently armed, trained, and advised by the United States; as Bendaña (1978) points out, the government was managed "like an extension" of the Guard.

In the countryside open repression was coupled with ideological repression carried out by the Catholic church, which acted as an authentic state apparatus in this regard until the 1970s. "For a hegemonic regime as weak as the Somocista one, the contribution of the Church, with its roots deep in the popular classes, was hardly an insignificant ideological support" (Samandú and Jansen 1982). Among the most backward of the continent, the hierachy and the clergy spread a Christianity of submission to the temporal order. The dictatorial power was in effect presented as a product of a divine will, and any effort to rebel against it as insubordination to God. With the exception of some young priests, "the rest of the Catholic leaders either collaborated actively with the governing elite or at least passively tolerated government excesses" (Alonso 1973). But ultimately this ideological repression could not supersede the contradictions generated by the vicious exploitation of the rural masses. As the masses moved ever closer to the FSLN, open repression was again the procedure adopted by the state to confront the protest and popular activism. While this expedient was never absent, it took on far greater proportions from 1975 on, and was executed through rural judges, local detachments of the National Guard, or directly by the private guards of the local landowners (see Amnesty International 1976; Guido 1981).

Whatever variations of repression were employed had as a common denominator permanent concession to the interests of the Somoza family. The state was not only a political-economic agent of capital, it was also an instrument of enrichment and accumulation for the Somozas and their most loyal allies. Exclusive exercise of state power and umbilical links with the United States, control over the National Guard and the Liberal party, friendship with the succession of U.S. ambassadors, and use of public resources, foreign financial aid, and technical assistance in their own benefit all offered the opportunity for a spectacular accumulation of wealth. At the time of the Sandinista revolutionary triumph the Somoza fortune was estimated at between U.S. $500 million and $900 million (López et al. 1979: 345; Black 1981: 34–36, 62–64).

The formation of this immense patrimony is intimately linked to the process of capitalist accumulation (Diederich 1981). At the end of World War II Anastasio Somoza García was already the largest cattle rancher and one of the largest coffee and sugarcane producers. After the war the family extended its activities first to mining concessions—in alliance with U.S. firms—and beef exports, followed by cement, textiles, milk products, shipping and airlines, ports, tobacco, slaughterhouses, fishing operations, securities, construction, finance, manufacturing industry, and real estate speculation. By the

Table 2.17
Nicaragua: Participation of Different Areas of Property
in the Economy, 1978 and 1980
(in percentages)

| Sectors of activity | 1978 | | | 1980 | |
| | | | | Private area | |
	Public area	Private area	APP	Large enterprise	Small enterprise
Agricultural	—	100	21	29	50
Manufacturing	—	100	25	45	30
Construction	40	60	70	5	25
Mining	—	100	95	5	—
Subtotal of material production	8	92	25	37	38
Services	31	69	56	22	22
Gross national product	15	85	41	34	25

Source: Ministry of Planning.

middle of the 1970s the Somoza family formed the third financial group in the country (Strachan 1976): the "loaded dice group" (Wheelock 1976).

Somoza used his absolute control of the state to push this accelerated economic growth: privatization of public funds, tax evasion, manipulation of information, inflationary selling, speculation with public funds, among others. In this he operated in common with other dictators, notably Trujillo in the Dominican Republic. But unlike Trujillo, he did not confine this process to his own family: a network of families and high-ranking guard officers enjoyed these benefits to a lesser extent, in exchange for their loyalty to the regime, and became through the course of half a century a true *Somocista bourgeoisie* (Torres Rivas 1980). Names like Hüeck, Sengelman, Urcuyo, Pallais, Montiel, and others achieved political and economic prominence in this way. Some of them were related to the Somoza family (the Sacasas or the Pallais family, for example), but others came to their family relation through political and economic relations. This family clique *(familismo),* which has been noted as a characteristic feature of the dictatorship (Alonso 1973), became more a product of the social and political structure of the regime, and less its cohesive element, in the measure that capitalist development was becoming more complex and deeply rooted.[19]

This style of political domination of the development of capitalism reached a crisis in the early 1970s. What had been until then the motor force of capitalist expansion would be transformed into a source of contradictions, preparing the ground for a gradual political differentiation among important sectors of the bourgeoisie as the popular challenge progressed and gained in strength.

The spectacular process of enrichment of the dictatorship and the contradictions that this generated in the final years with the local large bourgeoisie came to create an image of the subject that proved not totally correct. Table 2.17 shows the relative weight of the area of people's property (APP), the large bourgeoisie, and small production in the Nicaraguan economy at the beginning of 1980. Given that by this date the APP consisted fundamentally of the properties confiscated from the Somoza family and its allies, the difference beween 1978 and 1980 gives a good approximation of the magnitude of control by the regime over the national economy.

It is evident that the image of Somoza as owner of "half the country" was not quite exact, but it is equally clear that Somocismo was in fact owner of half, or nearly half, of everything of any magnitude.

3

Economy and Politics in the Popular Insurrection

The literature on revolutionary potential in agrarian societies offers two strategic perspectives. The first emphasizes the role of the medium-sized peasant as a driving force of social change, ready to confront exploitation and oppression from the state as well as the large landowners. The second, derived directly from the Marxist tradition and above all from Lenin's (1981) analysis of Russian society, emphasizes the role of the revolutionary vanguard of the agricultural proletariat and of the minifundista peasants, already in a process of losing their lands. If in the first perspective the revolution is the task of those who still have something to lose and thus to defend (cf., e.g., Moore 1966; Wolf 1969), in the second it is the task of those who have already lost everything but their chains.

Both perspectives are relevant to Nicaragua. The course of capitalist development in the countryside over the last thirty years linked the medium-sized peasant producers of the interior to the growth of export agriculture, primarily in the Pacific region, generating a mass of agricultural proletarians and semiproletarians. Thus, whereas throughout the 1960s the FSLN carried out a rural guerrilla struggle among the peasants in the interior, using the cities as rearguard and source of assistance, in the 1970s they began to pay more attention to the Pacific region—above all the departments of Chinandega, León, Carazo, and Managua—both to the agricultural proletariat and semiproletariat as well as to the urban working masses. The Frente promoted the claims, strengthened the organization levels, and articulated the demands of broad sectors of the population, all within the project of anti-dictatorial struggle. Thus three major factors came together in the triumph of the Sandinista Popular Revolution:

1. An accelerated process of capitalist development which, in the course of only a single generation, drastically altered the living conditions of the rural and urban working masses, stripping them of their land and their jobs, liquidating their small shops, drowning them in misery, and increasing their exploitation;

2. A dictatorial state, the direct product of imperialist military domination, which reproduced this social exploitation, expressing it as class domination and stimulating its development, but which was progressively isolating itself from society and which, by limiting the project of accumulation to a tiny fraction of the bourgeoisie, ended by antagonizing the rest of capital; and

3. A vanguard organization, forged in two decades of struggle, which was receptive to popular demands, articulated current struggles with the anti-imperialist tradition of the people, organized them and projected them to higher levels of consciousness and efficacy, and which knew how to capitalize on the internal contradictions of the dominant groups to the benefit of the popular project.

CRISIS OF THE ECONOMY OR CRISIS OF THE SOCIETY?

A number of authors have argued that the nature of Nicaraguan dependent capitalism, and its articulation with the world economic crisis, was decisive in the downfall of the Somocista regime. According to this interpretation, the development and advance of the popular struggle—as well as the collapse of the dictatorship—resulted from the development of profound economic crisis, on top of which the FSLN offensive operated (Bendaña 1978; O. Núñez 1980a; Castillo 1980b; Black 1981; H. Weber 1981).

A different interpretation argues that the development of this economic crisis, rather than pushing the Somocista regime to bankruptcy, allowed it to consolidate itself through the strengthening of its reformist or modernizing fractions (Vargas 1978, 1979). In both cases, the economic crisis appears to have produced political consequences, although opposite ones.

Apart from the fact that the concept of *economic crisis* itself is not clear in these works—save for generic references to the *permanent*

Table 3.1
Evolution of the Gross Domestic Product, 1970–78

| Years | Millions of 1980 cordobas | Rates of growth (%) | | |
		Overall GDP	Agricultural product	Industrial product
1970	20,098.3	—	—	—
1971	21,088.9	4.9	8.0	5.0
1972	21,759.9	3.1	0.9	5.2
1973	22,867.7	5.1	5.8	4.0
1974	25,773.2	12.7	8.7	12.7
1975	26,339.4	2.2	6.5	3.2
1976	27,667.9	5.0	1.7	4.5
1977	27,926.0	0.9	3.8	10.3
1978	25,977.5	−6.9	8.7	2.4
Average 1971–78		3.3	5.5	5.9

Source: World Bank 1981.

crisis of dependent capitalism, or to the *general* crisis of capitalism—and that the effects predicated by the two focuses are obviously antithetical, examination of the actual evolution of the Nicaraguan economy and the way it was tied into world capitalist economy at different periods, shows it to be insufficient in itself to produce a crisis. Rather, the fall of the Somocista dictatorship was the product of a *revolutionary political crisis,* which at a certain point in its evolution activated an economic crisis.

Table 3.1 shows the evolution of the gross domestic product (GDP) and two of its productive sectors during the period prior to the revolutionary triumph. From it, we can see that the Nicaraguan economy grew, although not at spectacular rates. Its rhythms were unequal and erratic, but it did grow, above all in the sectors of agricultural and industrial production.

During the second half of this period, however, we can see strong deceleration of growth. From an average annual rate of 6.4 percent in 1971–74, it dropped to 0.3 percent in 1975–78, and in the last year fell in absolute values. In the productive sectors, however, the deceleration was much less noticeable: from 5.8 percent to 5.3 percent in the agricultural sector, and from 6.7 percent to 5.1 percent in the manufacturing industry.

The slowing tendency in the dynamism of the national economy occurred over the long term. Between 1960 and 1965 the GDP grew at an annual average rate of 10.2 percent while in the isthmus as a whole it was 6 percent; in 1965–70 Nicaragua's GDP grew 4.2 percent, the regional GDF at 5.4 percent, and in 1970–78 the rates were 4 percent and 5.4 percent, respectively (Rosenthal 1982). But it is evident that deceleration of growth and the tendency toward stagnation are one thing, and stagnation itself and recession are another. If economic crisis is understood to mean stagnation or recession, it would seem hard to argue that there was an economic crisis in Nicaragua.

Table 3.2 shows the direction of investments during the same period. This variable does not seem to have altered in any relevant way during the years prior to the final insurrection and the fall of the dictatorship. The investment coefficient remained generally stable except in 1978, but even then the cut relative to GDP growth is much less impressive: 18.5 percent average in 1971–74 and 17.2 percent in 1975–78; the investment coefficient of 1977 is not comparable with any of the preceding years. If economic crisis is understood to mean a strong movement of decapitalization, or inversely, decapitalization is interpreted as a cause or at least an indicator of the crisis, one cannot properly speak of an economic crisis in prerevolutionary Nicaragua in this sense either.

Table 3.3 confirms this overview with respect to agrarian capital.

Table 3.2
Evolution of Investments, 1970–78

Year	Fixed gross investment	Private investment	Investment coefficient*
1970	3,268.0	2,448.6	17.5
1971	3,373.6	2,295.4	17.2
1972	2,997.8	1,946.8	12.5
1973	4,109.6	2,822.8	20.6
1974	5,023.9	3,497.0	23.9
1975	4,561.1	3,041.8	16.4
1976	4,820.4	2,884.7	16.3
1977	6,184.0	3,138.9	25.1
1978	3,436.4	1,895.9	11.0

Source: World Bank 1981.
Figures are in millions of 1980 cordobas.
*Gross internal investment/GDP × 100.

Table 3.3
Some Indicators of Agricultural Production, 1973–79

Agricultural year	Cotton	Sesame	Coffee	Sugarcane
1973–74	259.3	6.1	204.2	44.5
1974–75	254.3	6.7	231.5	50.1
1975–76	204.6	9.2	254.1	60.8
1976–77	283.0	7.9	190.9	56.6
1977–78	310.8	12.1	193.3	57.3
1978–79	248.1	13.7	195.7	56.7

Source: Compiled from Banco Central de Nicaragua.
Figures are thousands of manzanas in use.

The 1977–78 agricultural year was, from this perspective, excellent, and confirms the view that despite the insecurity and the "crisis of confidence" that the Nicaraguan bourgeoisie must have experienced in this period, even in mid-1977 it was thinking of the economy, not of politics, and was placing heavy bets on a favorable year.

These three economic indicators, far from demonstrating an economic crisis, suggest that the notion should be discarded. The most that one could say, based on facts, is that there existed a *tendency* toward a deceleration of economic growth, which is shown most clearly in the second half of the 1970s. But in this the Nicaraguan economy is not significantly different from the rest of Central America.

Table 3.4 looks at the impact of the international market on the national economy. It shows neither cuts nor breaks, nor, on the contrary, a reiteration or accumulation of negative tendencies that would permit an identification of the crisis or any way of tying it to the growth of the revolution. The years prior to the final stage of the liberation war were not awful, and the accumulated balance of the sub-period 1975–78 showed positive effects, while that of 1971–74 was negative. In other words, the shift is there, but in the sense of a slightly positive reinforcement to the local economy. In the final analysis, the comparison of Nicaragua with the situation of the other non-oil-producing countries of Latin America shows that in general terms, the impact of international commerce on the national economy was no worse than in the rest of the continent.

Table 3.5 shows the rise in the cost of living from 1972 to 1979.

Food prices climbed more than the general index, and to the extent that participation of this category in such an index is greater when the income level is lower, it indicates that the popular classes felt the price increase more than anyone. But the increase was slow, even in food. It does not appear evident that the cost of living was more intolerable or desperate than at the beginning of the decade.

A similar conclusion arises from a consideration of wage levels in Table 3.6. There is no doubt that the *absolute* wage level was low. In 1972, for example, the legal daily minimum wage was under 11 cordobas, the weekly wage was under 76 cordobas, the bimonthly 164 cordobas, and the monthly 323 cordobas; in 1975 these figures were 13 cordobas, 92 cordobas, 200 cordobas, and 401 cordobas, respectively.[1] Furthermore, legalities were one thing—often promulgated to show a good face to international organizations—and capitalist practices, particularly Somocista capitalist practices, were another. Although there is no available information in this regard, the levels actually paid were doubtless inferior to those fixed by legal norms. Even so, it is clear that relatively speaking, real wages stayed at the same level, and, according to the data consulted, workers' purchasing power did not deteriorate significantly in the period prior to the final stage of the struggle.

This evidence casts doubt on the argument about an acute deterioration in real wages as an expression, if not a cause, of the economic crisis. Nevertheless, its value is more generic than specific for the

Table 3.4
Nicaragua and Latin America: Percentage of Change, Terms of Trade,
1972–79

Year	Nicaragua	Latin America*
1972	10.4	3.6
1973	−4.6	10.3
1974	−4.4	−2.4
1975	−16.3	−9.1
1976	17.7	2.0
1977	27.4	9.0
1978	−11.3	−19.0
1979	−11.9	−6.0

Source: CEPAL figures.
*Includes only those countries that are not oil exporters.

Table 3.5
Consumer Price Index, 1972–79

Year	General index	Growth (%)	Food, drink, and tobacco	Growth (%)
1972	100.0	—	100.0	—
1973	127.02	27.0	141.17	41.2
1974	143.94	13.3	162.83	15.3
1975	154.77	7.5	175.44	7.7
1976	159.13	2.8	177.44	1.2
1977	177.26	11.4	203.75	14.8
1978	183.34	4.5	211.02	3.5
1979	274.64	48.1	344.66	63.3

Source: INEC.
Base: May–October 1972 = 100.

concrete case of the Nicaraguan economy, as are all considerations that try to reduce the question of the working masses to a salary problem.

In the first place, this is because salaried workers constitute only one part of the workers as a whole; although their volume is greater than that suggested in most common estimates, we noted in the previous chapter that a large number of the Nicaraguan workers were not salaried. "Self-employed" workers constitute two-fifths of the urban economically active population (EAP) and semiproletarian peasants a third of the rural EAP. In the second place, only a small portion of the salaried workers received their wages monthly: in the middle of the 1970s around 80 percent of the workers were paid daily, weekly, or bimonthly (Vilas 1982b).

In these conditions the value of a decrease in real wages, or an increase in the cost of living, as indicators of the impact of the economic crisis on this type of working mass is much less than is generally believed. For a seasonal worker, for example, the crisis can mean more time without work or more time surviving in some "informal" activity, rather than going from a situation of employment to one of unemployment. For the artisan or the "self-employed" worker, the crisis can be translated into a prolongation of the labor time *necessary* for his or her material reproduction, rather than closure or cessation. Those who receive income directly through sales—artisans, workshops owners, small merchants, street sellers—can in principle manipulate their prices to mitigate or transfer the inflationary impact. This is true in other cases as well. In all of them it is clear that the impact of the crisis varies with different types of capitalist development and for their distinct classes, groups, and fractions.

Table 3.7, per capita GNP, tries to overcome the limitations of real wages as an indicator of the crisis from the perspective of the working masses in a barely industrialized society. Here one can very neatly see the deterioration in the standard of living. Even more, there is a very marked break between the two sub-periods of the decade; while in 1971–74 the per capita GDP grew at an average annual rate of 3.1 percent, in 1975–78 the average annual rate was exactly the opposite: −3.2 percent.

It is worth pointing out that the growth in the first half of the decade was transformed into a reduction in the second, although to be sure the earnings and losses were not shared in the same way, in that those who reaped the benefits of the growth were not the same ones that experienced the losses. One does not need to be too imaginative to realize that the earnings were concentrated in the higher sections of the income scale while the losses were monopolized by the popular classes, specifically (to the extent that it is possible to make inferences from the combination of tables 3.6 and 3.7), by the nonsalaried workers and those who did not have monthly incomes. In 1977, 1.2 million people (almost half the population of the country) had a monthly per capita income of less than $25.

Beginning in the second half of the 1970s there was, then, a deepening process of pauperization of the popular classes, which

Table 3.6
Average Monthly Salary (1972 = 100)

Year	General average	Agriculture	Manufacturing industry	Commerce	Services
1972	100.0	100.0	100.0	100.0	100.0
1973	85.5	89.3	84.6	74.6	80.3
1974	86.6	92.6	86.2	75.6	83.6
1975	66.0	89.3	82.3	75.5	82.5
1976	87.8	91.5	86.4	75.7	83.2
1977	86.3	103.0	84.6	73.9	78.9
1978	86.3	97.6	85.3	71.8	78.5

Source: Author's elaboration based on figures from Banco Central de Nicaragua and INEC.

Table 3.7
Per Capita GDP, 1970–79

Year	U.S.$	Rate of growth (%)
1970	1,095	—
1971	1,116	1.9
1972	1,113	−0.2
1973	1,135	2.0
1974	1,235	8.8
1975	1,218	−1.3
1976	1,233	1.2
1977	1,201	−2.6
1978	1,078	−10.2
1979	777	−27.9

Source: World Bank 1981.

doubtless played a role in their integration into the revolutionary struggle. This aggravation of general living conditions must have been more intense for the urban popular classes than for those of the countryside, for those without work and those that worked in nonproductive activities than for those in productive sectors, and for the nonsalaried than for the salaried.[2]

But the impoverishment of the masses, the degradation of their levels of existence, including the brutal aspects of the last stage of the dictatorship, are not enough to form an economic crisis. Nor does the economic crisis signify much in itself when the political conditions do not exist to make of it a factor that pushes the revolution. Left to spontaneity, the masses can generate violent explosions, bursts of anger that make the regime tense but which do not translate into a politically effective means of toppling it; or they can seek individual solutions, such as moving to another country, seeking other horizons. Without the confluence of certain political conditions, which are not generated spontaneously or automatically by the dynamic of the economic situation, the crisis can even be reabsorbed by the dominant classes and converted into the point of take-off for a new stage of social exploitation and political oppression of the masses.

The contradiction between popular and dominant classes is a way of expressing the contradiction between the development of the productive forces and the existing relations of production. It is, therefore, the contradiction that gives way to "an era of social revolution" (Marx 1859), but it is also the contradiction that is at the base of the expanded reproduction of the capitalist system. What operates in a given situation depends, in the last analysis, on the political "use" of that contradiction by the forces in struggle. An economic crisis generally can merely create a more propitious terrain for the diffusion of certain ways of thinking and acting, for posing and resolving the central questions of the social struggle. Just as important as the crisis is the way in which the antagonistic forces—the state on one side, the revolutionary vanguard on the other—face it and function within it.

Analysis of Nicaragua's economic development shows that it was not free of problems and contradictions, but that these did not constitute in themselves a true *crisis*. The very impoverishment of the masses is more a result of the process of capitalist accumulation itself than an indicator of the crisis.

I would argue instead that in mid-1977 a true *revolutionary crisis* opened up in Nicaragua, of which the economic crisis unleashed in 1978—*and not before*—is but one dimension. The deterioration of living conditions of the masses, which was accelerated by 1976–77, and the genocidal repression launched against them by the dictatorship beginning with Monimbó (February 1978), was combined with the revolutionary advance of the FSLN which articulated military struggle with mass organization and an opening toward democratic fractions of the bourgeoisie and the international front.

The dictatorship's accelerated collapse in the face of the FSLN advance, as well as the erosion of its own social bases, is the context in which the economic crisis was activated. It evolved at a dizzying rate as the revolutionary struggle grew and moved ever closer to victory. The economy became autonomous of the state and its policy instruments, as well as of international financial assistance, because it was being converted more and more into a dimension of the liberation struggle.

The economic crisis that was unleashed in 1978 and reached its culmination in April–May 1979 was not a product of the "natural" development of the Nicaraguan economy, nor of its contradictory articulation to the world market, but of the political reorientation of a growing part of its resources (the external debt, for example) to try to stop the revolutionary ascent; this, combined with the flight of capital, the expatriation of assets, and in the end, the progressive paralysis of the economy in the face of defeat, accelerated the breakup of a system of iniquitous domination.

Two factors seem to have been of special relevance in the economic debacle. On the one hand was Somocismo itself, which subordinated the whole economic system to the development of the war against the FSLN and to the wanton practices of enrichment and accumulation. On the other hand was the fear and insecurity of the bourgeoisie, especially after the assassination of Pedro Joaquín Chamorro. This was not because the most important opposition business leaders had adhered to Chamorro's political positions or to the organization that he led (UDEL), but because the crime brutally demonstrated that no one was immune to Somocista repression. The bourgeoisie's lack of horizons grew even graver as it became evident that not even an FSLN victory augured a brighter future.

With no political experience, and with fragile and recently formed organizations, the bourgeois opposition had no choice but to put its money on a system of "Somocismo without Somoza"—but with the National Guard, due to jockeying by U.S. mediators. In its search for imperial support it had to compete with the efforts of Somoza himself, as well as with the neutralization strategy of the FSLN. Capital flight, liquidation of assets, and general retraction of productive activity were the economic expressions of this insecurity; as its own future as a class became more problematic, it reproduced the decapitalizing activities of its old allies and protectors.

We will study the political behavior of the Nicaraguan bourgeoisie further in Chapter 4. Here it is sufficient to point out that these contradictions between a state that functions as a mechanism of enrichment and accumulation for the groups that directly control it and bourgeois market fractions are nothing new in Latin America. By themselves they do not lead to a revolutionary process. In the Dominican Republic, for example, this contradiction was acute in the last presidential term of Joaquín Balaguer (1974–78), but the disorganization of the popular classes and the lack of a political-military vanguard, among other things, meant that it was resolved on terms proposed by the reformist fractions of the bourgeoisie (Vilas 1980b).

What is specific to Nicaragua is that the contradictions of the dominant groups—Somocista and non-Somocista, dictatorial and democratic—were in reality the product of the antagonistic contradiction between the state and the FSLN, and ultimately became subordinated to it. This occurred at a stage in which that contradiction was already the political-military expression of the fundamental antagonism between the people and the dominant classes. By then this expression of the basic contradiction of Nicaraguan dependent capitalism had taken on all the explosiveness of a revolutionary crisis.

As such, the contradiction between the productive forces (the people) and the relations of production (dominant classes) was always present, but it was the political action of the masses, and their incorporation into the Sandinista struggle, which made it a revolutionary crisis. The people who went into the streets to fight did so because the political conditions created by almost two decades of Sandinista struggle already existed, permitting them to foresee the efficacy of their participation and to believe in the probability of triumph. It was that Sandinista struggle that made possible the conversion of daily elements of life of the Nicaraguan masses—hunger, misery, lack of stable work, hatred of the National Guard—into combat forces for the war against the regime. To reduce this general, organic crisis of Nicaraguan society to an economic crisis is to confuse lightning with the tempest. There wasn't an economic crisis; there was a revolution.

THE WORKING MASSES AND THE URBAN POOR

In the previous chapter we saw how capitalism developed in the countryside starting in the late 1950s, articulated to simple mercantile forms of production. In the following decade industrial growth within the regional integration scheme introduced few modifications in the general functioning of the urban economy, which continued to be characterized by the large weight of commerce and services, particularly by an enormous number of small units of activity. With marked limitations, the tertiary sector continued to absorb the population growth in the cities and, above all, in the capital.

Between 1950 and 1971 Managua almost quadrupled its population, going from less than 110,000 inhabitants to almost 400,000. The lack of productive sectors that could employ this growing population, the lack of infrastructure, and so on, accelerated the growth of slums in the city and reinforced the process of pauperization of the majority of the population.

The earthquake of December 1972 further complicated this urban panorama. In addition to the thousands of dead and injured, the catastrophe left almost 52,000 people without work (57 percent of the city's economically active population) and forced the displacement of some 250,000—60 percent of the total population of Managua. Twenty-seven square kilometers of the city were affected, with thirteen square kilometers totally destroyed and the rest damaged, including the greater part of the sewerage system and water and light distribution. Seventy-five percent of family housing units were destroyed, the majority belonging to middle- and low-income families. Ninety-five percent of the small workshops and factories (carpentry shops, presses, shoemakers) and eleven large factories were lost or suffered serious damage. The same occurred with 400,000 square meters of commercial buildings and warehouses and with 340,000 square meters of public and private offices. Four hospitals with 1,650 beds were lost or seriously damaged, and 740 schoolrooms were left unusable (INCAE 1973).

The catastrophe left the working masses of the city and vast sectors of the petty bourgeoisie in the street—without housing, without work, without personal belongings, but with a tremendous emotional tension, thanks to the bullying actions of the National Guard.

All of these actions were blatantly open; people could see the dead—mothers and children—and daily endured the scarcity of food, of water. There was no protection by the Somocista authorities, who instead dedicated themselves to taking everything that arrived to help Nicaragua. The following testimony is typical: "We went to Chinandega and arrived at a school where there were already lots of people from Managua. The people in those days were traumatized, anxious, sick, and instead of coming to give relief the Guard arrived to tell us that we had to work, that we couldn't live there forever. The Guard itself threw us out. They gave us twenty-four hours to get out and we had to leave and sleep in the street. We all slept in the streets until we found somewhere to go, each on our own. They said they were building some houses for the homeless, but it was all promises; the houses were given to people close to them, not to the poor. The terrible situation we lived in, going around without a roof over our heads, lasted almost a year. Here it's been a breeding place for cockroaches, for rats, for everything. Here there is malaria, there is a lot of poverty."[3]

The urban employment surveys taken in the mid-1970s permit a relatively reliable approximation of the occupational profile in the principal cities, and an idea of the real nature and magnitude of the process of proletarianization of the labor force. Table 3.8 shows the kind of employment that prevailed in the early period of the development of agroindustrial capitalism in Nicaragua: a large number in services and mercantile activities (together a third of the employed population), a marked presence of artisanal jobs, possibly with a solid tie to small commerce—testimony to a minimal social division of labor—and an extremely small proletariat. Informal activities clearly dominated, those that relied on the personal initiative and resources of each agent.

Occupational diversification, as an expression of the dominant type of social division of labor, is also manifested as a gender differentiation. Women, who made up 30 percent of the economically active population in Managua in this period, constituted 70 percent of the service workers, 55 percent of the sellers and merchants, 37 percent of the office workers, 24 percent of the artisans and operators, and only 14 percent of the workers and apprentices, clearly accentuating the preindustrial features of urban occupation.

Table 3.8
Urban Employment in the Mid-1970s, by Occupational Category

	1974[a]		1975[c]
Categories	Total[a]	Managua	Managua
Professionals and technicians	11.0	12.1	10.7
Managers, administrators, and directors of public administration	2.9	3.3	4.0
Office employees and related	11.0	12.2	15.8
Growers, cattle ranchers	2.2	0.8	1.1
Traders, vendors, etc.	14.4	14.0	15.4
Transportation conductors and related	6.6	6.2	6.3
Artisans, operators, and others (spinners, dressmakers, carpenters, bricklayers, mechanics)	27.1	26.0	22.2
Workers and apprentices	6.5	7.6	6.8
Service workers	18.0	17.7	17.6
Others[b]	0.3	0.1	0.1
Total	100.0	100.0	100.0

Sources: 1974: INCAE (1975); 1975: OEDEC (1975).
   [a] Managua, Masaya, León and Estelí.
   [b] Includes those seeking work for the first time.

Table 3.9
Rates of Urban Unemployment, 1973–76 (in percentages)

Year	National rate	Managua	Other cities
May–June 1973[a]	14.03	16.39	11.45
June 1974[a]	6.88	8.04	5.12
September–October 1974[b]	16.50	17.00	15.20
June 1975[a]	9.62	11.11	6.64
June 1976[a]	8.72	9.80	6.70

Sources: [a] OEDEC (1975, 1976).
          [b] INCAE (1975).

This activity profile is articulated with relatively high rates of unemployment (Table 3.9). Urban unemployment, nonetheless, made itself felt much more forcefully in some activities than in others—above all in the productive sectors. In 1975 almost half of the unemployed were artisans, and workers and apprentices, and more than half in both categories were from the male work force.

Occupational instability joined with, and reinforced, income instability. Almost 40 percent of all salaried workers received remuneration for their labor power daily or weekly, but this was true of almost 85 percent of the factory workers and apprentices and for more than 70 percent of the artisans and operators. Income insecurity, thus defined, seems to have been greater in the male work force than in the female, since the forms of bimonthly and monthly payment covered 51 percent of the men and 76 percent of the women.[4]

Incomes are unstable and, for added measure, low and unequally distributed. Table 3.10 shows the situation of weekly incomes, which constituted the form of remuneration of one-third of the urban occupied population. More than two-thirds of those incomes did not reach 300 cordobas (a little more than $40), but in some occupational categories the renumerations were even further below this level: 83 percent of the artisans, 86 percent of the service workers, and 96 percent of the workers and apprentices.

The concept of *poverty,* as a combination of fierce unemployment, unstable employment, bad housing, lack of basic services, and low and insecure incomes, expressed the living conditions of the great majority of the urban working masses of Nicaragua. Such poverty also defined the process of proletarianization that the dependent and agroindustrial capitalism being staged in the country in the

mid-1970s imposed on these masses. It was a process of proletarianization in which a small working class, laboring in a few
modern business units, is not yet fully differentiated from the rest of
the urban workers either by mode of insertion in the relations of
production or by general living conditions, and where a vast and
complex differentiation, and articulation of activities, positions, services, and abilities, formal and informal, express the subordination
of the working masses to the dynamic of capital.

What is generally called "proletariat" even today in Nicaragua
responds to this moment of the proletarianization of the labor force
and is thus constituted primarily by these working masses rather
than by a working class in the strict sense. Compare the following
examples:

> He came from a peasant family, humble and hard-working. Like all the
> proletariat class of our people under the corrupt and exploitative re-
> gime of the Somocista dynasty, his life passed in an ebb and flow of
> poverty. Compañero T. was a vegetable merchant between the capital
> and Bluefields. . . . T's wife and children still live . . . near the market
> where T. worked to maintain them (Smutko 1980:9).

> The class extraction of M. was proletariat; don Ricardo (his father)
> was an electrical technician and his mother a seamstress (IES
> 1982b:213).

> . . . both were of proletariat extraction and worked for years as
> laborers in the city, and in the countryside when there was no work in
> the city. They had no access to higher education. . . . H. was a cotton

Table 3.10
Distribution of Urban Occupation According to Weekly Income,
1974 and 1975 (in percentages)

Income[a]	1974		1975	
	Total[b]	Managua	Total[b]	Managua
Less than 100	32.1	26.3	25.5	19.2
100 to 299	45.0	46.4	46.1	46.2
300 to 999	17.5	20.0	22.4	26.7
1,000 and above	5.4	7.3	6.0	7.9
Total	100.0	100.0	100.0	100.0

Source: INCAE (1975 and 1976).
[a] Cordobas per week.
[b] Managua, Masaya, León, Estelí.

gin mechanic, welder and cotton picker. . . . His father . . . was a stonecutter and his mother . . . a housewife. R. . . . was a carpenter, bricklayer, shoemaker, picker, planter, and tobacco wrapper. His father . . . worked in carpentry. . . . His mother was an illiterate peasant (*Barricada*, February 2, 1983).

His maternal grandmother sold meat and his mother . . . continues in this same work in Managua's enormous Oriental Market. His father is also of proletarian origin: as a youth he worked as a shoeshiner, bricklayer and later foreman (testimony taken from Randall 1980: 39).

To spend these five years as the campesinos live, to eat, to expose ourselves as they do, increased our love for the proletariat . . . (Martínez 1980).

I am of a working class family: my father is an electrician and my mother a dressmaker (testimony taken from Randall 1980: 197).

. . .thousands of workers, among them more than 5,000 hospital workers from the Nicaraguan Institute for Social Security, indefinitely paralyzed activity (IES 1982c: 91–92).

Eight ex-employees of Managua's Commercial Center played the lead in setting a dignified example for this country's working class. . . . The group of workers declared that very soon the working class would show that it could exercise its power in the means of production. . . .[5]

My father was a law student, of proletarian extraction, son of a domestic worker. . . . My mother was also of proletarian extraction, daughter of a carpenter and his wife. My mother was very poor, so she worked as a salesperson in a store; . . . She had a little store. (testimony taken from Randall 1980: 95).

This characterization, this way of seeing these groups and fractions as proletarians, depends in turn on a class perspective. If from the popular and revolutionary angle they are seen as proletariat, from the perspective of the bourgeoisie they are focused on as businesspeople. Enrique Dreyfus, president of the Nicaraguan Development Institute (INDE), stated in early 1983:

We want to stress again that of the economically active population of the country, which is 800,000 people, more than 200,000 are self-employed or owners of a land parcel or of a taxi or truck; small industrialists or artisans; owners of small stores or shops; or simply professionals. All belong to the private sector. . . . At the same time the private sector plays a very important role in Nicaraguan commerce. The shopowner of Matiguas helps generate employment at the same

time that he distributes products and even collects taxes for government expenses. More than 65,000 small shopowners and street merchants exist in the country. All of them carry out not only the economic
function of buying and selling, but also a social function that is rooted
in our history. . . . The small entrepreneur . . . is a vital part of our
economy. Nicaragua is made up of small entrepreneurs.[6]

A year later he added:

> . . . we consider an entrepreneur to be anyone who creates a good or
> a service for the community in an organized way, no matter the size of
> the operation. The woman who sells in the popular markets is as much
> an entrepreneur as those who produce. The person who manages a tiny
> grocery store is as much an entrepreneur as the manager of a super-
> market chain.[7]

This clash of contradictory characterizations is one way the confrontation of antagonistic classes of capitalism expresses itself in a
socioeconomic formation where the capitalist polarization of classes
is far from having culminated, and where the proletariat and bourgeoisie are still in a process of differentiation with respect to the
agents of social development. Proletarian from the revolutionary
viewpoint, bourgeois from the employers' perspective, both characterizations illustrate the essential ambiguity of these "intermediate"
groups of small property and small production, the lack of their own
horizon and their real subordination to the fundamental classes of
capitalism.[8]

In this structural ambiguity, the factors of change and of continuity, of rebellion and of submission, are articulated and coexist.
Some prevail over others according to the evolution of the contradictions between the antagonistic poles of the society, and to the political practice of the organizations that express and promote them.
According to Cmdte. Carlos Núñez:

> The petty bourgeoisie is totally identified with the revolution . . .
> insofar as the revolutionary movement, the workers' movement and the
> popular movement as a whole is enormously strong. . . . insofar as the
> revolutionary movement grows stronger or weaker the petty bour-
> geoisie wavers. When the revolutionary movement is strong it always
> tends to embrace the revolutionary interests so if we engage in educa-
> tion to inculcate in them the discipline, the example, the technique, and
> the self-denial of the proletariat, we can have them permanently at our
> side (C. Núñez, 1980a).

Table 3.11
Age and Sex of the Participants

Age	Men	Women	Total Number	Total Percent
Less than 15	10	1	11	1.4
15 to 19	187	14	201	31.0
20 to 24	229	14	243	40.0
25 to 30	113	10	123	19.0
31 to 40	48	1	49	7.0
41 and older	11	2	13	1.6
Total	598	42	640	100.0
	(93.4%)	(6.6%)	(100%)	

THE SOCIAL SUBJECT OF THE POPULAR INSURRECTION[9]

This is the real profile of the Nicaraguan people. A complex working mass of artisans, peasants, semiproletarians, sellers, tradespeople, people without trades, day workers, students, the poor of the city and the countryside from whose center the proletariat is becoming slowly differentiated; the forge from which emerged the *social subject* of the Sandinista revolution and the popular insurrection.

The creation, after the revolutionary triumph, of a program of pensions and subsidies for family members of combatants and supporters who fell in the liberation struggle against the Somocista dictatorship provided a great deal of information about the social origin of the participants and their families (their occupation, lifestyle, formal education, etc.), and made it possible to reconstruct the concrete physiognomy of the protagonists of the final stage of the revolutionary struggle.[10]

The extreme youth of the participants is shown in Table 3.11. Seventy-one percent were between 15 and 24 years old when they died, a proportion almost three times higher than the weight of this age group in the demographic pyramid (20 percent). The predominant role of youth in the struggle against the Somocista dictatorship has already been analyzed (see, for example, O. Núñez 1982a: 125–27), and needs only a few additional comments.

The predominance of men is impressive and contrasts with the prevailing image about the level of participation of women in the revolutionary struggle, especially in the final insurrection. While that participation was a real one, the figures in Table 3.11 suggest that their incorporation in the struggle was carried out primarily through *different* forms and modalities, which are not registered by the kind of information being analyzed here. More than in direct combat, women's participation seems to have taken place fundamentally in support tasks: as message carriers, providing safe houses, providing food and medicines, hiding and moving arms, clandestine hospital attention, and the like.[11]

More than half the participants (54 percent) were children born out of wedlock; almost half (47 percent) were raised and lived during their formative years (first 12 years) in families with a single head of household—the mother in the majority of cases.[12] The head of household also had to spend the greater part of the day outside the home, for occupational reasons. The children were raised together with other children—brothers, friends, cousins—under the distant gaze of a neighbor, or in the jumble of the marketplace where the mother—and many times the children as well—worked.[13]

The proportion of families with a single head of household—above all with a female head—is very high even given the patterns of family structure prevalent in Nicaraguan society. According to the National Demographic Survey of 1978, from a total of 6,600 heads of family researched, some 1,500 were women—around 23 percent. That is, among the combatants in the insurrection there were *double* the youth from families with one head of household than in the population as a whole.

Undoubtedly, the issue has a class framework. In an investigation of the "marginal" barrios of pre-earthquake Managua it was found that 48 percent of the interviewed heads of households were women (Tefel 1978: 52, 58). More recently an investigation about working minors in the streets of Managua (house-to-house sellers, car watchers, etc.) shows that, of 334 heads of household, 58 percent are women and only 54 percent of the child workers live in a house with both parents (CTM/INSSBI 1983).

These data suggest some hypotheses that, although they cannot be developed within the scope of this work, are important to make explicit. If, as psychology asserts, the family is the environment where the human being comes into contact with authority for the first time and at a very young age, it seems possible that a very high proportion of the participants in the insurrection and in the final stages of the struggle had their first experiences of social and psychological development in families where the authoritarian component expressed itself in a way distinct from the dominant stereotypes of the bourgeois or the patriarchal family. The authoritarian pattern of adult-child relations of a vertical and immediate type seem here to have been displaced by or at least interwoven with a pattern of horizontal relations among equals—relations between children taking up the greater part of the day—in families with a single head of household as the authority image. Furthermore, this head of household spent a great deal of time outside the home or dedicated to activities that detracted from direct attention to the children, so that this attention was usually delegated to the grandmother or other adult. As a consequence, these children lived a good part of their infancy basically interacting with other children, in the house, the street, or the market, but in any event with relatively little adult control—either spatially or affectionately.[14]

The specific modality of this type of family in its function as generator of images of authority is articulated with the weaknesses of other traditional agencies of social control. The high degree of illiteracy and high dropout rates put schooling outside the reach of the popular classes; the figure of the teacher—the conventional image of the *second mother* in the educational ideology of the Latin American bourgeoisie—as a referent of authority was far from the early experiences of the popular classes.

Something similar must have occurred with the church. According to an investigation in the poorest barrios of Managua (Tefel 1978), the prevailing attitude in the population seems to have been between indifference and criticism:

> In total 39.9% of the heads of family answered that they only went to church or temple "once in a while," and 13% never. The religious practice of those that attended church occasionally, rather than demonstrating a profound conviction, obeys a social ritualism that revolves around certain important events, such as baptism, marriage or death. A considerable part of the heads of family have a critical attitude toward the hierarchical Church, although perhaps not with the rigor and crudeness of the youth.
>
> A socioreligious survey reveals "an unfavorable public opinion" toward the ecclesiastical structures. Thus they saw the hierarchy as "stony, conservative, static, advanced in age, indifferent, negative, divided, barely accessible to the people, part of which didn't know the

hierarchy and didn't want to." The opinion expressed through this survey about the diocesan clergy is also critical. Outstanding is "the lack of dialogue and its lack of *aggiornamento,* remaining in a state of ideological paralysis; marginalized by the hierarchy and by the people." It also notes that "they only seek their own economic interest" and that they have "little social sensitivity to the problems of their faithful."

The criticism is not only for the hierarchical church but also for the church as "people of God." Upon reading the assertion that "the majority of those that go to church do not practice what they listen to," 68.8 percent of those interviewed said they agreed and 15.9 percent were dubious. Only 11.7 percent rejected the assertion (pp. 136–37).

It could be argued, given these considerations, that the capacity of the church to play a role as the agent of ideological reproduction of the existing social order seems to have been small in the case of these popular sectors. After the Managua earthquake, the development of pastoral practices inspired by the new currents of Latin American Christian thought, the shakeup within the priesthood, and the attention given by the FSLN to the Christian base organizations lessened this capacity even more, and in turn opened up an atmosphere of questioning about the Somocista dictatorship and social injustices (see Argüello 1979; Molina 1981).

The picture with regard to political and community organizations is similarly desolate. Tefel's investigation in the Managua barrios reveals the dearth of "community" or cultural organizations, or complete ignorance of them by the people of the barrios; youth clubs and the like were similarly nonexistent. Not even the political parties had base organizations of a permanent sort in these zones of the city:

> The new parties had not yet penetrated in a massive way into the belts of misery, and the historic parties—Liberal and Conservative— due to their "electoral" nature, only mobilized themselves during the electoral campaigns where they created ephemeral committees in the barrios which disappeared after the elections. Party activity in the barrios is extremely low and limited (Tefel 1978: 159).

The hypothesis could therefore be posed that contact with authority among the popular sectors must have come primarily through the repressive apparatuses of the Somocista state—as victims or forced witnesses to their bullying, their corruption, their abuses— and at ages in which the basic structure of the personality is already shaped. Omar Cabezas writes:

Table 3.12
Occupation of the Participants

Occupation	Percentage
Students	29.0
Tradespeople	
(artisans, workshop owners, food vendors, ironers, transport workers, mechanics, carpenters, tinsmiths, mattress makers, shoemakers, plumbers, repairers, etc.)	22.0
Workers and journeymen	16.0
Office employees	16.0
Technicians, professionals, teachers and professors	7.0
Small merchants and traders	5.0
Peasants, farmers	4.5
Others	0.5
Total	100.00
	(n = 542)
Unknown	98

When I was a kid in my barrio there was a canteen that belonged to a big fat woman—she used to hit her husband—, they called it the canteen of the Dimas. So since there were often drunken fights in this canteen, the Guard would come and beat up on the drunks. This was the first impression that I had of the Guardia. They beat them, they were like savages beating them in the face with their rifle butts. You could see the blood . . . (1982: 11).

The isolation of the National Guard from the popular masses must have increased the weight of their repressive presence in the eyes— and on the backs—of the people. Booth (1982a: 57) has called attention to the Somocista strategy of isolating the Guard from the civil population. Members of the Guard (troops and officers) and their families generally lived in distinct neighborhoods and fundamentally maintained social relations only among themselves in order to increase internal unity and, according to Booth, to lessen their scruples regarding repression of the civilians, converting themselves in their acts into "a detested and feared occupation army in their own national territory."

Obviously these sociopsychological elements are not sufficient to explain the rebellion of the people, their incorporation into the struggle. But it is possible that in these conditions the oppressive social and political order could make one more receptive. The arbitrariness of the exercise of political-military power by the dictatorship, the indiscriminate—and finally, genocidal—character of the repression, was felt in a more direct and generalized way among the popular classes and converted active rebellion and participation in the revolutionary struggle into a defensive question—life or death.[15]

Table 3.12 shows the occupational profile of participants in the insurrection. Students constituted the primary force, followed by tradespeople, those who are self-employed in a multiplicity of occupations, skills, and productive and repair tasks.[16] Salaried workers constitute 32 percent of the total, but it does not seem appropriate to include office workers and employees in the same category with laborers and apprentices; the occupational differences express deeper class differences. On the other hand, an important proportion of the "laborers and apprentices" are those for whom the salary relation does not imply a divorce from instruments of production. The presence of laborers is low not only with respect to students and self-employed workers, but also with respect to what could be expected according to some characterizations of the insurrection. It is important to point out, nevertheless, that the proportion of workers and apprentices in the struggle is more than double their participation in the urban occupational structure (cf. Table 3.8). Finally, the small number of peasants and farmers is consistent with the eminently urban character of the final stretch of the struggle.

This picture is consistent with that which emerges from an additional sample of 113 cases taken from biographies of Sandinista militants and leaders, lists of Samocista prisoners, and testimonies of participants and observers, shown in Table 3.13. It is interesting to see the greater weight that the intellectual groups acquired here—students, but above all teachers, professors, technicians, and professionals—and those of peasant origin, while worker participation is much lower than in Table 3.12. One possible explanation involves the *different type of participants* in both cases: while Table 3.12 refers fundamentally to what could be called the rank and file of the insurrection, Table 3.13 shows a greater presence of leadership cadre and notable militants, in a period that begins much before the insurrection.

The marked occupational and income instability of the working masses is neatly shown in the profiles of the participants. One combatant was, in the space of no more than three years, a bread

Table 3.13
Occupation of a Selected Group of Participants

Occupation	Percentage
Students	31
Tradespeople, artisans, household workers	17
Technicians and professionals, teachers and professors	17
Peasants and farmers	13
Workers and journeymen	8
Small entrepreneurs, traders, and small merchants	8
Office employees	6
Total	100
	(n = 113)

deliverer, jeweler, seasonal worker in the banana companies, postman. Another was a carpenter, bricklayer, seasonal agricultural worker, shoemaker. The mother of one combatant who fell in Masaya "rents magazines and gives injections." A peasant mother of eight children and widow of a combatant combined growing corn on her little farm with the preparation and sale of food and temporary work as an agricultural laborer on the coffee farms. A combatant killed in Masaya was a primary school teacher, bread vendor, apprentice shoemaker, and professor of secondary education. Another was a rural teacher and motorboat employee on the Rama river. Yet another was a cabinetmaker, factory worker, bricklayer, furniture maker and, at the time of his death, owner of a small mechanic shop. Another was a mechanic, a seasonal agricultural worker, and a welder.

The predominance of artisans and self-employed in general becomes accentuated when we look at the occupation of the participants' parents. The presence of the small merchant and the peasantry is substantially greater among the parents of the participants than among the participants themselves, and inversely, the proletariat component is noticeably less.[17]

Table 3.14 shows the occupational situation of the parents of participants. In every case the predominant origin is artisanal or self-employed; add to this the merchant and small-business origin, and you have between half and two thirds of the participants in each of the principal occupational groups.

Among the students petty-bourgeois and middle-class extraction is greater—more than 80 percent. This suggests their incorporation was not the exclusive effect of well-known elements—the natural rebellion of the younger generation, their greater exposure to critical ideological processes, the instability of those who still lack a mode of insertion into the social order—but must also have been an expression of the contradictions of their class origins, with all the attendant mediations—familial, psychological, and so on.

The broad presence of students is consistent with the historic origins of the FSLN and with the wide space for political recruitment which was won, at an early stage, in the educational centers. The student body was seen by the FSLN as a particularly strategic element of agitation and mobilization, given the small character of the industrial proletariat, the weakness of its organizations, and the economic focus that prevailed within it:

> In our country there exists a very young industrial proletariat which, in the overwhelming majority of cases, finds itself without trade union organization, and this limits its current capacity for struggle. The peasant movement with classist demands is also of a recent vintage. For reasons of a dialectic process, then, it is the student sector of the people which welcomes in the first stage of revolutionary ideals with the greatest enthusiasm. For a certain period, the students are the force

Table 3.14
Occupation of the Parents of Participants

Parents' occupation	Participants			
	Total	Students	Self-employed	Workers/apprs.
Self-employed	39.0	35.0	45.5	46.0
Peasants, farmers	19.0	13.0	15.0	15.0
Small entrepreneurs and merchants, traders	17.0	15.0	16.5	16.0
Office employees	9.5	14.0	11.0	—
Technicians, professionals, teachers, professors	9.5	17.0	—	—
Workers and journeymen	5.0	4.0	5.0	12.0
Others	1.0	2.0	7.0	11.0
Total	100.0 (n = 390)	100.0	100.0	100.0

that will have to be at the head of the popular struggle (Fonseca 1981: 137).[18]

Furthermore, schools and universities constitute the point of encounter of the petty-bourgeois student masses which otherwise have no common meeting ground, due to the individual character of their work. School becomes the space where these sectors can overcome their reciprocal isolation; in this sense it is equivalent to that of markets in the sphere of mercantile circulation.

For their part, 62 percent of the proletarian participants were also children of the self-employed and merchants, traders, and small entrepreneurs. In a certain sense, this permits one to see a concrete moment in the process of proletarianization of these "intermediate" or petty-bourgeois fractions in two generations of each family; they are consistent with what we pointed out in the previous chapter about the progressive reduction of the artisan sector and in general of urban petty production through the process of industrial expansion.

Finally, Table 3.15 looks at the occupations of the participants by region. The results are what we would expect: students are the principal force in seven departments: Managua and León, seats of the National University; Rivas, theater of operations of the Southern Front, where student recruitment from Costa Rica seems to have been high; the rest, departments whose capitals had important contingents of secondary students. Self-employed people predominate in four departments, although they are primary in only two (Masaya and Zelaya). Laborers and journeymen, and peasants each appear as an important force in three departments. Middle-class and petty-bourgeois intellectual groups had a very low profile in all departments, although not as low as sellers, small merchants, and the like.

It is important to point out that the only three cases in which laborers appear as a relevant force with relevant weight are in agricultural departments: this suggests that they are rural or agroindustrial workers (coffee in Matagalpa and Carazo, sugar and cotton in Chinandega) rather than industrial workers. In some sense this unequal involvement of the urban and rural proletariat reflects FSLN activity: the organization of the rural workers was indisputably developed by the FSLN some years before the revolutionary triumph. Carazo and Chinandega figure precisely among the departments where the political work of the FSLN with the agricultural

Table 3.15

Occupation of the Participants, by Department (in percentages)

Occupation	Managua	Estelí	Masaya	León	Rivas	Chinandega	Matagalpa	Zelaya	Carazo	Nueva Segovia	Others
Students	32	21	16	28	32	21	29	15	33.0	12	15
Technicians, professionals, teachers, professors	6	6	9	8	4	4	6	15	—	—	15
Office employees	19	11	17	16	12	15	18	8	8.5	—	5
Workers and journeymen	13	15	10	16	11	26	24	8	33.0	—	15
Peasants and farmers	2	30	15	10	18	13	6	15	8.5	76	25
Tradespeople	22	14	29	19	18	19	11	31	17.0	12	15
Small merchants and entrepreneurs, traders	6	3	4	3	5	2	6	8	—	—	10
Total	100	100	100	100	100	100	100	100	100.0	100	100
n	(143)	(54)	(62)	(51)	(48)	(42)	(57)	(22)	(24)	(16)	(20)

Figures are percentages.

workers began the earliest; the Association of Rural Workers (ATC) was created in 1978 in the Department of Carazo, and from the beginning promoted intense mobilizations, in accord with the orientations of the FSLN. On the other hand, political work within the industrial workers' movement received less and later attention (Talavera 1979; Rivas 1983), and furthermore had to confront the reticence or opposition to a strategy of revolutionary struggle among trade-union and political leaders of the traditional left and the Social Christian party. According to Cmdte. Bayardo Arce:

> Our history registers efforts at direct ties with the working classes of the country since 1963, with the dockworker strikes of Corinto, and in the very textile factories of Somoza. But at that same time, once those who saw themselves as having patents on the unions identified the political inclination of our organizations, they did not hesitate to point out as FSLN militants in public assemblies those that were trying, they said, "to carry the workers to sure death in an adventurous method of struggle," and in this manner managed in some cases and for a certain period of time to prevent the integration of the workers into the revolutionary process (1980a: 19).

FSLN leader Gladys Baez remarks on these early differences: "I had very strongly rooted concepts of the Frente, concepts the [Socialist] party leaders themselves had taught me: that those of the FSLN were opportunists, adventurers, crazies, tramps, and worse" (Randall 1980: 228). And Omar Cabezas explains:

> And assaults and executions were carried out, which the press reported because they were direct actions against the dictatorship; that was boundless audacity, political heresy within the framework of the bourgeois political parties, Conservative and Liberal, and of course also for the Social Christians and Socialists. These latter catalogued us as adventurers, petty bourgeois, and in the university assemblies they recited paragraphs to us from that book of Lenin, *Leftism, and Infantile Disorder* (1982: 27).

In such conditions of manifest hostility, the approach of the FSLN to the workers, their recruitment into the revolutionary struggle, had to occur more in the barrios—which, for reasons pointed out above, appeared as an open camp for Sandinista political work—than in the factories: more in the centers of reproduction than in those of production.[19]

The social subject of the insurrection and of the final stretch of the struggle thus emerged with a more *popular* character, in the broad sense of *working masses,* rather than *proletarian* in the narrow sense. Proletarian components were interwoven within a broad spectrum of generalized and acute poverty, of *real* more than *formal* subordination to capital, and of instability and insecurity in all dimensions of life—consistent with the type of capitalism that was developing in the country.[20]

Petty producers and unsalaried workers—who in this chapter, for lack of a better name, have been called *tradespeople*—emerge clearly as the principal social force in the insurrection. They constituted the greater part of the direct participants as well as of the socio-occupational sectors that engendered participants. It is true that students topped them as a direct participant group, but for the most part these students were children of that social fraction.

By contrast, the proletariat does not seem to have been a quantitatively determinant force. Nevertheless its participation must not be minimized. Worker presence in the insurrection was *two times greater than in the urban occupational structure,* which is not true for the self-employed or those of small property. Worker presence was thus greater in the revolutionary struggle than in the economy; more determinant in the production of the new society than in the reproduction of the old. This imbalance in participation between the tradespeople and workers can be explained, I believe, by the elements pointed out above: the arena and mode of recruitment, and the unequal level of political work.

The nonproductive sector of the salaried workers (employees, officer workers, etc.) participated in the same numbers as the proletariat, and in some departments—Masaya, for example—constituted the second group in order of magnitude. The intellectual groups—professionals, teachers, technicians—and, above all, the small merchants who register so strongly in the Nicaraguan urban landscape—shopkeepers, small sellers, etc.—were barely relevant as participants in the insurrection.

The social subject of the Sandinista revolution in the stage that culminated with the July 19, 1979, triumph comes much closer to that of other third-world revolutions of national liberation than to the prevailing image in some leftist academic circles of a proletarian revolution in the sense of a revolution *by* proletarians. Popular and anti-imperialist revolution, based in the broad majority of the people, is in the framework of national liberation that gives anticapitalist tasks the possibility of development.

This social subject is not the survivor of backward or precapitalist forms of production, but the product and central protagonist of the type of capitalism that developed in Nicaragua through imperialist domination, and of the way in which that system articulated with pre-existing forms of production and reproduced them. In this system the proletarianization of the labor force took place through its formal subordination to capital, and not only by way of the salarization of the "freed" worker. A large proportion of workers went on being tied to their land, to their instruments of work, and to sources of subsistence, thereby remaining available to capital at moments when they were needed and dispensable when no longer required.

The concept of *poverty* that circumscribes this broad spectrum of occupational groups, classes, and fractions is not reducible to low income levels, illiteracy, or lack of higher education, or to miserable housing; that is, to say they *have little* is a simplistic description of the problem. Rather, the poverty shapes a social situation whose protagonists experience intense pressures, profound or at least brusque changes within the space of a single generation—migrations, catastrophes, economic degradation, loss of housing, of employment, and so on—which impact directly on their daily lives. These experiences are translated into an insecurity, general instability, and, at bottom, a lack of any place in the sun.

The capitalist development of the 1950s onward delivered a strong blow to the popular masses—a phenomenon which, though "normal," is no less relevant. The elevated growth rates of the gross domestic product, the rapid formation of new fortunes, the modification of the rural and urban landscapes—not only by the earthquake but also by the construction of new neighborhoods, factories, and so on—and the general modernization of economic activity and of social life, translated, for the immense majority of the population, into a more profound disarticulation of their living conditions. The peasants lost their lands and had to migrate toward the frontier zones or to the cities. In the latter, the advance of industrial and commercial capital reduced the economic space of the artisans, small merchants, and self-employed individual workers, all without generating alternate forms of employment: as was pointed out in Chapter 2, the process of proletarianization of the labor force was more effective in impoverishing the working masses and degrading their general living conditions than in salarizing the "freed" workers.

The dictatorship was more than the *form* of this kind of capitalism and this mode of labor proletarianization. The Somocista state operated on top of the structural tendencies of the Nicaraguan society that aimed at the disarticulation, disorganization, and isolation of the workers, reinforcing it all through repression. But at the same time, the dictatorship unintentionally contributed to the progressive development of a popular consciousness in which the rejection of misery, of lack of work and land, of a life without dignity, was articulated with the repudiation of the extra-economic components of Nicaraguan capitalism: police and military arbitrariness, all-embracing power of the bosses, daily insecurity. As a Managua worker told me: "Before, if you wanted to assert your rights, they made mincemeat out of you. They wanted you to work for peanuts."

Labor instability, under these conditions, mixed with and reinforced instability of income, of housing, and of the family; with hard and uncompensated labor; with the oppression of a dictatorship that controlled everything; with the arbitrariness of a public administration (the *private* stock of the governing clique) that corrupted everything. All of this was played out on the state of a society whose historic backdrop was also painted without any horizon for its popular classes; just foreign invasions, seasonal work, growing impoverishment, and a mean life.

The rise of the revolutionary struggle and especially the indiscriminate—and finally genocidal—nature of the dictatorial repression made it possible to overcome the internal divisions and reciprocal isolation among these sectors and unify them in the confrontation with the oppressor state. Active rebellion and personal and direct participation in the revolutionary struggle were converted into a defensive question, one of life or death. When being a victim of repression ceases being what happens to *someone else*—because that someone else is a *Sandinista,* or an *agitator,* or a *subversive,* or is *sought out* for a role in a situation far from one's own—and starts being what happens to *anyone,* even when that anyone remains passively at home, then remaining passively at home no longer serves as a defense. Fear of repression as something outside of daily life is transformed into a daily certainty of repression and opens the way for the necessity of an active defense. The following testimony illustrates this change:

> I told my aunt: "If they'll let me fight in this condition [pregnant], I'll fight," because even if I stay home a bullet or a rocket or a bomb'll get me. So either way I die (Maier 1980: 122).

I went into the Front because I thought otherwise we were just going to die as jerks (Maier 1980: 123).

Every action of the Front . . . brought the incorporation of dozens of youth who were ready to die fighting rather than stay behind and be killed with impunity (told to anthropologist Bernardo Albrecht).

We said goodbye to our wives, sisters, and mothers with tears in our eyes thinking we would never return, but always thinking that it would be better to die fighting than to die on our knees asking clemency (ibid.).

. . . and I told my children that it would be best for them to go into the Frente because, even if they didn't, the Guard would kill them anyway—just for being young, y'know (testimony of a mother of Estelí).

VANGUARD AND MASSES

The rejection of social exploitation and political oppression does not imply the automatic incorporation of the masses into the revolutionary struggle, or even acceptance of the idea that revolutionary change was necessary. Nor was the economic crisis or the exercise of repression enough. Left to their own instincts, people can produce violent explosions which are spectacular but are a political dead-end. Or they can opt for an evasive answer: migration, flight. It is the articulation of the masses into a revolutionary political organization that opens up the possibility of effective struggle, and provides a transformational potential to popular rebellions and protests.

The political terrain of Somoza's Nicaragua reinforced the social contradictions for the masses. The succession of pacts between the Conservative party and the dictatorship demonstrated that it was not through the traditional opposition—more traditional than oppositional—that the popular masses could express their yearning for emancipation.

The incapacity of the traditional left to root for itself in the masses and pose a viable revolutionary strategy—and the lack of interest of Social Christians in such a project—further restricted alternatives. In this regard, it is possible to see a relatively marked ideological gap between the popular bases and the established leadership. In some cases the problem seems to have stemmed from leaders actually having a different project; in others, it was their incapacity to link themselves effectively to the way in which the masses experienced

social exploitation and political oppression and thus recognize the
real level of conflict locked up inside them.[21]

The assassination of Pedro Joaquín Chamorro (January 10, 1978)
was the detonator that set off the popular explosion. The death of
someone who up to that moment seemed like the most dedicated
personal critic of the dictatorship sent the people out into the streets
in a violent expression of their accumulated fury—marching, shout-
ing, breaking, burning, hurling their anger in front of them with a
mixture of consciousness and instinct, in a single-minded attack
against the persons and property of the dictatorship:

> I started to participate after the death of Pedro Joaquín. Before that,
> no one really knew those that did; the ones who joined were very silent
> and specific. There weren't these masses like now . . . all this. So it
> began with the death of Pedro Joaquín. Well, it was just huge! Suddenly
> people weren't afraid anymore, there was one demonstration after
> another; they even burned houses and factories and everything (Maier
> 1980: 93).

Mobilizations in the street were nothing new in the struggle
against the dictatorship. Above all during the 1970s, the FSLN had
initiated student marches, peasant mobilizations, takeovers of
schools and churches, and the like. Notwithstanding their propaganda value, these forms of protest were basically an effort to recruit
specific sectors of the population and as such, had defined objectives: freedom of political prisoners, denunciations of torture and
disappearances, and so on. Though these forms of protest were
increasingly rooted among the people, fear still prevented broad
sectors of the masses from accepting the risks that incorporating
oneself into them implied—to be taken prisoner or disappear, to be
beaten, tortured, to die.

The assassination of Pedro Joaquín Chamorro put an end to all
that. Something definitively snapped: for vast numbers of people that
death was the final, brutal, overwhelming proof that no one was safe
from the dictatorship, that there was no way out apart from eliminating the dictatorship and direct action by the masses themselves. It
wasn't just the leader of UDEL, or the director of *La Prensa,* or an
internationally respected person who had been assassinated. As a
leader of the United People's movement told me: "That night, I had
the sensation that they had killed not only Pedro Joaquín but the
opposition to Somoza."

In any case, it was a particular kind of opposition that died with

Chamorro: that of change within the existing system. For the masses, what died was hope—or the fantasy—of change without their own efforts, the illusion that outside effort would be sufficient. The death of this illusion gave violent birth to a new conviction: the only effective opposition was that which the FSLN had been articulating for almost twenty years.

From that moment forward, the people never left the streets. A month later in Monimbó, the repression of a mobilization to commemorate the assassination of Augusto C. Sandino initiated the popular insurrection that would definitively unite the popular majority with the revolutionary vanguard; if the masses first poured spontaneously into the streets, they were consolidated there and triumphed against the dictatorship through Sandinista organization and arms: "The truth is that the masses were always considered, but they were viewed more as a support for the guerrilla, so that the guerrilla as such could break the National Guard, and not as happened in practice: it was the guerrilla that served as support for the masses so that they, through the insurrection, could demolish the enemy" (H. Ortega 1980.)

What in October 1977 were vanguard actions, and in January 1978 was an explosion of the masses, would become, starting with Monimbó and Masaya, a revolutionary insurrection. As a woman from Masaya explained:

> At that time we already knew that the Frente Sandinista moved through here, but some of us imagined that they would come in columns, or something. It was only later that we realized that we were the Frente; that they would give orientations, but that we were the ones, alongside them, who would have to fight. That day the red and black handkerchiefs came out. For the first time we all began to participate in the struggle. I remember that they put us all to work building barricades so that the Guardia couldn't come in; the problem was that we didn't have any weapons, but that didn't matter. We just said "Either we win or they'll kill us all."
>
> Our struggle was the struggle of all the people. We believed only in the Sandinista National Liberation Front. We never saw these bourgeois folks in combat who now say they helped. We never saw those that say they are for Human Rights. We never saw anyone but our own children, who were and are the Frente (*Los Muchachos*, 9 February 1983).

In order to explain Nicaragua's dizzying revolutionary surge between 1977 and 1979, it has been sometimes asserted, particularly in academic circles, that Somoza was a sort of "*ideal* enemy": the profoundly and increasingly corrupt character of his regime ended up isolating him from the rest of society and from a good part of the international community. This must have then made things easier for the FSLN, which could thus act within the space opened up by the errors, or the obstinacy, of its enemy.[22]

The argument, of course, is trivial. From this point of view, Trujillo must have also been an "ideal enemy": Why then did Dominican history evolve in such a different way from that of Nicaragua? Nor was the "final insurrection" an unknown phenomenon in Latin American popular struggles; among others, Colombia in 1948 and Argentina in 1970–71 lived through insurrectional explosions of extraordinary magnitudes. Why in these cases did popular rebellion not lead to the destruction of the oppressor state and to the constitution of a new kind of political power?

The answer is not given by the *primitive* character or the *errors* of the enemy, but by the capacity of the popular forces to find the strategies and instruments to give effective power to their struggle. What differentiates Nicaragua from these other cases is the existence of a revolutionary organization *consolidated* and *legitimated* by two decades of struggle against Somocismo. The impact within the consciousness of the people of this testament of struggle against the dictatorship, against exploitation, against oppression, is always enormous. The response of the masses may not be immediate, but the heroism, the boldness, the sacrifice of those who were first, progressively created the conditions for the incorporation—slowly at the beginning, massively at the end—of the people.[23] And at the same time, the active presence of the revolutionary organization meant that, when the people finally took to the streets, there was a structure that served as support to the rebellion, organized it, armed it, gave it continuity, and elevated it to higher political levels.

Elements of spontaneity undoubtedly existed among the people at the beginning of the final leg of the struggle. An IES report states: "The February (1978) revolt in Monimbó had . . . a highly spontaneous character. . . . The Frente Sandinista did not conduct the people's struggle in those actions, and at the beginning it was more a vital action of a community that spontaneously revalidated its tradition of struggle than it was any decision of the vanguard" (IES 1982c: 54).

Nonetheless these outbreaks took place in terrain prepared by the mass mobilization, propaganda, and armed actions of the FSLN. After the Monimbó insurrection, the FSLN decided to transfer its guerrilla cadre to the front of the mass struggle. This meant, as Cmdte. Humberto Ortega explained: "Comrades forged in the guerrilla, experienced in the military art, in ambushes . . . brought to mass work a solid military experience. Then, in September the signal had already been given for the insurrection among a large part of that guerrilla" (1980: 30).[24]

At the beginning of January 1979 the FSLN began to plan the complex military operation of the insurrection in Managua, which would be launched six months later. In a meticulous study of the terrain, they determined in which barrio or barrios the insurrection would be initiated, which barrios would act as support, diversion, or rearguard, where and how the trenches and barricades would be constructed, and so on. Little or nothing was left to improvisation or chance.[25]

The history of the FSLN is without doubt a history of armed confrontations with the Somocista dictatorship, but it is also a history of peasant and worker organization, of neighborhood and trade-union struggles, of the defense of human rights and civil liberties, of student mobilizations and cultural demands. The protagonist role of the masses that began at the start of 1978 both was the fruit of prior work and examples, and prepared the ground for more organized and massive forms of struggle.[26] The reflection of Cmdte. Henry Ruiz about the incorporation of the campesinos into the Sandinista struggle is also valid for the city: "The peasant . . . responded as if by magic, when there was really no more magic than the permanent activity of the years we spent in the mountains" (Ruiz 1980a).

4

National Unity
and Mixed Economy

One of the most frequently noted aspects of the Sandinista revolution is the participation of bourgeois sectors. This was made possible by the material structure of society, the way in which the Sandinista National Liberation Front (FSLN) articulated its revolutionary strategy to this structure, and finally, the nature of the dictatorship.

The Nicaraguan bourgeoisie's opposition to the Somocista regime had its ups and downs, but it originated fundamentally in the middle sectors rather than among large capitalists. The contradictions that differentiated Nicaraguan capitalists—particularly that between Somocista and non-Somocista capital, and between local and foreign (primarily finance) capital—acted in such a way that economic differences impelled political differences, gradually forcing the subordinated fractions to a political confrontation with the dictatorship.

This difference in the heart of the class was nourished by the evolution of the contradiction Somocismo/Sandinismo. Insofar as Somocismo was the political synthesis of the dependent capitalism evolving in Nicaragua, and Sandinismo the most advanced form of the popular struggle, the confrontation of these bourgeois fractions to the dictatorship was, at bottom, derived from the fundamental class antagonisms of Nicaraguan society rather than an autonomous element.

This is definitely not the opinion of the bourgeoisie itself, which tends to give its struggle a much more belligerent and decisive character—even though an analysis of its pronouncements and direct actions shows a moderate tone in both its ends and its focus.

Despite this, some academic left observers also concur with this image:

> The unleashing factor of the revolutionary process was initially the *interbourgeois crisis*, a product of the specific form that the repercussions from the prolonged capitalist recession took in Nicaragua, combined with the changes in the country's economy over the last 15 years (Gilly 1980: 134).

> *There can be no doubt, however, that in Nicaragua the bourgeois opposition itself opened up the crisis of the Somoza regime and actually led the first phase of the revolution. It was only at the end of the process, with the help of Somoza's intransigence, that the FSLN captured the leadership of the struggle* (H. Weber 1981: 33; italics in the original).

These appraisals show the influence not only of distance and haste—and an arbitrary reduction of a two-decade process of Sandinista struggle to its last twenty-four months—but also some elements of the FSLN's own political discourse in this last phase. Seeking to accelerate the general crisis of the dictatorship, the Sandinista Front defined a strategy of approach to democratic sectors of the Nicaraguan bourgeoisie in mid-1977. This urged their open incorporation into active opposition and emphasized the value that their contributions could have. Finally, the contrast of the collective actions adopted by these bourgeois fractions with their previous passivity and lack of understanding, together with their fear or insecurity, inclined the bourgeoisie to experience their actions as if they were extremely bold.

Dispassionate analysis accords the opposition activity of the bourgeoisie a minor relevance. Its participation in the defeat of Somocismo was real, but its efficacy was minimal insofar as it aspired to a primary role in the popular struggle. The participation of these sectors made sense to the extent that they inserted themselves into the rising revolutionary struggle and were subordinated to it.

FROM THE AMERICAN DREAM TO THE REVOLUTIONARY NIGHTMARE

The "pact of the generals" between Anastasio Somoza García and Emiliano Chamorro in 1950 (referred to in Chapter 2) welded the alliance between the two Nicaraguan bourgeois political forces: the Liberal party and the Conservative party. Their differences were more historical and geographic than economic. Thus there was no clear difference in their material bases—as, for example, between landowners and industrialists, producers and wholesalers, or whatever. Nor did they espouse different political-ideological projects. The point of conflict was simply over exclusive control of the state apparatus by the Somoza family and its friends and, through this, the privileged relationship with the United States, in a stage of Nicaraguan capitalist development in which both appeared as necessary conditions for the consolidation of the material bases of social domination. The pact of 1950 assured the Conservatives of subordinate incorporation into the Somocista state and to its benefits and sinecures, and guaranteed that from then on the disputes about the question of power would be settled by means other than armed confrontations. Explicit adherence to the anticommunist doctrine of the cold war demonstrated the *good intentions* of both parties with respect to the primacy of U.S. interests in the region.

The execution of Somoza García in 1956 by Rigoberto López Pérez initiated a succession of armed attempts by petty-bourgeois groups and small sectors of the middle bourgeoisie to put an end to the dynastic dictatorship. In the end they all failed: either because they could never root themselves in the population, or because of the repression that came down on them. In the late 1950s some Conservative party youth attempted an action of this kind in the zone of Olama y Mollejones, which was frustrated almost immediately. The attempt, led by Pedro Joaquín Chamorro among others, apparently counted on the tacit support of the highest authorities of the party and the cooperation of José Figueres from Costa Rica (Talavera 1978).

That was the end of bourgeois direct actions until the mobilizations and bosses' strikes of January–February 1978. During the two intervening decades the bourgeoisie integrated itself actively into the state-led capitalist expansion process taking place in the country, significantly tempering its political resentments. Its position toward the dictatorship changed radically. During the 1960s the market rather than the state absorbed the efforts of the bourgeoisie; its capacity to recruit broad sectors of the popular masses was used to guarantee itself better treatment in the accumulation process. In the 1970s, especially after the Managua earthquake, contradictions between the bourgeoisie and Somocismo became more acute, but did not move beyond the arena of production and circulation or generate a political alternative. The bourgeoisie's disputes with Somocismo were always economic, while it agreed to leave political management to the regime.

The Nicaraguan bourgeoisie thus collaborated with the timid reformist orientations of the state in the developmentalist decade of the 1960s, through a group of institutions for "common good," "development of the community," "social promotion," and the like. Usually endowed with abundant U.S. financing (Wheelock 1976: 150ff), these organizations were oriented mainly to community development schemes promoted by the Alliance for Progress, to the provision of small loans, and to other such measures. They mixed benevolence with interest and objectively helped foster both expectations of individual progress and fantasies of an alternative to the regime among the most impoverished groups of the popular masses. The following commentary of a high officer of one of these organizations—FUNDE (Nicaraguan Development Foundation)—is representative of the basic overall conception:

> Said institution presented the formula to make a bloodless revolution, and to incorporate the discontented—the great majority in our Latin American countries—into the development of the country.
> In Managua a group of 22 entrepreneurs met and launched the idea, very concerned about the change of mentality in help for the marginalized. . . . They chatted, you might say, about a continent where the cry for justice and the petition for opportunities is igniting a tremendous clamor that threatens to go beyond such issues. The 22 business leaders of FUNDE decided to call their new movement: *New Alternative,* based on the idea that "really and truly," as one of its directors said, "one cannot be rich when there is poverty all around" (Báez Sacasa 1970).

The bourgeois position changed with the Managua earthquake and the practices of the dictatorship regarding reconstruction. In effect, Somoza made privileged use of international credits to move into banking and construction, dominated up to that point by capitalists integrated into the two large financial groups that existed in Nicaragua: BANIC and BANAMERICA (Wheelock 1976; Strachan 1976; Diederich 1981). Government corruption reached unprecedented levels, and although the international crisis began to be felt a few years later through the increase in industrial costs and the fall in demand for traditional exports, the reactivation of the economy sparked by the reconstruction, though limited, basically fed the waters that turned Somoza's own economic mill, leaving the financial groups' own large bourgeoisie with the bitter taste of lost business. From then on, the *disloyal competition* of the regime would be the fundamental charge of the local capitalists unable to use the state apparatus for their own profits.

The question of *disloyal competition* expressed the unfolding contradiction between a bourgeois fraction that accumulated capital and diversified its interests through the state apparatus, and those fractions that were supported by market forces. This contradiction is not peculiar to Nicaraguan capitalism, but rather to the kind and level of capitalist development taking place in that period in Nicaragua. What is notable in the Nicaraguan case is the cohesion with which the fractions affected by this contradiction responded to the Somocista clique, confining themselves to the corporative plane until the regime's general crisis became fully evident. But before turning attention to the strategy of these fractions, it is necessary to note that the state-market contradiction is only *one* dimension of the internal divisions in the Nicaraguan bourgeoisie—basically those at the highest levels. In the middle-bourgeois fractions, and above all among the agrarian bourgeoisie, this contradiction is articulated with those analyzed in Chapter 2, that between the productive capital of the small and middle bourgeoisie, and large financial capital—which was as much Somocista as opposition.

The first confrontation of the subordinated bourgeois fractions took place in March 1974, with the First Grand Convention of Nicaraguan Private Enterprise. Convoked by the Higher Council of Private Initiative (COSIP)—an organization of the country's large financial groups—the meeting was viewed by many observers, as well as participants, as the beginning of a firm stance against Somocismo. It called attention, in the words of one participant, to "the need for profound social changes that would benefit the great dispossessed majorities" (Dreyfus 1980).

My opinion is less categorical. The meeting unquestionably pointed out various doubts about the regime, but it lacked the aggressiveness and profundity with which it has since been adorned. It touched on a tenuous confrontation in which spokespersons of the medium bourgeoisie assumed the most active role. The business leaders presented themselves as a business association with strict economic demands, therefore sidelining any introduction of the question of power. They discussed improvements in the functioning of the existing economic system, increasing its efficiency levels, and particularly obtaining more equitable participation in its benefits for all fractions of the class.

The demands by the "private sector" centered on two principle issues: (1) guarantees of the correct and efficient utilization of public resources; and (2) strengthening of the system of public bidding to assure the correct use of public funds destined for national projects—in other words, guarantees of an *appropriate* use of the social surplus to benefit capital in general rather than certain capitalist fractions exclusively. At the same time, they incorporated the demands of particular business sectors—cattle ranchers, medium-size farmers, and so on. They also proposed the need to raise salaries and the advisability of recognizing workers' right to unionize.[1] In terms of overall proposals, they advocated properly integrated agroindustry, above all in food and natural fiber products—that is, cattle and cotton.

The Nicaraguan entrepreneurs saw four legitimate functions of government: (1) maintenance of constitutional order; (2) provision of physical and social infrastructure; (3) definition of rules of the game between the public sector and private business; and (4) maintenance of the macroeconomic equilibrium—to assure that price and income levels would be maintained, and so on (Cruz 1974: 16–17). At the same time, private business clamored for participation in the management of public affairs. But the limits of that participation were clearly suggested by its social function as private enterprise; thus it would be limited to orienting and prosecuting state actions and demanding the complete fulfillment of the state's obligations regarding business (Cruz 1974: 18–19).

The kind of state demanded by the Nicaraguan bourgeoisie was thus a modern capitalist state that would efficiently fulfill its political-economic functions (cf. O'Connor 1973; Altvater 1977). Only the capitalist backwardness of the Somocista state—the captive bounty of one clique—and the lack of precedents for this type of claim could lend this entrepreneurial outline the aggressive character with which it is sometimes presented.

The first attempt to transform this corporativist pressure into an opposition took place at the end of that same year. In December 1974 the Democratic Union for Liberation (UDEL) was created. Decisively pushed by Pedro Joaquín Chamorro, UDEL united various parties and political groups of the middle class and medium-sized bourgeoisie—the Independent Liberal party (PLI), the Social Christian party (PSC), the Conservative National Action (ANC—Chamorro's own group), the Constitutionalist Liberal Movement (MLC), and others.[2] It also included the Nicaraguan Socialist party (PSN) which, following the line of similar Latin American parties, considered the realization of bourgeois-democratic reforms to be a necessary condition for the development of a revolutionary process later on. Two trade unions also participated: the Nicaraguan Workers' Confederation (CTN), oriented to the Social Christian party, and the General Workers' Confederation (Independent), which responded to the PSN. UDEL was distinguished from previous party initiatives (such as the National Oppositional Union of 1967 or the National Oppositional Coalition at the beginning of the 1970s) by promoting a whole package of social reforms and progressive measures, including agrarian reform, free elections, and national self-determination (Chamorro 1982). Nevertheless, the Conservative party resented UDEL's—and particularly Chamorro's—effort to try to go over its head, and the large bourgeoisie showed little confidence in its pluralist composition and its openly reformist political program (Bendaña 1978). It is evident that the bankers and industrialists were still not interested in a frontal break with Somoza, and remained unconvinced that an effort of this kind could count on U.S. support.

Furthermore, these groups considered it beyond all doubt that repression would triumph over the revolutionary movement. Two weeks after the creation of UDEL, the FSLN carried out its operation against the residence of Chema Castillo, ending the stage of "silent accumulation" (see Wheelock 1979). In addition to the operational efficacy of the FSLN, the action showed the enthusiastic support of the population for the Sandinista struggle (Diederich 1981). But the establishment of the state of siege, martial law, and press censorship immediately afterward, as well as their class prejudices, led these groups of the large bourgeoisie to conclude that the regime was consolidating itself. Why then involve themselves in a confrontation with such a small chance of winning?

The repressive measures lasted thirty-three months, until September 1977. During that time the persecution and massacre of peasants, students, and the general population suspected of collaborating with the FSLN knew no bounds. Somocista aircraft bombed rural populations while the National Guard attacked trade unions, "disappeared" worker and student activists, and persecuted priests and religious workers who were denouncing the atrocities being committed against the population. At the same time, the brutality and breadth of the repression opened the space for a strengthening of the capital accumulation process. Trade-union repression made more intense exploitation of the labor force possible, and Nicaraguan business interests found excellent opportunities to make more money. On the other hand, the rise of international prices for some export products—coffee, in particular—acted to center the attention of the bourgeoisie and middle groups even more on the economic question, without looking too much into the social and political cost of the bonanza.

This bonanza, nonetheless, was not without tensions or aggravations for the bourgeoisie. The existence of the state of siege gave Somoza and the National Guard a free hand to truly pillage the economy, leaving the non-Somocista bourgeoisie unable to do anything, or even to criticize the situation through its traditional voice—the newspaper *La Prensa,* directed by Pedro Joaquin Chamorro. The *disloyal competition* was aggravated during this period. At the same time the tight alliance of Somocista capital with foreign capital and with large local financial capital deprived the middle bourgeoisie of any opportunity for the extraordinary earnings generated by the rise of international prices, as we saw in Chapter 2.

Finally, the exacerbation of Somocista repression failed to liquidate the Sandinista struggle, which continued to make itself felt in the countryside and mountains as well as in the city, despite the blows it received (IES 1981: 45).

The lifting of the state of siege unquestionably reflected the persistence of popular demands, but it also reflected the pressure of the opposition bourgeoisie, suffocated in its democratic aspirations and unable to extract substantial benefits from the state of siege. In turn, the outbreak of business pressure for the return to institutional *normality* was decisively supported by the changes in international politics that took place at the end of 1976, with the election of U.S. President James Carter. Carter's focus on the issue of human rights—independent of his ideological slant or ulterior motives—broadened the space for representatives of the Nicaraguan bourgeoisie, clerical elements, and sectors tied to the revolutionary movement to denounce Somocista atrocities to the U.S. Congress. The election thus suggested to the most dynamic and democratic bourgeois groups the possibility of winning a powerful ally for a strategy of posing an alternative both to Somoza and to the revolutionary project. At the same time, the rise of social democracy in the region posed the possibility of winning additional support for a strategy of democratic reforms led by the business sector. In October, with the intermediation of the Catholic church hierarchy, the bourgeoisie convoked a *national dialogue* on the situation of the country, initiating an association with the hierarchy that has lasted to the present time.

But by then the FSLN had advanced its own approach to elements of business and the middle classes: the Group of Twelve. Formed between August and September of that year, the Group of Twelve consisted of intellectuals, professionals, priests, and businessmen, some of whom were already collaborators with the FSLN, and others whose children were in the Frente; its objective was to constitute a provisional government and to broaden the relations of the FSLN with the bourgeois opposition and in international circles. None of the large economic or financial interests was represented, and the two or three business functionaries that participated did so in their own names. The Group of Twelve was basically made up of personalities with national and international prestige in their respective fields, which permitted the FSLN to significantly broaden its internal and foreign political relations (López et al. 1979; Briones Torres 1980). Above all it allowed the Frente to build a bridge toward the "official" opposition.

The Group of Twelve came into public light in October 1977, coinciding with the launching of the FSLN's military offensive in San Carlos, Ocotal, and Masaya. In a public communiqué in *La Prensa* (October 21, 1977) the group denounced the repressive character of the dictatorship and underscored the general yearning for "a new form of democratic and social organization." Soon after, the Twelve declared that the crisis could not be resolved without the participation of the FSLN, and called for the creation of a broad anti-Somoza front that would include it.

This was the first time that representatives of the middle-class and medium-sized bourgeoisie had taken an open stand against the dictatorship *claiming the revolutionary positions of the FSLN*. By that period two clear positions existed within the Nicaraguan bourgeoisie: (1) that of the Group of Twelve, which presented the revolutionary positions of the Frente Sandinista and advocated its recognition and incorporation into broad opposition groupings; and (2) that of a broad spectrum of political and corporativist associations, which called for "national dialogue" without referring to Sandinismo and rejected revolutionary struggle. The latter included UDEL, INDE (Nicaraguan Development Institute), the Confederation of Chambers of Commerce, the Authentic Conservative party, and others (Lozano 1980).

This second position would predominate in the antidictatorial struggle of the bourgeoisie in that period. The greater weight and respectability of the class *organizations* involved contrasted favorably with the *individual* character of the prestige of members of the Twelve; recognition of the legitimacy of armed struggle against the dictatorship was still too large a step for the bourgeoisie to make. Nevertheless, "national dialogue" headed quickly toward failure due to the intransigence of the dictatorship and the hesitations of the bourgeoisie itself, while the creation of the Twelve showed the Sandinista will to establish ties with all the opposition bourgeoisie, without abdicating its revolutionary perspective or its strategy of armed struggle.

The assassination of Pedro Joaquín Chamorro—to silence the denunciations of Somocista corruption coming from his newspaper—accelerated things for the bourgeoisie. The Higher Council of Private Initiative (COSIP) called for a national strike supposedly to get some explanation from the dictatorship; but the real objective was to get Somoza to leave, either through his resignation or by way of a military coup. All the business sectors accepted the call and, to ensure the indispensable cooperation of the workers, opted to pay outstanding salaries during the stoppage. But when after three weeks Somoza had not resigned and a military coup had not taken place, and the costs of the tactic had already become burdensome, the bourgeoisie opted to give up and go back to normal.

The decision to lift the strike made the political weakness of the bourgeoisie vis à vis the dictatorship all too evident, to say nothing of its inability to get the United States to relax its support for Somoza. At the same time, it showed the passivity of the workers toward the bourgeois calls: they joined a paid bosses' strike, and just as easily accepted the reinitiation of activities. From then on, insecurity would penetrate deeply into the bougeoisie; it was evident to them all that the ally and competitor of yesterday was today an enemy that it would be impossible to ease out with their own efforts. The inefficiency of collective action quickly gave way to individual strategies: between early 1978 and July 1979 capital flight abroad has been estimated at some U.S. $1,500 million, of which at least $600 million belonged to the large bourgeoisie and the rest to the governing clique (although after the revolution the bourgeoisie itself would characterize this "every man for himself" approach as a planned strategy of *economic destabilization* against the dictatorship) (Dreyfus 1980).

After the failure of the bosses' strike, the first *political* organization of the bourgeoisie as a class was created in March 1978: the Nicaraguan Democratic Movement (MDN), headed by Alfonso Robelo, a businessman with strong ties to the BANIC financial group and to U.S. capital in the country. The creation of MDN suggested that the bourgeoisie had determined what was fundamental in its opposition, and realized that UDEL had barely begun to represent the higher fractions of the class.

Two months later, in May, the MDN, UDEL, the PLI, the PSN, the PSC, and other lesser traditional opposition parties, as well as the CTN, the CGT-I, and the Confederation of Trade Union Unity (CUS), created the Broad Opposition Front (FAO). The Twelve participated at the beginning; after all, the FAO was taking up an initiative proposed by the Twelve in October 1977, which the bourgeoisie only recently had decided it could swallow. But by its composition the FAO expressed the prevalence of the timid view of that class, which was quickly reflected in its positions; furthermore, absent from this proposal was the Twelve's call for a broad front to include the FSLN. The FAO's Democratic Government Program included a combination of political and social reforms of a democratic kind: reorganization of the national army, separation of army and politics, prohibition of civil trials by military tribunals, elimination of corruption, abolition of repressive laws and elimination of intelligence services, free trade-union and popular organization, agrarian reform, literacy programs, fiscal reform, urban reform, and free elections (López et al. 1979: 357–59). After almost four years, the bourgeoisie insisted on the UDEL program, both in its reach and in its limitations. As in 1974, the demands for reforms were accompanied by a careful omission of any reference to the revolutionary struggle of the FSLN. As then, the reformist bourgeoisie *still* could not count on U.S. support, but unlike in 1974, it *could no longer* aspire to head up the protest of the masses. May, June, and July 1978 showed the clear signs of a rapid evolution by the people toward Sandinista positions.

Within a short time the Twelve quit the FAO and in July the FSLN created the United People's Movement (MPU): a broad alliance of political, trade union, women's, and student organizations.[3] If the FAO was a bourgeois effort to consolidate class unity in its confrontation with the dictatorship, the MPU testified to the effort to reach unity in the popular camp within the framework of a revolutionary strategy to overthrow Somocismo. It talked not only about reorganizing the national army, but about abolishing the existing army and creating an Army in Defense of National Sovereignty that would guarantee the active defense of the sovereignty, independence, democracy, and the process of social development of the country. This army would be integrated by (a) combatants who participated in the defeat of the Somocista dictatorship; (b) soldiers and officers who joined the struggle to overthrow the regime and those who rebelled against the orders to fight against the people; and (c) citizens that complied with obligatory military service, which would be duly re-established.

In other words, the MPU explicitly proposed the constitution of a new army based on the revolutionary combatants—a clear allusion to the FSLN—and the definitive liquidation of the National Guard. At the same time the program postulated the confiscation and nationalization of Somocista properties; the nationalization of natural resources and of enterprises that exploited them; the nationalization of maritime, air, and urban public transport; an agrarian reform program that would promote and diversify production, limit landowning property and nationalize idle latifundios; freedom of trade union organization; reforms in labor legislation; and so on (see López et al. 1979: 360–72).

The FAO signified, with all its limitations, the culmination of the autonomous political initiative of the Nicaraguan bourgeoisie (Lozano 1980; Gilbert 1983). In September 1978 it called a second national strike. By then the general political climate was extremely active, following the Sandinista operation of August 22 against the National Palace; spontaneous uprisings occurred in Matagalpa and at the beginning of September the FSLN launched the insurrection in various cities of the country. At the end of September a coup movement within the National Guard, led by Colonel Bernardino Larios, was aborted.

The bosses' strike thus passed almost unnoticed in the middle of political polarization and a consequent elevation of the revolutionary popular struggle. The business offensive was overpowered in *civic* as well as *military* terms, by Somoza's fierce resistance, by the loyalty of the National Guard, by the incorporation of the majority of the people into the Sandinista revolutionary strategy, and by the continuing U.S. government resistance to supporting the departure of the dictator.

This resistance, however, was overcome by October, and through so-called *international mediation* the United States moved to openly support the business interests' demand for Somoza's negotiated departure. During that period it was evident to everyone that his remaining in power would guarantee the advance of the revolutionary struggle and quickly reduce the possibilities of triumph for the bourgeois option. The United States at that point abandoned its creature of the last half-century in order to help the bourgeoisie cut a path for itself through the revolutionary advance.

From that moment on the bourgeoisie was thrust into a policy of winning over the lesser groups and fractions of capital, toward whom they had never before had a defined policy, and whose contradictions with the large bourgeoisie facilitated their approach to the popular opposition. In August 1978—that is, *almost thirty years after* the initiation of cotton raising—the first cotton producer organizations were created: the León Cotton Growers Association (ADAL), the Chinandega Cotton Growers' Association (ADACH), and the Western Cotton Growers' Association (ADADO). The leaders of these associations came from the most traditional landowning families of the sector, although they were subordinated to commercial-financial-processing capital; the lesser fractions of the bourgeoisie—what are sometimes called the *chapiolla* bourgeoisie—and the well-off strata of the peasantry were weakly represented in these organizations (Baumeister 1982).

At the beginning of 1979, with the backing of INDE, the Union of Agricultural Producers of Nicaragua (UPANIC) was created, with the goal of grouping all the agricultural and cattlemen's associations into one organization (Dreyfus 1980). And soon afterward, also with the help of INDE, the Confederation of Professional Associations of Nicaragua (CONAPRO) was created, aiming at these respective sectors of the urban middle class.

This decision also tailed the Sandinista initiative, since it sought to give corporativist expression to particular business fractions—in a way that subordinated them to large capital—when the FSLN was already offering them political expression in the context of the revolutionary project. In February 1979, in effect, the National Patriotic Front (FPN) was created at the request of the Frente Sandinista. In addition to the MPU and the Twelve, it included organizations that until then figured among the allies of the bourgeoisie: the PLI and the CTN, as well as the Popular Social Christian party (PPSC), the Union of Radio Journalists of Managua—particularly strategic in the battle for the means of communication—and the Workers Front, traditionally identified with extreme left positions and thus critical of the FSLN strategy.

The FPN was constituted around three principles: (1) national sovereignty, (2) effective democracy, and (3) justice and social progress. It rejected any kind of foreign intervention that tried to "impose formulas for our political, economic, and social life," an unmistakable reference to the negotiations of the FAO with the U.S. government and the Organization of American States regarding so-called *collective mediation* and to the intervention of an "inter-American" armed force. It advocated the overthrow of the Somocista dictatorship and the eradication of all its vestiges, rejecting any maneuver that would signify "Somocismo without Somoza" in order to open the way for the democratic transformation of Nicaraguan society; it thus repudiated the efforts of the FAO and the U.S. Embassy to safeguard as much as possible the control of the National Guard with the exception of those most compromised by their association with Somoza. It put forward the creation of the new National Army proposed by the MPU, dedicated to safeguarding the sovereignty and territorial integrity of the country, as well as socioeconomic changes proposed by MPU (López et al, 1979: 372–78).

From this point on the bourgeoisie resigned itself to following in the footsteps of U.S. policy toward Nicaragua. It accepted the U.S. initiative of broadening the Junta of the Government of National Reconstruction (JGRN) created by the FSLN, simply to share with the U.S. Embassy the defeat that resulted from the Sandinista refusal; its recognition of this junta came too late. It played a marginal role in some programmatic points of the future Government of National Reconstruction, and during the insurrection it limited itself to pronouncements and declarations without involving itself directly in the struggle, swallowing its frustration.[4]

The strategy of the antidictatorial struggle designed by the FSLN put into bold relief the lack of political options of a bourgeoisie that had confronted the Somocista state in such a weak way that up to the last moment it lacked its own political program, and depended for its survival on the White House. At the same time it revealed the U.S. involvement with the dictatorship up to the moment it appeared unsalvageable, and its failure, when the revolutionary triumph appeared inevitable, to separate itself from Somoza and generate a non-Sandinista alternative: what in the political language of the FSLN was called "Somocismo without Somoza." The failure first of the "collective mediation" of the United States, the Dominican Republic, and Guatemala (end of 1978), later of the OAS initiative (beginning of 1979), and finally of the special mission of Ambassador Bowdler, marked Washington's inability to detach itself from an ally whose fall threatened to go much further than a simple change of personnel in the exercise of government.

It is evident that the U.S. strategy was elaborated much more as an alternative to the FSLN's revolutionary strategy than as a product of a foreign policy aimed at supporting nondictatorial forms of political power. This may not have been the fault of the Carter administration alone, but the inevitable product of U.S. involvement in Nicaragua over the past half-century—an involvement, from the outset, in an adventure of personal power and dictatorial domination. The comfortable relations with the Somozas developed by the United States lulled any notion in the Department of State or the White House that the Somoza family might not reign eternal. When the Sandinista struggle entered its final phase, the United States comprehended that such a theoretical possibility had become an irrefutable reality. Not only the military but the political initiative of the anti-Somocista struggle as well had belonged to the FSLN for some time. Given this, it took a lot of imagination to entertain the notion of replacing Somoza without significantly affecting his scheme of power—especially the National Guard.

A related question refers to the relation of the Nicaraguan non-Somocista bourgeoisie to U.S. policy. In effect, Washington's strategy was supported by the opposition to Somoza in the heart of the business classes, above all after the assassination of Pedro Joaquín Chamorro. At that point the bourgeoisie threw itself into open actions against the dictatorship, trying to thus define a nonrevolutionary option for getting rid of the dictator. It seems clear that this strategy depended on gaining the support of the U.S. Embassy, which it essentially did.

The relationship of the non-Somocista bourgeoisie to the United States is important for our political understanding. On the one hand it shows that the denunciations about the long-term U.S. involvement with the Somocista regime were not simply an FSLN slogan, but a basic part of the reality with which the bourgeoisie had to deal. As a class this bourgeoisie was able to participate in some of the benefits of the system of power that the United States contributed so decisively to structuring—notwithstanding the subordination it had to accept as the *cost* of those benefits. Everyone knew that if the Somoza family achieved absolute control of Nicaragua, it was thanks to the military support of Washington. And if Somoza Debayle was maintained in the government despite the opposition of these bourgeois fractions, that was also thanks to the fact that the United States had not decided, or did not know how, to get rid of him.

On the other hand, the negotiations of these bourgeois fractions with the United States shows that the opposition that grew out of them was by nature *internal* to the system of domination established in Nicaragua a half-century before by the United States itself. U.S. endorsement represented the common denominator of all the projects of bourgeois political domination in Nicaragua; neither Somocismo, nor bourgeois anti-Somocismo, was conceived of as viable without U.S. support. The defense of national sovereignty, the liberation from all forms of external domination, appeared once again in the history of Nicaragua as the heritage of the revolutionary struggle of its people.

Thus a bitter competition developed between Somoza and the anti-Somocista bourgeoisie over U.S. support, a competition fed by fear of the program of social transformations promoted by the FSLN. Somoza tried to retain for himself the role of champion of anticommunism, denouncing the complicity of his bourgeois enemies with the FSLN, but this cold war argument was less useful in the era of *detente*. For its part, the non-Somocista bourgeoisie tried to raise a nonrevolutionary alternative to the regime, but without proposing its total dismantling.

The alliance that the non-Somocista bourgeoisie tried to establish with the U.S. Embassy had to compete with the revolutionary struggle of the FSLN and its frontal opposition to the Somocista regime. The open participation of the popular classes in the Sandinista struggle was on the rise, particularly after 1977, while the FSLN gained support from friendly governments in the region, notably

Panama and Costa Rica. Failing in its mass actions, the bourgeoisie opted for palace strategies: a military coup, pressure from the U.S. Embassy. But this could not win out over the FSLN's strategy that combined mass insurrectional action, popular organization, rural guerrilla warfare, conventional military combat, international diplomacy, and the opening toward all forces opposed to Somocismo on the basis of an uncompromising program. The Nicaraguan bourgeoisie—a class of recent origins, weak in the face of a state from which it had been benefiting up until a short time earlier, with no autonomous political experience—could not present itself to the peasants, workers, students, unemployed, the poor of the countryside and the city, in other words the majority of the country, as a real alternative to the FSLN.

Lulled by the fantasy of U.S. imperial omnipotence, mortgaged to a strategy of smooth whispering and lobbying, accustomed to considering politics as something outside their class, and lacking a national project, the wealthy classes of Nicaragua were in no condition to understand that more was at stake than a man and a name in the government. And when they did understand it, their own subordination to the Somocista state effectively eliminated them from any possibility of action.

NATIONAL UNITY AND POPULAR HEGEMONY

The Frente Sandinista knew how to unite under their leadership all the forces exploited and oppressed by the dictatorship. This included the local bourgeois fractions that opposed Somocismo because of its monopoly of political power, favoritism, corruption, and generalized repression. The contradiction Somocismo/anti-Somocismo could thus be expressed as the contradiction Somocismo/Sandinismo. It was, in the first instance, a political contradiction. But it was more than that: it combined the contradiction of imperialism and the class contradiction.[5]

The triumph over the Somocista regime took place within the development of a clear anti-oligarchic and anti-imperialist consciousness promoted at the base of the popular classes by FSLN political work. Popular victory signified not only the fall of the dictatorship but also the violent and total destruction of the dependent capitalist state. Lacking any base of legitimacy or consensus, the Somocista state collapsed quickly and in fact disappeared after the dictator's flight and subsequent dissolution of the National Guard.

Posing the struggle against Somoza as a stage in a broader and deeper process of popular struggle determined that the defeat of the dictatorship was also the defeat of the substitution projects promoted by the bourgeoisie and imperialism. Sandinista strategy permitted a glimpse therefore that the popular victory was not the end of the process, but defined a new and more advantageous position from which to pursue the development of the revolution (H. Ortega 1981: 79–80).

This specific configuration of the Sandinista struggle helps delineate the *democratic, popular and anti-imperialist* character of the current stage of the revolution, at the same time that it highlights the profound class differences that separate the Nicaraguan process from traditional bourgeois-democratic revolutions. The latter are directed against the continuance of the feudal order, while the Sandinista struggle liquidated a clearly capitalist domination—notwithstanding the comparatively backward character of its material base. Bourgeois-democratic revolutions, furthermore, appeal to the popular masses as a force to be maneuvered to impose a capitalist project, and therefore welcome their mobilization to the extent necessary to force absolutism to accept a transaction. The activation of popular rebellion is intermixed therefore with the efficacy—and the reality—of repression. The Sandinista struggle, on the other hand, testifies to the leadership by a vanguard that expresses the majority—worker and popular—component of the struggle, in an alliance with other sectors based on Sandinista strength.

The FSLN synthesized a complex matrix of contradictions into a strategy of struggle that would also begin to break apart the material bases of the dictatorship. The FSLN's leadership permitted these democratic and national contradictions to be articulated under the lead of the class contradiction, in a way that would express the historic hegemony of the popular classes.

The bourgeoisie grasped the evidence of its defeat only at the last moment. The Broad Opposition Front gave its support to the Sandinista-inspired Government Junta of National Reconstruction only on June 24, 1979, and the Superior Council of Private Enterprise (COSEP) not until June 27.[6] By so doing, these private sectors were able to join the victors in the stage that opened up on July 19. They did not do so as the hegemonic force, however, but rather as a subordinated element of a national liberation movement.

National unity under the hegemony of the popular classes did not constitute a novelty for the Frente Sandinista: in a 1970 text, Carlos Fonseca expressed it as follows:

> We are conscious that socialism is the only perspective that the people have to achieve a profound change in their living conditions. This does not suggest that we will exclude persons that do not think as we do, and although we think that the fundamental guide must be the principles of scientific socialism, we are disposed to march alongside people with the most diverse beliefs who are interested in the overthrow of the tyranny and in the liberation of our country. (Fonseca 1981: 219).

The Group of Twelve, the United People's Movement, the National Patriotic Front, and later the Program of the Government of National Reconstruction (July 9, 1979) expressed this proposal in terms of a popular democracy with a plurality of perspectives.

Nevertheless, the experience of four years of revolution demonstrates the disinterest of the different bourgeois sectors in accepting the subordinated role that the process has awarded them. In the period July–December 1979, elements representing different fractions of the bourgeoisie were incorporated into important positions in the governing junta and the appartus of the new state. The engineer Alfonso Robelo—president of the MDN, business leader, and large capitalist—was designated a member of the junta together with Violetta Chamorro—widow of Pedro Joaquín and with strong economic interests in the newspaper *La Prensa*. Economist Roberto Mayorga joined the Planning Ministry; businessman Manuel J. Torres, former president of COSEP, was at Agriculture; Noel Rivas Gasteazoro, also an important businessman, joined the Ministry of Industry and Commerce; the presidency of the Central Bank was given to Arturo Cruz, an economist of the Democratic Conservative party and former official of the Inter-American Development Bank; Dr. Luis Carrión Montoya, linked to the now confiscated financial group BANIC, was designated president of the National Financial System; the presidency of the Supreme Court of Justice was occupied by Dr. Rafael Córdoba Rivas, leader of the Democratic Conservative party and of UDEL; ex-Colonel Bernardino Larios, who in

August 1978 had headed a frustrated military coup within the National Guard, was named minister of defense. At the same time, a number of professionals linked to the MDN were given important technical positions. Other ministries were occupied by members of the Group of Twelve (Education, Justice, Foreign Relations, Finances), or by independent personalities or leaders of political or other kinds of organizations—although in their personal capacity (Labor, Housing, Health), and many vice-ministries were covered by leaders or members of non-Sandinista parties or organizations.

During this period only two members of the FSLN National Directorate occupied positions as ministers: Cmdte. Tomás Borge (minister of the interior) and Cmdte. Jaime Wheelock, at the head of the Nicaraguan Institute of Agrarian Reform (INRA). But three of the five members of the junta indicated the decisive weight of the Frente in that body: Cmdte. Daniel Ortega, Dr. Sergio Ramírez Mercado (of the Group of Twelve), and Dr. Moisés Hassán (of the MPU). Other ministries were occupied by members of the FSLN: Social Welfare, Culture, Transport and Public Works, and the post of commander-in-chief of the new Sandinista Popular Army was assumed by two members of the National Directorate of the FSLN: Cmdtes. Humberto Ortega Saavedra and Luis Carrión Cruz.[7]

The participation of diverse political social forces—including the bourgeoisie—in the institutionalization of the new state must be appreciated. Clearly this participation was subordinated to the FSLN project of popular hegemony; however, it could also be said that the bourgeois participation in government was far in excess of the role it played in the struggle against the dictatorship. In some ways this served the interests of the FSLN, immediately lessening the impact of their own lack of technical cadres and ties to the financial world. It may also have neutralized excessive pressures from the United States and other countries. But fundamentally everyone was clear what the political project postulated by the FSLN was, and that the junta would execute it as the government program—a program in whose elaboration the bourgeois representatives had had some role (INDE 1979: 11–13).

This project was not opposed, in principle, to the private appropriation of the means of production, although for political reasons the Somocista properties that were the product of a half-century of plunder were confiscated. In effect the legitimation of private property was founded on the notion of means of production as such, not as rental property. This implied the existence of a state to supervise the development of production, a normal aspect of any modern state (see, for example, Agnoli 1978), which appeared excessive to a good part of the property-owning classes of Nicaragua. On the other hand, within the popular camp, and even within the FSLN, some questioned even this level of private property in production, although they granted the temporary necessity.

The Nicaraguan bourgeoisie, furthermore, entered the new stage *deprived of military power.* Their defense of the National Guard right up to the last moment—with the exception of the officers most committed to repression and corruption, and the members of the Somoza family—was their way of defending the incorporation of their own armed class power into the new stage. The disbanding of the Guard and trials and imprisonment of its members, along with the creation of the Sandinista Popular Army, left them disarmed in the face of organized popular power. The bourgeoisie did not, however, give up trying to make its project felt, and to that end used its position in the new state. The period between July 1979 and May 1980 marked what at times was a quiet, at others an open bid to impose a political project that the majority of the population had repudiated in the streets, in the trenches, and at the barricades.

The FSLN triumphed in this confrontation, however, due to its monopoly of armed power, the strength of the newly created mass organizations, and its ability to ally with subordinate elements of the bourgeoisie. Each of these is worth looking at in some detail.

The Sandinista Popular Army, based primarily on the youth who joined the struggle, is both the national army and the army of a nation born out of a popular and anti-imperialist struggle. It is not a party army, but one that recognizes the political—and certainly class—content of the project of a nation that the Sandinista revolution is promoting. Any army is a *political army,* since it is the army of state, which defends and sustains a given project of social domination, and therefore of class. The army is *apolitical* only with regard to internal class differences: the armed forces stay apart from these contradictions between dominant fractions or groups as a condition of their effective political function.[8] What differentiates the *politicalness* of the Sandinista Popular Army is the character of the political project that it defends, and the explicitness of this political role. But to the extent that the *nation* was being shaped in the development of that popular, anti-imperialist struggle, it becomes, in the fullest sense of the concept, a *national army*.

Equally important in the rapid consolidation of Sandinista leadership was the development of the mass organizations. Initiated during the struggle against the dictatorship, they grew rapidly after July 19, 1979, and were quickly involved in a broad range of tasks. The different urban workers' organizations formed in the struggle against Somocismo came together in the Sandinista Workers' Confederation (CST); the Civil Defense Committees, created to support the insurrection, were converted into the Sandinista Defense Committees (CDS); the Association of Women Facing the National Problematic (AMPRONAC) gave way to the Nicaraguan Womens' Association "Luisa Amanda Espinoza" (AMNLAE): and the Rural Workers' Association (ATC) existed as such since before the triumph.

The process of strengthening and expanding the mass organizations was neither ordered nor easy. The urgency and complexity of the tasks that had to be assumed demanded resources and experience that could not be gained overnight. In the months after the revolutionary triumph, the fragility of the new state meant that the workers' organizations had to take charge of the farms and industrial enterprises abandoned by their owners; the CDS had to hand out documentary proofs of residence, take charge of basic provisioning of whole cities, and exercise security functions. Out of necessity, the people organized in these structures directly managed a whole array of tasks and activities that were beyond their experience in a true version of popular democracy. There was obviously a lot of improvisation and some abuses, but this should come as no surprise. With experience improvisation gave way to organization, and this helped put an end to abuses. More important than these limitations, of course, is the fact that this rapid incorporation of the population into the multiple tasks of the revolution, reinforced the conviction— acquired in the insurrection—that the revolution belonged to them. As a CDS coordinator in Managua told me: "Here at the beginning everything remained to be done, there had been a lot of destruction, and the only way of doing it was for us all to organize ourselves. At the beginning it wasn't easy, but we had the experience of the war, this helped us enormously."

Of increasing importance was the ability of the FSLN to carry out an implicit political alliance with middle-sized proprietors and producers, technicians, and professionals of the middle class, and the like. The emphasis on national, democratic, and development issues—characterized in Chapter 1—as a *principal aspect* of the class issue at this stage of the revolution permitted the FSLN to retain important fractions of these sectors in the revolutionary camp, thereby reducing the ability of the bourgeoisie to undermine the revolutionary project. Relevant to this was the creation of the Patriotic Front of the Revolution (FPR) in 1980.[9]

The bourgeoisie saw the advance of the revolutionary project as a violation of supposedly original accords, as an alleged *betrayal* of the *real* program of the revolution.[10] This remains today the central argument of the bourgeois opposition and its justification for the evolution of some of its members toward open counter-revolution.[11] The road these groups took was not straight, but it is possible to identify the course of their progressive confrontation with the revolution, which began in the period under discussion.

On November 14, 1979, COSEP sent the governing junta an extensive document in which it outlined its grievances with the revolution: the presence of the mass organizations, and particularly the CDSs, in a variety of aspects of national life; the lack of an exact definition of the reach of the area of people's property (APP) and of the functions of the state; the "marginalization of the private sector"; the reduced operational area of the judiciary. At bottom, what the private sector was criticizing was that its conception of the world and of life—and not only of economic life—was being bypassed; the break with its ideas of authority; the slow and complicated emergence of a new kind of state; and the rowdy and persistent presence of the organized population. All these aspects and dimensions of a society in revolution, shattered by a war, pillaged by a dictatorship, were seen by the bourgeoisie as yet more aggressions against their own survival.

At the end of December 1979 a drastic reorganization of the government accentuated Sandinista weight at its base and displaced various members of the bourgeoisie from their positions. Cmdte. Humberto Ortega replaced former Colonel Larios as minister of defense; Cmdte. Henry Ruiz took charge of the Ministry of Planning; the Ministry of Agriculture was united with the Nicaraguan Institute of Agrarian Reform and Cmdte. Jaime Wheelock was designated the head of both; the Ministry of Industry and Commerce was separated into two ministries and two well-known FSLN members were put at their heads; there were similar changes in the National Financial System and in lesser levels of the cabinet. The institutional participation of the bourgeoisie was thus reduced to the presence of Violeta Chamorro and Alfonso Robelo in the government, and to some technicians and professionals the Frente Sandinista was trying to win over.

Having lost the cabinet battle, the bourgeoisie faced the fight for control of the Council of State, a co-legislative body created through the Program of Reconstruction of July 9, 1979. Originally it had thirty-three members of different political and social organizations that participated in the struggle against the dictatorship.[12] The business organizations and the opposition parties had pressured for the immediate constitution of the council, hoping to thus achieve the necessary majority to stop the advance of Sandinista initiatives, and did not want it to change. But by 1980 its composition reflected a correlation of forces out of keeping with reality. Some of the organizations represented had since ceased to exist (for example, the MPU), while others, created afterward, had no representation at all (the CST, the CDS, and others). Since the new organizations testified to increased Sandinista hegemony, the FSLN was obviously interested in permitting them to join the Council. The Sandinista position predominated and in February the government junta broadened the council to forty-seven members.[13] The confrontation around the composition of the council hastened the slide of Chamorro and Robelo toward the opposition. Toward the end of April 1980, Mrs. Chamorro resigned from her post in the government, followed a few days later by Robelo himself. Robelo assumed that other functionaries in the MDN would also resign, leaving the state without technical personnel, but by then the FSLN policy of alliance with these sectors was well advanced and, to Robelo's surprise, only a small group joined him. The FSLN rapidly replaced the vacant seats with Rafael Córdoba Rivas and Arturo Cruz—both members of the Democratic Conservative party—and assured the participation of COSEP in the Council of State. With Cmdte. Bayardo Arce as president, the Council of State was solemnly installed on May 4 of that same year.[14] What was hoped to be a class imposition ended up being only a personal dirty trick.

The bourgeoisie was thus incorporated into the Council of State as a minority force, and used it fundamentally as a tribunal for their own propaganda. At the same time they turned their attacks against the Sandinista project toward the ideological: they repeatedly denounced aggressions against private property, reiterated their complaints about the actions of the mass organizations, and moved rapidly to embrace the Catholic church hierarchy, which would soon be converted into the political party of the bourgeoisie.[15] This strategy, however, did not gain the unanimity of the whole camp, and soon there appeared the first signs that bourgeois groups were opting for open counter-revolution, including armed actions, no doubt emboldened by the election of Ronald Reagan in the United States. In mid-November 1980 an effort of this type was detected, directed by the vice-president of COSEP and president of UPANIC—who was killed in the preliminary stages of the action. In the same days, members of the opposition bloc—COSEP, MDN, CTN, CUS, and PCD—jointly walked out of the Council of State, abandoning their seats.

From then on, and particularly starting in early 1981 with the new U.S. administration, the bourgeois confrontation has become ever more acute, going hand in hand with the increase in the predatory activity of the former Somocista guards operating from Honduras. Both activities are backed by U.S. maneuvers—at first destabilizing actions such as the suspension of food assistance programs and the international credit blockade, and later openly interventionist ones such as financing and advising the counter-revolution. Weakened by the split it had in fact experienced in April 1980, and by the resistance of many of its members to stand by the policy of their top leader, the MDN increased its political opposition until, in 1982, Robelo actively joined the external counter-revolutionary forces competing for White House support; since then the MDN has disappeared completely from the national political scene.[16]

This situation disarmed sectors of the bourgeoisie not yet ready to take such an extreme step—some because they did not want to risk the subsequent confiscation of all their belongings; others because they still had confidence in their ability to influence the course of the revolutionary process; still others because their ideological grief was not so deep that they refused to accept the incentives of the economic policy and benefit from them. Again the Nicaraguan bourgeoisie lacked any political base and had to confine its proposals to the arena of its business associations. And again it had to go in search of the foreign assistance savior: the United States obviously, but also Venezuela, Panama, Costa Rica, and European social democrats. Just as before the triumph, it had to compete at two levels. For European social democratic parties and the Latin American governments it had to compete with the diplomacy of the FSLN and the international solidarity that this generated; for the United States it had to compete with the openly counter-revolutionary project, toward which the Reagan administration showed much greater generosity: if the business organizations of the large bourgeoisie and the hierarchy of the Catholic church managed to get a puny $5 million, the sums effectively invested in the counter-revolutionary project at the end of 1983 surpassed $100 million.[17]

In these confrontations the revolutionary government has generally acted with moderation, trying to avoid irreversible ruptures and points of no return. Thus, in the midst of trade-union mobilizations against decapitalizing maneuvers undertaken by sectors of the bourgeoisie, the Forum for Discussion of the National Problematic (June 1981) defined an arena of frank discussion of the respective political perspectives.[18] But when in October of that same year COSEP sent out an international declaration accusing the FSLN of carrying the country to a "new genocide" promoting a "Marxist-Leninist project on the backs of the people," and holding them responsible for everything wrong with the economy, the revolution interpreted the document as a destabilizing maneuver.[19] Applying the State of Emergency law, it put the signatories in prison—together with a group of Communist Party trade-union leaders, authors of a document accusing the FSLN of playing the U.S. government's game and pushing a social-democratic project. But here too the revolutionary leadership showed moderation: the business leaders were sentenced to seven months in prison and benefited from a pardon in February 1982; the Communist leaders were sentenced to twenty-nine months but were pardoned in September 1982.[20]

The unfolding of this process led to a progressive reformulation of the original idea of national unity. While the bourgeoisie component began to shrink, the participation of small and medium private-sector property increased: small merchants, peasantry, small industry, technical and professional sectors, and others.

THE MIXED ECONOMY AND LARGE PROPERTY

The war against Somoza provoked enormous human and material losses, and the complete disarticulation of the economy. According to CEPAL (1981: 16), around 35,000 people died, between 80,000 and 110,000 were wounded, some 40,000 children were orphaned, and 1 million people required food assistance to survive; some 150,000 of these were left homeless. Material losses totaled some U.S. $480 million, and more than U.S. $1.5 billion had been sent abroad: this total of almost $2 billion was equivalent to the value of the Gross Domestic Product. Furthermore, the final stage of the struggle coincided with the season for preparing the land and sowing both export crops and those for the internal market. The internal displacement of the population fleeing the repression and the cities where there was fighting, the emigration—temporary or permanent—of many capitalists and their capital, the disruption of the financial system, the blockade of roads, the rustling of part of the cattle herd to Honduras, all of this seriously affected the agricultural sector and presented the specter of hunger to the young revolution.

The reconstruction of the economy and the infrastructure was thus a priority task, central to revolutionary transformation. Reconstruction and transformation, however, were not seen as separate processes. Rather the goal of economic recovery, of physical reconstruction, was to be integrated with the project of revolutionary change (cf. Jarquin 1980; Fitzgerald 1982b). Reconstruction did not consist in a return to the way in which the economy had functioned before, but in the recuperation of the productive system at the same time that changes were introduced into its basic relations and its way of functioning.

The central element of this task, and of the policy of national unity that would promote it, was the development of a *mixed economy* that would join an area of people's property (APP) and a private area (AP), oriented toward overcoming economic backwardness, breaking dependency, and "favoring changes in the distribution of the national income in favor of the popular majority" (JGRN 1982).

The idea of an economy controlled by Somocismo, large bourgeois property, and imperialism, on top of which a broad APP would be created that could be converted into the dynamic axis of a rapid recuperation, proved only partially correct. The participation of large capital—Nicaraguan and foreign—took place above all in processing, commercialization, and finance, and to a lesser degree in production. The creation of the APP could only reflect this situation: in 1980 it represented 41 percent of the gross product, but accounted for only 25 percent of material production. On the other hand, it represented 56 percent of the service sector (see Table 2.14). In other words, the direct participation of the state in the economy was of a magnitude similar to or even smaller than that of other Latin American and European countries: Mexico, Peru, Argentina, and France, among others.

The formation of the APP began immediately after July 19. On July 20 the government ordered the confiscation "of all the properties of the Somoza family, military and functionaries who have abandoned the country since December 1977," and the same day extended the measure to "persons allied to Somocismo." These and other measures—such as the nationalization of the financial system, of gold and silver mining—affected Somocismo first and foreign capitalists to a lesser degree. Included in this were banks, savings and loan companies, insurance companies, and the warehousing and foreign commerce of traditional export products (coffee, cotton, sugar, meat). The foreign-owned gold and silver mines passed to the state, as did the fishing and wood industries. The agrarian reform affected 1.2 million manzanas of land (a little more than 850,000 hectares), among them 27.3 percent of all farms of over 500 manzanas, which corresponds to almost 43 percent of the land that was in the hands of large landowners. Somocista capital was also turned into state property in the textile, chemical, and agrochemical industries, the construction and machine-metal industries, and the air, sea, and land transport industry.

This first stage of nationalizations and confiscations signified the execution of part of the program outlined by the FPN at the beginning of 1979. The second advance of the APP was initiated with the second anniversary of the revolutionary triumph (July 19, 1981), in the context of increased U.S. pressures, and given evidence of the weak business response to the state economic policy. Measures included the confiscation of enterprises that were decapitalizing, as well as of all fixed and movable property, security titles, and stocks of Nicaraguans that abandoned them by leaving the country for more than six months without justifiable cause; and the nationalization of the distribution of sugar, soluble coffee exports, rum, liquor, liquor concentrates and essences, and various chemical and other agricultural products—nontraditional exports with an approximate annual value of U.S. $45 million. Also confiscated were properties of those who joined counter-revolutionary activities. The agrarian reform also affected all farms of more than 500 or 1,000 manzanas—

according to their location—that were abandoned or underexploited by their owners.[21]

Table 4.1 shows the participation of the APP in the production of basic goods and services, and its unequal representation between and within sectors. In the manufacturing industry, for example, the APP controls 30 percent of the gross production value (GPV) and 33 percent of the aggregate value, while in some branches this participation is much greater: 67% of the GPV in cattle slaughtering and meat preparation and preservation (3,111), 49 percent in the fabrication of milk products (3,112), 40 percent in sugar refining (3,118), 67 percent in spinning (3,211), 84 percent in paint fabrication (3,521), 100 percent of cement (3,692), 72 percent in basic iron industries (3,710), 83 percent in the fabrication of metal products (3,813) (INEC 1981b).[22] In crop agriculture APP participation is more pronounced than in cattle, and within agriculture, a little more pronounced in agroexports than in production for the internal market; in this latter sector, the only category with significant APP presence is rice.

The image spread abroad by counter-revolutionary propaganda and by the Reagan administration—and fed by the fear of the large bourgeoisie—of an omnipresent state that is overpowering and strangling private activity, is therefore false. The reality is that the private sector is still the majority in almost all areas of the economy, and that the action of the state occurs mostly indirectly, through the financial system, the fixing of prices, agroindustrial processing, commercialization, and labor and salary legislation.

Despite this still relatively modest participation, the APP is seen by the FSLN as the focus of change in the economic structure and in the relations between classes. As Dr. Sergio Ramírez explained:

> we are looking toward a mixed economy system in which the popular strategic sector will have to continue defining its hegemony in terms of the total social dynamic imposed by the Revolution, but also in terms of a process of future economic accumulation that will give maximum production possibilities to the area of people's property. . . .
>
> Here then, we are not talking about coercing the private sectors from within the strategy of the revolutionary project to participate in production, even though, given the restricted and destroyed economy, national reconstruction urgently needs elements of reactivation. It is a question of a historic choice that the revolutionary process itself has made as a consequence of the radical substitution of the whole traditional power apparatus which, while obviously representing a model of repressive

Table 4.1
Nicaragua: APP Participation in the National Economy, 1982

Participation in the gross production value, by sector

Sector	Percentage of GPV
GDP	*39.6*
Agricultural	21.0
Cattle	18.5
Fishing	34.5
Forestry	76.6
Mining	100.0
Primary sector	*50.3*
Manufacturing industry	30.7
Construction	92.3
Secondary sector	*62.2*
Transport and communications	40.0
Water and electricity	100.0
Basic services	*70.4*
Commerce	32.2

Participation in the physical volume of agricultural production*

Product	Percentage
Raw cotton	22
Coffee	16
Sugar cane	31
Natural Sesame	4
Havana tobacco	100
Agroexports	*19*
Corn	6
Beans	5
Sugar	32
Sorghum	14
Blond tobacco	10
Internal market	*13*
Total agriculture	*16*

Source: Compiled from INEC, MIPLAN, and MIDINRA.
* Agricultural year 1981–82.

military dictatorship, also represented, in social terms, the possibility of sustaining alternatives of domination distinct from those of the dictatorship, but of the same class nature—even though that alternative project would have been of a bourgeois-democratic character (Ramírez 1980; see also Ruiz 1980b).

And more recently, Cmdte. Jaime Wheelock noted:

> the hegemony of the economic development process is in the new relations of production created by the revolution. It is a hegemony achieved with the nationalization of foreign commerce, of natural resources and of strategic industrial sectors, and with the nationalization of the banks. With these measures we have created a system of production and of management which predominates, which is hegemonic, which coexists with forms one could call capitalist to an appreciable degree, and with others that are backward or precapitalist. . . .
> Our tendency is that state and cooperative properties will be hegemonic, coexisting with medium and small, and even large, private production, in which the backward relations of capitalism will surely become secondary, subordinated (Wheelock 1983: 102).

The creation of efficient and dynamic production and circulation in the APP is a long and complex process that is still going on, especially in the industrial sector. The enterprises incorporated into the area generally had a backward if not obsolete technology, the machinery had not been adequately maintained, many were outsized for the national market, and in others the war had left them deteriorated and destroyed. Furthermore, many technicians abandoned the enterprises when they became integrated into the public sector, either for ideological reasons or in search of higher salaries or more attractive working conditions. Others remained, but frequently using authoritarian criteria in their relations with the workers and the unions. For their part, many of the new administrators lacked experience; in not a few cases they tended to reproduce the behavior of the old bosses. The workers, on the other hand, tended to take a relaxed attitude toward labor discipline, above all in the months immediately following the triumph: the break with capitalist criteria of labor discipline, based on the exploitation of the labor force, did not imply their immediate substitution by alternative criteria of discipline—based on the patriotism of the workers, on their class consciousness, and so on. As a result, labor productivity in the APP was lower and evolved with a slower rhythm than in the private area in the first years of the revolution.

These problems are common, and in some respects normal, in any process of creating a public sector in an economy undergoing socio-economic transformation, especially one so little developed as that of Nicaragua. On the other hand, the lack of information about real levels of productive efficiency and the evolution of productivity before the respective firms were incorporated into the APP, makes it impossible to compare performance. The argument reiterated by the private sector that the APP is characterized by inefficiency and the squandering of resources (INDE 1981) has not yet been accompanied by consistent empirical data that show these organizational deficiencies to originate in the APP as opposed to a continuation of existing problems.

The practice of almost five years indicates that in principle there is no confrontation with large private property as far as it accepts the government's economic policies. The contradiction occurs when the private owners engage in underproduction or absenteeism, abandon the country, or collaborate with the counter-revolution.

The initial proof of the revolution's good will toward large business was the suspension of Decree No. 38, on August 8, 1979—in other words, scarcely twenty days after being put into effect. This decree extended the confiscations to those "related to Somocismo"; the measure provoked insecurity in the large bourgeoisie, because of the interests that many of them maintained with the Somoza family or with functionaries of the regime and officers of the National Guard. The existence of Decree No. 38 therefore implied the possibility of unlimited expansion of the nascent public sector, affecting the interests of some bourgeois groups politically opposed to the dictatorship but with economic, financial, commercial, or other ties to it.[23]

The agrarian reform ratified this moderated position. The law, sanctioned in 1981, outlined among its objectives the necessity of overcoming absentee [*rentista*], extensive, or inefficient forms of property and exploitation of the land and the vicious exploitation of peasant labor by means of sharecropping, tenant farming, and similar forms; and encouraging production and productivity, guaranteeing the most adequate and rational use of the land, as well as soil protection and the best use of water and other natural resources (see MIDINRA 1982a).

As a consequence it guaranteed "ownership of the land to all those who work it productively and efficiently" (Art. 1) and that the agrarian reform would affect only idle lands, underexploited or leased land (according to criteria specified in Article 66) or that of property owners with more than 500 or 1,000 manzanas (350 and 700 hectares respectively), according to the region.

Although the law originally approved by the Council of State did not contemplate indemnification in the case of idle land, the government ultimately decided to change this, giving indemnification also to these landowners, in order to reduce the confrontations with the bourgeoisie.[24]

These criteria for modernization, efficiency, and protection of natural resources were enough to profoundly alter the land tenure structure and the social profile of the countryside. Large agrarian property has been reduced to between half and two-thirds of its size before the revolution; only 680 property owners remain who have more than 500 manzanas.

The *antilatifundist rather than anticapitalist* character of the Sandinista agrarian reform shows also in the fact that of the total amount of land affected up to December 1983 (some 421,000 manzanas), 63 percent consisted of idle or deficiently exploited lands; another 18 percent pertained to properties that were not directly exploited—leased properties or those maintained by peasant producers under *precarias* or tenant farm forms—and the remaining 19 percent originated from situations of abandonment.

Just as productive large property remains outside the agrarian

Table 4.2
Nicaragua: Land Tenure by Area of Property, 1979 and 1983

| Areas of property | Extension | | | |
| | 1979 | | 1983 | |
	Manzanas (×1,000)	%	Manzanas (×1,000)	%
Individual producers				
More than 500 mz	2,920.0	41	880.4	12
200 to 500 mz	980.0	14	730.0	10
51 to 200 mz	2,100.0	30	2,100.0	30
10 to 50 mz	910.0	13	1,000.0	14
Less than 10 mz	170.0	2	284.0	4
Production cooperatives	—	—	485.6	7
APP	—	—	1,600.0	23
Total	7,080.0	100	7,080.0	100

Source: MIDINRA.

Table 4.3
Nicaragua: Evolution of Investments, 1977–83

Investment	1977	1978	1979	1980	1981	1982	1983*
Total investment	7,008	2,875	−304	3,499.7	4,967.3	3,391.7	4,460.0
Fixed investment	6,186	3,436	1,404	3,032.2	4,473.1	2,893.7	3,955.0
Private	3,139	1,895	726	622.2	1,093.1	796.7	711.9
Public	3,047	1,541	678	2,410.0	3,380.0	2,097.0	3,243.1
Stock exchanges	822	−561	−1,752	467.5	494.2	487.3	505.0
Percentage structure of fixed investments							
Private	51	55	52	21	24	27	18
Public	49	45	48	79	76	73	82
Total	100	100	100	100	100	100	100

Source: MIPLAN. Private investment figures are estimated.
Figures are in millions of 1980 cordobas.
*Preliminary estimates.

reform, urban industrial capital that accepts the government's economic policy is supported and guaranteed financial resources. More than 70% of the value of the tax exemptions authorized for imports have benefited the industrial private sector, particularly the largest companies. At the same time, the National Financial System finances *100 percent* of the working and investment capital requirements of the private sector with negative real interest rates. This contrasts sharply with Somoza's financial policies, which never financed more than 70 percent of these needs, and with positive or neutral interest rates in the best of cases (Vilas 1982b).

In January 1982 the Second Sandinista Assembly ratified the continuation of the mixed economy project and the necessity of perfecting it, stimulating the convergence of the public and private sectors.[25] To undertake this, a broad array of financial incentives were defined for agriculture and industry that substantially raised the surplus appropriated by private enterprise.[26] Foreign enterprises have received the same treatment as nationals, and occasionally have benefited from some subsidies (Nolff 1982).

Despite this, with few exceptions, private enterprise has not responded according to expectations. Private investment has undergone a strong retraction; in the 1981–83 period fixed private investment in constant prices was between one-third and one-half of the 1977–78 level (see Table 4.3). At the same time, the investment structure changed markedly; in the total revolutionary period more than 70 percent of total fixed investment was under the administration of the public sector.

The low private-sector investment is basically led by the large producers. According to the Ministry of Planning:

despite the fiscal and financial incentives offered by the Revolutionary Government, the labor normalization process, the rapid expansion of the national market and of prices, there is evidence that the large private producers have not shown themselves disposed to support the reactivation with their own investment. Thus, although earnings have objectively recuperated much more rapidly than salaries, the cooperation of the private sector has been limited to raising production, but its attitude with respect to investment has been ambiguous (MIPLAN 1981: 121).

This behavior cannot be reduced to a single cause, but results from multiple if related factors. The nature of the internal economic situation and the external crisis—the growth of inflation and foreign indebtedness, plus a lag in the rate of exchange—counterbalanced the stimulant effect of the incentives to private business fixed during 1980 and 1981; investment retraction during these years responded more to these factors than to a class decision to block the recuperation of the national economy. The adoption of new incentives in February 1982 indicate that this view prevailed within the FSLN and the government—although it may not have been unanimous. The abnormality of 1982 due to the damages provoked first by Hurricane Alleta, later by the prolonged drought, the retraction of inter-Central American commerce due to the regional economic crisis, and increasing counter-revolutionary attacks from Honduras—which particularly affected agroexport zones—all meant that an evaluation of the effect of these incentives on bourgeois decisions could not be carried out. Table 4.4 nonetheless suggests that at the start there must have been a positive response, at least in global terms: comparing 1982 with 1981 private participation in total fixed investment grew, and the reduction of its absolute value was proportionately less (27 percent) than that experienced in the public sector (38 percent).

At the same time it is possible to hypothesize that the Sandinista revolution is creating a socioeconomic system that despite broad space for medium and large private enterprise is not attractive to the type of bourgeoisie *effectively developed in Nicaragua.* This bourgeoisie maintains its means of production—within the limits mentioned—but the economic and financial policy reduces its margin for maneuvering and introduces elements of insecurity into its future evaluations. At the same time, the stimulus to trade-union organization, the increase in labor legislation as well as new labor contracts, and the growing trade-union participation in the development of the enterprises reduce the levels of exploitation of the labor force and questions the bourgeois principle of authority in the enterprise. The growing U.S. aggressions against revolutionary Nicaragua—a vessel on which the bourgeoisie has embarked but can never steer—put before their eyes levels of confrontation with their traditional ally that they possibly never imagined. And finally, the dominant political discourse that emphasizes the class content of the process—or at least of its long-term goals—the rejection of the absolute sovereignty of owners in the economic process, and the political obligation to produce, disconcerts and frightens a class traditionally accustomed to commanding and being obeyed. The conservation of the means of production takes place in the context of a political system that ideologically emphasizes the higher values of socialism and the proletarian *ethos*.

Thus it should not be surprising that private sector production has increased less than the increase in financial facilities accorded it by the government. Available evidence indicates that the financing handed over was converted into dollars and taken out of the country through the free foreign exchange market—a market lacking any effective regulation before September 1981; productive capital slowly moved toward the sphere of commerce and speculation; the cattle herd was rapidly reduced by indiscriminate slaughter; overpricing of imports and underpricing of exports permitted the illicit flight of earnings and the consequent reduction of the tax base. Many companies did not create depreciation reserves, and a tendency to decapitalization can be seen in many sectors of private enterprise. All this was in the framework of a financial system that advanced all necessary working capital and reduced all operative risks to a minimum.

The result was a transfer of surplus from the public sector toward the private sector, and from the productive sectors toward the nonproductive ones, contrary to what had been expected. While the nationalization of the financial system limits these movements somewhat it has not been able to eliminate them totally. Nationalization seems not to have been sufficient to eliminate the bourgeois ability to maneuver, an ability that derives from its ownership of the means of production. Aggravating these tendencies, however, was the lack of practical experience of technical cadres in these first years.[27]

The retraction of the bourgeoisie prolonged and deepened the economic crisis that has wracked the country since 1978, combining with the economic results of the U.S. blockade of credit assistance in international lending agencies, difficulties in the normal supply of parts and spare parts, and so on.

This is certainly not the situation of the whole class; there do exist bourgeois groups, including those of the large bourgeoisie, that have actively accepted the new rules of the game and have participated in the plans for expanding production (MIDINRA 1982b: 25–26). But they are small and unrepresentative.

Large property has in fact remained in the middle of a camp of increasingly polarized forces. On one side there is the revolutionary project, with its mass organizations, Sandinista Popular Army, class discourse, opening toward the socialist countries and the national liberation movements, and national unity with popular hegemony; this project makes demands on large owners that they do not know how to or cannot satisfy so far. They deprecate the institutional guarantees that the new order offers them and are aggravated by the lack of a "state of law"; they are frightened by the development of the APP as a response to their own capitalist retreat and rail about the "confiscatory appetite" and the effort to "destroy private enterprise." The organization of the people in defense, production, health care, and popular education motivates their appeals for a stable "social peace" and their indignation at the fomenting of "class hatred."[28]

On the other side, there is the counter-revolution—the return of the assassins, the thieves, the scum of the past society. These are the veterans of the National Guard who took refuge in Honduras, supported and financed by the United States. It is an option that is still excessive for the democratic bourgeois subjectivity of a good part of the medium and large capitalist entrepreneurs, but one that *objectively* approximates their conduct in the economy.[29]

This conduct puts the government in a complex situation: in effect, it is in a crisis fed by the bourgeois recession, although, due to the popular character of its social base and its social project, it does not have recourse to the conventional bourgeois "technology" for treating the crisis: elimination of consumption subsidies, reduction of employment levels, freeing prices, and so on—which increase earnings. The government is also unable to take more drastic steps regarding the medium and large bourgeoisie, given the existence of the principle of a mixed economy, the conservation of broad alliances at the international level, and the limitations existing in the area of people's property itself.

The leadership of the machine and large bourgeoisie realize this dilemma and, to the extent possible, exploit it. They combine the capacity for economic decision-making that they still hold with political pressure through their external allies and the church hierarchy, hoping that the current economic difficulties will oblige the government to modify its political and economic project. The government in turn knows the doubts and inhibitions of the private sector, its internal differences and fears, and takes advantage of them: it combines denunciations, mobilizations, and the actions of the mass organizations with economic incentives, always offering a new opportunity, deferring, for the sake of national unity, the moment of rupture.

MIXED ECONOMY AND SMALL AND MEDIUM PROPRIETORS

Small- and medium-sized proprietors have shown more enthusiasm and a better capacity to respond to the revolutionary program, and they appear to be the principal type of private property owners to emerge in the context of the mixed economy. From the beginning of the revolutionary struggle the claims of the peasants found an echo in Sandinismo. The peasantry constituted one of the pillars of the Army in Defense of National Sovereignty, which, under the leadership of Augusto Sandino, defeated the U.S. invasion in the early 1930s, and forced the departure of the U.S. Marines from the country. Thirty years later the peasantry was the first arena of the FSLN's political work, the *sea* in which the Sandinista fighters moved like *fish;* the peasantry gave the FSLN their first collaborators, provisions, and the space and conditions necessary for their consolidation and growth.

Today, while the current stage of the revolution reflects the broad popular base with which the FSLN defeated the Somocista dictatorship and the bourgeois opposition bloc, it is possible to detect a special emphasis in the revolutionary policies toward the small and medium rural owners, and toward their urban counterparts.

In the countryside, the agrarian reform responded to the demands (for land, credits, inputs, technical assistance, prices) of the peasant and medium-sized producers, articulating a broad sector of individual and cooperative small production with large units of state production and with the medium and large agrarian bourgeoisie. According to a report of the Ministry of Agricultural Development and Agrarian Reform (MIDINRA):

> the agricultural sector will consist of four socioeconomic sectors: (a) the APP, which will represent between 20 and 25 percent of the agricultural lands of the country, concentrated in the agroindustrial linkages and the most capital and technology intensive production; (b) the cooperative sector, which will represent around 40% of the agricultural area; (c) the individual peasant sector, which will continue to count on the Revolution's economic support, seeking its gradual evolution toward associative forms of production; (d) the private business sector, sustenance of the mixed economy and national untiy (1982b: 18).[30]

The agrarian reform up to now has gone through two stages. The first, from the revolutionary triumph to its second anniversary (July 19, 1981), shaped what one revolutionary leader has named the "anti-Somocista phase" of the agrarian reform (Wheelock 1983: 86). Through decrees 3 and 38 the revolutionary government recovered Somocista lands, while decrees 230 and 263 (January 5 and 31, 1980) reduced the lease prices of lands destined for cotton and basic grains cultivation. In cotton the new lease contracts displayed a preference for the small farmers associated in cooperatives, medium farmers that sowed up to 200 manzanas, and those that sowed in the 1979–80 agricultural cycle; in basic grains it favored farmers associated in cooperatives, "or in production units," and small farmers. These dispositions were a hard blow to the renting landlords, one of the traditional problems for small and medium rural production.

The same period saw the normalization of the relatively confusing tenure situation with regard to the confiscated lands. Many farms had been occupied by peasants and agricultural workers during the insurrection; in various cases rudimentary administration forms had been established by the occupants themselves, although their lack of experience made the development of real economic management difficult. At the same time many farms had been abandoned by their owners as a result of the insecurity that spread through the large bourgeoisie in the last stages of the dictatorship. Many of these landowners had opposed Somoza and were not included in the confiscation decrees, a distinction that seemed senseless to the workers who had occupied the lands with the departure of their owners; these workers resisted turning the lands back when the landowners returned.

On the other hand, the dismantling of the state apparatus in the last months of the dictatorship, the lack of land registries, the inexperience of the new cadres, and the amount of work to be done meant that a large effort went toward endowing the APP with a minimum organization and efficiency, as well as a degree of centralization of decision-making. Meanwhile, decisions in the first months were administered as much by the state as by the mass organizations, spontaneous groupings of peasants or agricultural workers, and regional or local FSLN or state authorities (see Karmowitz and Thome 1982).

The second stage of the agrarian reform began in July 1981. While the agrarian reform law had been announced a year before in celebration of the first anniversary of the revolution, the elaboration of the project took another year. In the interval intense discussions took place about the character that the reform should have: antilatifundist? anticapitalist? peasant-oriented? proletarian-oriented? There was also heated discussion about the kind of production organization that should be promoted: state farms? cooperatives? small individual farms? Also discussed was whether or not to pay indemnification for the affected properties. At the same time there was an effort not to produce a legal instrument that would alarm the bourgeois sectors of the mixed economy. The question of the latifundias gained priority, especially with regard to idle, abandoned, or inadequately exploited lands. The goal was to point the way toward stability for the small and medium producers, promote a process of voluntary cooperativization, and foster the articulation of the four types of agrarian property already mentioned.

By December 1983 the handing over of agrarian reform lands reached some 421,000 manzanas (roughly 295,000 hectares). The goal of this second phase is to adjudicate 2 million manzanas.[31] If the current rhythm is maintained, this goal will be reached in 1986.

Cooperative production has received a very strong push. Eighty-three percent of the land was allocated to cooperatives and only 17 percent to individual farmers; some 15,000 peasant families benefited, of which more than 13,000 (around 87 percent) were cooperative members. Almost nonexistent before the revolutionary triumph, at the end of 1982 there were some 3,200 cooperatives, with more than 70,000 shareholders.[32] Nonetheless they represented only 56 percent of the small producers, thus leaving a broad sector outside this kind of organization. Incorporation into a cooperative is voluntary, but the law tries to create conditions to encourage this decision by the peasant, confident that the superior results of associated production will be the best propaganda about its benefits.

In some regions the stimulus to cooperative production had to deal not only with the preference of the peasants for individual production, but also with the activities of the business organization FUNDE (Nicaraguan Economic Development Foundation). In the departments of Matagalpa and Jinotega, FUNDE began to promote the cooperative organization of small farmers, trying to attract broad sectors of small and medium rural production to their non-Sandinista positions. The selection of these departments seems to have been owing to their greater concentration of middle and wealthy peasants, unlike the Pacific region, where the predominance of the poor peasant is very marked.

The confrontation took place not only around the two different types of cooperative organization, but around two different political projects. FUNDE's cooperative recruitment was carried out through a political discourse that emphasized the peasant as property owner, appealing to the virtues and superiority of private initiative; the cooperative organization was presented as a chapter of the true democracy oriented toward the celebration of elections and opposed to *totalitarian collectivism;* an important part of FUNDE's cultural activities in these zones consisted in sponsoring visits and conferences by members of the church hierarchy, U.S. Embassy personnel, COSEP directors, opposition leaders, and the like (INDE 1980, 1982). Clearly this contrasted strongly with the type of cooperativism promoted by the agrarian reform, which tries to emphasize the elements of collective production, projecting the importance of collaboration in the context of the revolutionary process. This includes participation in adult education, integration into the Sandinista Popular Militias, participation in the Popular Health Campaigns, and so on.

FUNDE's cooperative project was thus seen by the revolutionary government as eminently demobilizing and at bottom counter-revolutionary; 1982 saw denunciations about the collaboration lent by directors of these cooperatives to the counter-revolutionary bands operating in the region. Although the directors of FUNDE, INDE, and COSEP have rejected these charges, evidence exists that various of these organizations have effectively served as support structures for these bands; and of the U.S. $5.1 million that the U.S. government offered the church hierarchy and private enterprise in 1982–83, $1.4 million was precisely destined for FUNDE.[33] The politics of the revolution in handling this issue has been to try to differentiate the participation of the leaders and peasants in counter-revolutionary activities from the base membership and from the poor and middle peasants in general. But the FSLN National Directorate itself has recognized errors and abuses—unjustified confiscations and excessive pressures—which in some cases have undermined the support of these sectors for the government.

The agrarian reform comprises two types of cooperative organizations: the Sandinista Agricultural Cooperatives (CAS) and the Credit and Service Cooperatives (CCS); both are the product of a prior process of experimentation that had varied results—labor collectives, "dead furrow" cooperatives, and so on. Currently two-thirds of the cooperatives are of the CCS type, and one-third are CASs; the former socialize the receipt of credit, technical assistance, and other services, but land ownership remains individual; the latter represents a more advanced form of association since the ownership of the land is collective.

The unequal development of the two types responds generally to the greater or lesser regional weight of the different peasant fractions. In the Pacific region, with a higher concentration of poor peasants, a greater number of CASs are found, while the CCSs predominate in the interior, owing to the strong presence of middle and wealthy peasants. In general the CASs are small; they suffer from a certain internal instability due to the initial difficulties of the collective organization of labor. Their productive activity is oriented predominantly to annual crops. Seventy-nine percent of the land assigned to the peasantry has corresponded to the CASs.

The CCSs, by contrast, are larger with between twenty-five and thirty members on the average. Their principal orientation is toward annual crops, although they have an important component of permanent crops and cattle.

Since mid-1983 a new kind of cooperative has begun to be developed in some regions of the country: the Production and Defense Cooperatives. In the regions of the north most exposed to attacks from the Honduran Army and incursions of the former Somocista

National Guardsmen from Honduran territory, these cooperatives have the dual objective to guarantee the defense of the zone and to assure the continuity of production. Many of their members are individual peasants who have grouped together out of the necessities of self-defense; others are militia members who returned home with the collective experience of the war. In both cases, to continue producing in individual fashion was to expose oneself to kidnapping, assassination, the rape of family members, and crop destruction, so that many peasants began to move away and resettle as a group, and then to defend themselves and produce as a group.[34]

This type of cooperative is being developed mainly in regions I (the departments of Nueva Segovia, Madriz and Estelí), VI (Matagalpa and Jinotega), and in Special Zone III (Rio San Juan). The agrarian reform provides land and technical assistance, and the EPS the weapons and other military material for defense. The special nature of these cooperatives and the difficult conditions in which their activity must take place has meant more flexible criteria in allocating lands; a high proportion of the land consists of lands that previously belonged to the APP and were being exploited as Units of State Production (UPE), that is, state farms.[35]

While an evaluation of these cooperatives is still premature, their very existence highlights the capacity of the Sandinista revolution to respond to the challenges of the changing conditions in which they must evolve. For the moment, the synthesis of the experience is left to one of its beneficiaries: "We all come from where the land is a real nightmare, where you have to use a hammer and nail to get the seed into the furrow; now we have these nice lands . . . and also these rifles."[36]

The allocation of lands has been accompanied by a broad distribution of credit. If 1980 and 1978 are compared, the number of peasants included grew 327 percent, with a land coverage 440 percent more extensive and a 739 percent larger amount of credit (UNAG/ATC/CIERA 1982: 30). The cooperatives have played an important role in this growth of credit; 70 percent of the 57,000 new clients of the National Development Bank are cooperative members. In 1978 small production controlled only 4 percent of total agricultural credit, and in 1983, 23 percent were participating. Nevertheless, some MID-INRA studies suggest that individual peasants have received more credit than the cooperative members, and that the CCSs have received more than the CASs.

In the first year of the revolution credit was lavishly provided with scant attention to the productive or payback capacity of the recipient; what counted was peasant need rather than management capability. The result was that production experienced less growth than credit. A high proportion of the farmers used the money for the immediate satisfaction of largely stifled consumer needs; others, in part for lack of advice, were not able to effectively invest it. On the other hand, the availability of money seems to have played a strong role in the retraction of the poor peasantry from the export harvests. Together with other pressures on the labor market, the availability of money for these semiproletarian workers meant having in advance income that in previous years required working for salaries in the coffee and cotton harvests. This seems to have been one of the principal causes for the lack of manual labor experienced in agroexports in the 1980–81 agricultural year.

These factors led to a restriction of credit in 1981, above all that destined for the peasantry that produced individually; total credit was reduced 27 percent with respect to 1980, but rural credit (that is, to small farmers) was restricted 43 percent (MIDINRA 1982b: 24). At the same time the stimulus to join associative production forms was reinforced, and the supervision in the use of credit was improved by the financial system. In any case, this veritable credit inundation to producers who for various reasons were unable to manage it adequately—through lack of experience, the poor quality of their lands, lack of appropriate productive technology, or whatever—created serious problems of indebtedness in broad sectors of the peasantry, which led in 1983 to the adjustment and partial condoning of the peasant debts. Around 40,000 peasants benefited from this decision, in the amount of 266 million cordobas (U.S. $26.6 million at the official exchange rate), but here again more attention was given to the situation of the cooperativized peasants than to individual producers, and within that, CAS shareholders received more benefits than CCS members.[37]

The process of economic development of small and medium agrarian property has gone hand in hand with the promotion of the class organization of this sector. Originally the peasant was incorporated into the Rural Workers' Association (ATC), the organization of the agricultural proletariat. But it was soon clear that the existence of two different classes within the same organization was very difficult, given the diversity of interests and perspectives, even though both were forces of the revolution. The ATC fundamentally expressed its worker component; the historic demands of the peasantry for land were different from the worker demands for salary; with the agrarian reform, the agricultural proletariat was fundamentally interested in the question of the state farms, while the farmers paid more attention to the question of the cooperatives and the future of the individual parcel.

This initial lack of a revolutionary organization for the small and medium producers contrasted with the existence of UPANIC—the grouping of the large agrarian bourgeoisie created by COSEP at the beginning of 1979 to capture the support of the peasantry. Based on the corporativist unification of large and small producers in their common condition as *farmers,* UPANIC appeared in principle to be much closer to the demands of the peasantry than an organization of workers—albeit agricultural workers. It is probable that the recognition of the existence of structural differences within the popular camp, and the perception of the bourgeois competition *for the same social sectors,* combined to stimulate the creation of an organization specifically for the small and medium agricultural producers: the National Union of Farmers and Cattle Ranchers (UNAG).

UNAG was constituted in April 1981 after a long process of discussion in all regions of the country; in addition to the creation of the organization, these discussions approved a *struggle plan* that collected and systematized the demands of the small and medium producers: financing, technical assistance, commercialization, roads, services and supplies, labor productivity, participation in the state institutions; curiously, *they did not include the demand for more land* (UNAG 1982: 3ff). UNAG rapidly grew into one of the most dynamic organizations and one with the greatest mobilization capacity in support of the revolution.

The response of small rural property owners has been a growth of participation in production, in contrast to the apathy and even retreat of the majority of the large agrarian bourgeoisie. Table 4.4 shows the great weight of this fraction in national agricultural production, and its tendency to grow even in such traditional export crops as cotton and coffee.[38]

Table 4.5 shows the growth of small individual and cooperative cotton production. Even in the years in which the total land sown was less, the peasantry more than tripled its land sown in absolute terms, behavior that contrasts neatly with the increasing retraction

Table 4.4
Nicaragua: Agrarian Participation by Smallholders
(in percentages)

	Agricultural year	
Category	1980–81	1981–82
Corn	87	84
Beans	81	92
Industrial sorghum	12	12
Millet	77	77
Rice	13	20
Vegetables	90	95
Coffee	32	40
Cotton	9	15
Sesame	64	80
Cattle	69	69

Source: UNAG

of the large bourgeoisie. At the same time small production has shown greater efficiency in this crop than have large property owners in the period after 1979.[39]

The integration of small and medium rural property into the current stage of the revolution is not limited to production, however. The small and medium peasantry has been incorporated into defense, popular adult education, and in general into the tasks that require their cooperation. Not only in political discourse, but in the reality of daily life, the peasantry is without doubt one of the basic forces of the Sandinista revolution.

In contrast to the ideology of private ownership, the revolution emphasizes the contradictions within private ownership of the means of production and the unity of the classes of the popular camp. As UNAG itself outlines it:

> We understand National Unity as the Unity of all the producers of the wealth of the country that are willing to reconstruct our country:
> . . . The Unity with the workers of the countryside and city, with the technicians, professionals, students, small and medium merchants who work for the development of our country, some raising crops, others making tools, clothes, shoes, in factories or shops, others helping to improve our technical and cultural level, and our living conditions, because we need each of them and because all of us joined together will make the reconstruction of our Nicaragua a reality.[40]

The rapid advance of the revolutionary peasant organization contrasts with the situation among small urban owners. The efforts of the revolution to endow this sector with the principles of organizing are still modest and are principally directed toward small production: artisans, small industry, and cottage production. Through credit, exchange, and tax incentives, there is the political will to induce these producers to incorporate themselves into some form of association such as production cooperatives, or labor or service cooperatives. The advance has been slow but real. As of May 1983 some 4,600 workshops were organized into seventy-seven service cooperatives and a preliminary form called "precooperatives," and fifty production cooperatives. At the same time fifteen state production collectives have been constituted; in these, the means of production are the social property of all the people, administered by the state,

Table 4.5
Nicaragua: Evolution of the Cotton Area Sown
by Property Owning Sector, 1980/81–1984/85

	1980/81	1981/82	1982/83	1983/84	1984/85
Thousands of manzanas					
Small individual and cooperative production	12.5	15.2	19.1	41.4	44.5
Large producers	99.4	92.1	77.2	77.6	76.0
APP	22.8	25.4	32.9	47.2	44.5
Total	134.7	132.7	129.2	166.2	165.0
Index numbers (1980/81 = 100)					
Small individual and cooperative production	100	122	153	331	356
Large producers	100	93	78	78	76
APP	100	111	144	207	195
Total	100	98	96	123	122
Structural percentage					
Small individual and cooperative production	9	12	15	25	27
Large producers	74	69	60	47	46
APP	17	19	25	28	27
Total	100	100	100	100	100

Sources: MIDINRA; Banco Nacional de Desarrollo.

the collective's workers, and the mass organizations.[41] The aggravation of the external crisis and the growing scarcity of foreign exchange have seriously affected a good part of small production, dependent in large measure on external supplies. The response of the economic authority has been to guarantee a minimum availability of foreign exchange for fundamental imports. For a large part of artisan production of shoes, clothes, and furniture, however, the crisis has created tensions that are difficult to overcome.

The treatment of small merchants has been carried out indirectly. Through the mass organizations—above all CDS and AMNLAE—there has been an effort to guarantee effective price controls and availability of goods, together with the creation of a network of local provision stores under the Ministry of Interior Commerce. The current objective is to regulate the development of the sector, neutralizing possible negative effects on supply and popular incomes, guaranteeing the observance of tax obligations, and eliminating the black market in foreign exchange. In this last aspect, subsequent foreign exchange regulations provided for monthly amounts of foreign exchange, at official rates, to those small import merchants who agreed to also act as export merchants. Measures to stimulate cooperative organization in the light urban and interurban transport sector—small movers, taxi owners and so on—have also been adopted, with mixed success.

The revolution has not proposed the nationalization of small production or small commerce. The experiences of other revolutions suggest that a measure of this type is enormously complex; in the specific case of Nicaragua, the strong dependence of consumers on these sectors would risk having to confront a strong disarticulation of the urban market until superior criteria of production and circulation could be developed (see Wheelock 1983: 101–2). Besides, it is evident that the APP is still in no condition to extend its activities in this way, beyond what it has achieved already, with the establishment of popular stores and the nationalization of supermarkets that had belonged to those close to Somoza.

5

The Working Class
in the Popular Revolution

The national unity that the Sandinista revolution recognized as one of its basic principles implies bringing together contradictory interests to overcome the two most urgent contradictions: economic reconstruction (the development question) and sovereign self-determination and defense against imperialist aggressions (the national sovereignty question). In class terms national unity is not neutral; it is led and made coherent by a popular project, which must confront a bourgeois project that proposes different ways of treating these crucial issues.

Popular hegemony in national unity means that it is fundamentally supported by the popular classes and prioritizes their interests and demands. Yet as we have seen, "the people" as a category is not homogeneous; it covers a diversity of groups and sectors unified by exploitation and oppression and by their struggle against the dictatorial power. We have looked at the role of small production and small proprietors, especially in the urban areas, and examined the significance of the peasantry and other small property groups in the current stage of the revolution. Now then, what role does the working class play in this process? What demands does it make? How does it articulate its interests in the context of national unity? Together with the peasantry, the working class is considered the motor force of the Sandinista revolution; only they "will go all the way to the end." What does this mean in the current stage of the revolution, and in a society where the process of proletarianization of the labor force has been so unequal and limited? This chapter tries to answer these questions.

175

UNION ORGANIZING . . .

The structural features of the Nicaraguan economy, linked to the repressive characteristics of the Somocista dictatorship, have produced a union movement that is small, weak, and barely developed (Gutiérrez Mayorga 1978; Guevara and Pérez Bermúdez 1981; Rivas 1983). According to Labor Ministry figures, in July 1979 only 138 unions existed, with a total of 27,020 member workers, equivalent to around 11–12 percent of the salaried population. While this is much more than the 6–7 percent usually estimated, many of these unions had a purely formal existence, with no activities for a number of years.[1]

Since that time unionization has grown very rapidly. Between August 1979 and December 1982 almost 1,200 new unions were registered with the Labor Ministry. The predominant form of new organization was the enterprise-wide union, with 72 percent of the new unions and affiliated members.

Half of the new organizations are found in the agricultural sector, and a little more than 20 percent in the industrial sector, with similar percentages of membership. In total, they account for more than two-thirds of the new organizations and affiliated workers, but the sequence of the unionization movement was not similar in the two cases. The first year and a half after the triumph was clearly the period of industrial unionization, with almost 40 percent of the new organizations and workers (compared to only 8.5 percent and 11.4 percent of unions and workers) in the agricultural sector. On the other hand, in 1981, 79 percent of the new unions and 73 percent of the workers were in agriculture and only 6 percent of unions and 10 percent of workers were in industry. The extent of rural unionization expresses the organizational deficit of this sector before the triumph, the intense mobilizations of agricultural workers against de-capitalization, and the impact of the agrarian legislation (the agrarian reform law, creation of agrarian reform enterprises) approved during the course of that year.

The predominance of union by enterprise tended to be accentuated during the entire post-1979 period, so that by 1982 they represented 80 percent of the unions and 70 percent of the workers, compared to 59 percent and 64 percent respectively, between August 1979 and December 1980. This boom was complemented by a reduction of the average union size, which shrank 33 percent between 1979 and 1982: from an average of 87 workers to 58 per union (see Table 5.1).

The reduction in union size has been most notable in the agricultural and construction sectors. In agriculture the average size was reduced almost 62 percent between 1979 and 1982 (from an average of 117 workers to 45 per organization) and in construction 18 percent (from 92 to 75 workers), while industry saw an accumulated growth of 19 percent (from an average of 87 workers in 1979–80 to 116 in 1981 and 100 in 1982).

The change is hard to explain. One hypothesis is that it reflects the incorporation of successively smaller economic units: union pressures might have begun in enterprises of greater worker concentration, and extended toward smaller ones. Evidence supports this hypothesis in the agrarian sector but not in the manufacturing sector, and in any case is limited to one type of organization—the enterprise-wide union.

Whatever the case may be, since 1981 the principal union confederations and the FSLN have been trying to reverse this tendency toward organizational atomization, both promoting the creation of trade unions by branch of activity and encouraging a single trade-union federation.[2] A countertendency can be discerned in the sugar and oil agroindustries, the textile industry, and in pharmaceutical products, and has its first successful result in construction.

Almost 90 percent of both new unions and members belong to the Sandinista Workers Confederation (CST) and to the Association of Rural Workers (ATC), both of Sandinista affiliation. The participation of each reflects this intersectoral movement of the unionization process in the stage following 1979. In 1979–80, years of rapid urban-

Table 5.1
Average Size of New Unions

| Period | Total | Type of union | | | |
		By enterprise	Several enterprises	Several activities	Guild
August 1979 to Dec. 80	87	94	84	60	76
1981	70	69	88	39	45
1982	58	62	38	*	43

Source: Based on Ministry of Labor figures.

industrial unionization, 75 percent of the new organizations were affiliated to the CST, while in 1981 and 1982, years of rapid rural unionization, 76 percent and 72 percent respectively were affiliated to the ATC, and only 17 percent to 20 percent to the CST.

Only 14 percent of the new unions affiliated with the other union confederations.[3] This situation testifies to the *political* character of the development of worker unionization, in that the institutional possibility of such development is clearly a product of the revolutionary process itself.

It is not possible to determine the precise impact of this rapid growth of worker organizations on the rate of unionization. Union registries frequently differ from Ministry of Labor information; estimates of the number of salaried workers differ according to the sources and methodology.[4] Without denying the extent of the unionization process over the last four years, it is evident that current figures are too high and do not have a reliable statistical basis.

According to Pérez-Stable (1982), by July 1980, of a total of 457 urban unions, 369 were affiliated to the CST. This means that more than 200,000 urban workers belonged to Sandinista unions, while over 300,000 urban and rural workers belonged to Sandinista unions.

These figures suggest a 74 percent rate of urban unionization, 77 percent of the salaried rural economically active population (EAP)— *despite the fact that it was only in 1981 that unionization in the countryside acquired real significance—* and 75 percent for the total salaried EAP. And this takes into consideration only the Sandinista unions.

In 1981 newspapers estimated that the ATC had 100,000 members, although no official records yet existed.[5] This appears to have been excessive: while the most reliable recent figures are around 43,000, this does not cover all rural workers: in the sugar agroindustry, for example, field workers are affiliated to the CST, which also covers the refinery workers.[6]

These estimates contrast with the Ministry of Labor picture. Adding the 27,020 workers who belonged to the unions that existed before July 19, 1979, and the 89,016 affiliated to the unions inscribed afterward, the total is 116,036, equivalent to 30–35 percent of the total salaried work force. It is possible, nonetheless, that this figure in turn underestimates the reality. For legal reasons, the computations of the Ministry of Labor only consider an organization a *union* if it has complied with all the requirements stipulated by the respective legislation. This leaves out organizations that for diverse reasons—pending negotiations, unfinished legal steps—have still not reached this level, but do reflect the organizational will of the workers. On the other hand, the unions do not inform the ministry of changes in their membership, which impedes a precise follow-up report about their actual size.

Taking into account all these circumstances, my own investigations in mid-1983 led to a total estimate of 145,000 union workers, equivalent to 41–43 percent of the total salaried EAP.

But regardless of the exact figure, it is evident that in the last four years union organizing has acquired a dynamic unparalleled in the history of the Nicaraguan working class. The resonance of these mobilizations in the revolutionary state and the FSLN, and the promotion accorded them, constitute the determinant factor for this dizzying growth in an economy as backward and unequally developed as Nicaragua's.

. . . OF A NEW TYPE

The period that began on July 19, 1979, was characterized not only by the quantitative growth of union organizations, but also by a marked change in the conception of what a union is and must be. This change in the political focus of unionization—*political* in the sense that it is seen from the perspective of constituting a new social order—took place amid intense struggles within the workers' movement and the revolutionary camp, and made up part of the process of consolidation of Sandinista hegemony in this arena.

In the view of the FSLN, unions are not merely trade-union organizations, but should articulate this activity with the advance of the revolutionary process in all its fronts, and should train the workers in progressively more complex forms of participation.[7] In particular, immediately after the overthrow of the dictatorship, the FSLN demanded of the union movement an active contribution to recovery. To the Frente this implied not only an attentive watch on the business behavior of the bourgeoisie and its administrators, but also a strengthening of *labor discipline* and of the subordination of salary demands to those of reconstruction.

This was a blow to the workers' expectations of rapid salary improvements and created a certain initial disorientation. The FSLN outlined the situation of the economy after the war, and the disarticulation and destruction of the productive apparatus, which did not permit the workers' immediate and total satisfaction of salary aspirations. Production had fallen sharply, the circulation mechanisms were broken, and in these conditions a rapid salary growth would only reinforce the inflationary process, which was already very high due to the effects of the conflict.[8] Many Nicaraguan revolutionaries undoubtedly remembered the tragic end of the Chilean Popular Unity government in which uncontrollable inflation, combined with declining production, hastened the deterioriation and fall of the popular government.

The economic policy promoted by the revolutionary state tended to respond to popular demands through consumption subsidies and expansion of social services—what in that period was called the *social wage*—more than through an increase in monetary salaries (MIPLAN 1980). This strategy created some conflicts within the workers' movement. At bottom, the way in which the contradiction between economistic demands and economic reconstruction was expressed manifested the contradiction class-nation within the revolutionary camp, and the way the forces involved understood this reflected their position with respect to the present stage of the revolution. From the Sandinista perspective, economic demands above a certain minimum level went against the economy's accumulative capacity and investment recovery, created insecurity in the bourgeois groups incorporated into the process, and created obstacles for the creation of the material base of the popular project. From a different perspective, the emphasis on such demands was one way of expressing workers' power at that stage, orienting part of the surplus toward the working class without further delay.

This explicit linking of issues and levels was strengthened by the close ties that existed between the union organizations and the political forces. The strong emphasis of such organizations as the Central Union for Action and Unity (CAUS) and the Workers Front (FO) on immediate economistic issues obeyed both a policy of rapid appeal to the worker base and their characterization of the new stage. Both organizations recognized the FSLN as the vanguard of the antidictatorial struggle, but denied its character as vanguard of the working class and of the revolutionary transformation. On the contrary, they interpreted the ties of some sectors of the FSLN with fractions of the bourgeoisie, and the initial presence of some bourgeois elements in the government, as proofs of its own bourgeois character. According to this thinking, Sandinista demands to moderate economic claims could have no other effect than to consolidate capitalist earnings and the political presence of the bourgeoisie. Regarding the public sector, the situation was the same: the state was behaving like a new boss, and therefore it made no sense to differentiate between the APP and the private sector. What for the FSLN was "national reconstruction" was interpreted by the CAUS, the Workers' Front, the Communist party, and the Popular Action Movement as the promotion of bourgeois class interests; labor discipline was seen as an increase in worker exploitation. The response of these organizations to the FSLN combined strong attacks against the CST and ATC for what they considered lack of combativity and betrayal of their bases with extreme economistic demands (Villagra 1980; M. Ortega 1983).[9]

In the case of the Nicaraguan Workers' Confederation (CTN) and the Confederation of Trade Union Unity (CUS), the promotion of this extreme economism was simply the continuation of the guild labor line, which reduced the union function to the achievement of immediate interests. Nonetheless, it flowed into the FO and CAUS strategies in the sense that it undermined the worker bases built by the FSLN in the heat of the revolutionary struggle—a struggle in which both had participated in secondary fashion and then only at the end. As the contradictions became more acute in the popular camp the General Workers' Confederation-Independent (CGTi) seemed to assume a less belligerent position with respect to the FSLN line. Notwithstanding divergent positions regarding specific issues, the CGTi loosely coordinated itself with the CST, creating a coordination body—the National Inter-Union Commission (CNI).

In this way the last months of 1979 and the beginning of 1980 showed an increase in political tensions within the workers' movement. Stoppages, factory and farm takeovers, mobilizations, and strikes expressed these struggles for political control of the rapidly growing unions. In these conditions, each participant put a strain on all its forces and employed all its resources; the FSLN used the prestige it had won in the struggle against the dictatorship, its deep roots with the masses, and the power of the revolutionary state.

In fact, in these first moments the FSLN position seemed less organically consolidated in the proletarian terrain than the other organizations that had participated less in the liberation war. The FSLN's political work among the working class had been initiated later than among the peasantry, the students, and the urban popular masses and the advances reached in these sectors were uneven. In the first months after the triumph the Sandinista political presence in the workers' movement took place mainly among the agricultural workers in agroexport, and was less solid in the urban economy. Here, the Frente's position seems to have been consolidated beginning with the incorporation into its ranks of the fraction that split from the PSN in 1977 to join the revolutionary struggle. This fusion, which took place a few months after the triumph, contributed a group of experienced trade-union leaders to the CST.

In the development of these contradictions, the FSLN combined ideological struggle with the benefits of the economic policies and the resources of the state apparatus. This permitted it to gradually gain the bases of those organizations and many of their cadres, at the same time that it neutralized or disarticulated their leadership groups. When in the beginning of 1980 the contradictions became unmanageable, the temporary jailing of leaders of the Workers' Front and the Communist party and the closing of the Workers' Front newspaper *Pueblo* and the Communist paper *Avance* concluded by also widening the space of the CST in the worker base of those organizations.

This process was closely tied to the development of the contradictions between the FSLN and the bourgeoisie, whose investment behavior was expected to be a strong impulse to economic revitalization. At the end of December 1979 members of this sector with important posts in the government were replaced in favor of a greater Sandinista cohesion of the revolutionary state. Only the engineer Alfonso Robelo and Mrs. Chamorro temporarily kept their positions in the government and the Frente acted to isolate Robelo from the bourgeoisie and neutralize the pressures coming from Washington. In this strategy, keeping workers' demands within certain limits, strengthening labor discipline, and the like, were essential to avoid excessively alarming the private entrepreneurs.

The view of the FSLN toward the worker question seems to have resulted from the relation of forces between the revolution and the bourgeoisie, the limitations imposed by the productive apparatus, and the tensions that arose from the international arena, all framed within a process that defined the worker-peasant alliance as its fundamental base and aimed at profound social transformation.

The FSLN focus on the issue implied that, in that stage, *popular power* was not reduced to *union power,* but comprised all arenas of revolutionary construction, especially the revolutionary state. The autonomy of the union organizations to make economic demands was therefore subordinated to the strategic interests of the revolutionary project. But this did not mean denying the legitimacy of union activism or of demands promoted within that framework. The FSLN position during this period is summarized in a report submitted by the National Inter-Union Commission (CNI) at the Assembly for Trade Union Unity on April 13, 1980, and in a speech presented by Cmdte. Carlos Núñez a week later.

The CNI document posits that the unions should be framed within two general lines of the Sandinista Popular Revolution: (a) to work arduously so that the revolution solidifies, consolidates, establishes its bases, stabilizes and is ready at any moment to defend itself politically, economically, or militarily; (b) to be at the head of the most felt demands of the workers, to make them the union's own, to channel and strengthen them so that these demands can be resolved and materialized into practical deeds by the revolution (CNI 1980).

These points express the need to reach a point of equilibrium—not, however, without contradictions—between immediate economic demands and the larger political project.

In general, workers accepted the initial restrictions that emerged out of the precarious economic situation. The case of the "Armando Jiménez" union of the La Perfecta milk complex is illustrative. To contribute to the recovery of the factory, the workers decided to take a half salary for a certain period during which distributors also stopped receiving their respective commissions; voluntary work campaigns were promoted, the workers stopped demanding better working conditions, and initiatives were proposed to state agencies to get production inputs and financing.[10]

In some cases this emphasis on economic recovery of the enterprises—not only of the APP but private as well—led some Sandinista unions to neglect workers' demands altogether, which left the field to the union confederations competing with the CST for leadership of the workers' movement. At the same time the workers' sacrifice contrasted with the attitude of many entrepreneurs, who made no effort to reinitiate the productive process, and who rejected economic petitions in the name of the bad general economic situation.

The presentation of Cmdte. Núñez points out these aspects of the issue, by projecting the legitimacy of such demands:

We wanted to generate the consciousness within the mass organizations that we had to work to preserve the revolutionary political project . . .; they had to also be instruments capable of autonomously expressing the demands of the social sectors they represented, so they had to make use of the most usual as well as the most unusual means (1980c: 16).

At the same time he criticized those who tried to postpone indefinitely the satisfaction of popular demands: "It was neither sufficient nor easy to say that the country was in ruins; effectively, at the level of the recently born state no line was implemented that would permit taking into account and receiving claims, criticisms, exigencies or demands of the masses" (ibid).

The FSLN National Directorate thus outlined the existence of a relative autonomy between the state and the mass organizations:

> . . . must the mass organizations revert to their own force, expression, and mobilization when their petitions are not heard, when the doors are shut on all sides, without finding an answer anywhere? We believe so.
>
> . . . the mass organizations must collect and make their own the demands of their members, of their social sectors, and struggle for their materialization through the new mechanisms that the revolution has instituted. But when these roads are closed, when they knock and no one hears, when they are reverted to and are not functional, whether because of bureaucracy, or liberal methods, or because the problems of the masses are not taken into account, etc., our organizations must move to other forms of political persuasion.
>
> This means that the mass organizations, framed within the general line of the revolution, have sufficient right, when these organisms are closed, to recur to internal criticism, to public criticism, to use all means of communications up to mobilization to demand the necessary measures to guarantee that their claims be heard (ibid.: 11–21).

The struggle plan promoted by the CST in February 1980 can be considered a practical example of the union struggle within this policy. Its basic points contemplated an increase in the minimum salary for the lowest paid workers; the revision of the salary table; reform of the Labor Code (sanctioned during the period of Somoza García); improvements in the social wage; and promotion of workers' participation in enterprise management. At the same time, the CST promoted the creation of occupational health committees to oversee work and safety conditions in the enterprises, and the systematic denunciation of owners and administrators involved in decapitalization practices or who in any way neglected the recovery of the productive apparatus or the normalization of distribution and provision channels.

Nonetheless, for many union leaders affiliated to the CST the FSLN demand for autonomy of the mass organizations was a difficult issue, as it put their organizations in inferior positions vis à vis the other confederations. The Frente also confronted some tendencies toward bureaucratization in certain union leaderships. In a self-critical document that appeared in *Barricada* (October 5, 1980), it was noted that the lack of cadres with sufficient union experience meant the risk of separating the leaderships from their bases; other times the leaders, in the case of a labor conflict, did not give adequate support, thereby creating the conditions for other confederations to capitalize on the workers' claims.

This situation was more conflictive in the APP than in the private sector. Promotion of the union movement was interwoven with the disappearance of the old bosses and their replacement by administrators that were presented as the representatives of the popular state. Expectations for immediate solutions to the labor problems were therefore stronger. A CIERA investigation into mining in the department of Zelaya is illustrative. After the nationalization of the mines a corporation was created to run them (CONDEMINAH); inexperience of its functionaries and of the union leaders, lack of clarity about the role of the union in the new situation, adoption of decisions without prior consultation with the bases, and reduced representation of the poorer paid workers in the direction of the union disoriented the majority of the workers, causing apathy and frustration (CIERA 1981: 200–208).

Toward the end of 1980 the FSLN began to emphasize the necessity of promoting union claims without interrupting the productive process, characterizing stoppages and strikes as means of last resort:

> labor conflicts must be resolved without paralyzing production, because it is evident that now strikes not only damage the economy in general, but also the workers in particular. Around these points we must be clear: the salary and right to strike restrictions must be viewed as measures freely, voluntarily, and conscientiously adopted by the workers themselves owing to the situation the country is living through. It is a question of defending the economy by conscientiously assuming the sacrifices and the efforts that this implies.[11]

This was the position outlined in April of that same year. By then it was evident that the representative organizations of the large bourgeoisie, particularly COSEP, had passed into open opposition. Cmdte. Jaime Wheelock said in November:

COSEP is converting itself ever more into a clique that wants to provoke problems for the revolutionary process and for National Unity, that has been converted practically into a clique of political types who are trying, whenever possible, to provoke situations and make us think that they represent the whole private sector. We want to tell them that we have been in communication with the private sector—with the small, the medium, and the large as well, even the largest. We have not been able to find in any of our conversations, of which there have been many, such an imprudent attitude, such a truly unreflective and irresponsible attitude as that which the gentlemen of COSEP are taking.[12]

Obviously the election of Ronald Reagan prompted some elements of the bourgeoisie to involve themselves in open counter-revolutionary activities. At the same time, the FSLN was trying both to generate political differences within the bourgeoisie and promote the unity of the workers' movement. From this process emerged the Trade Union Coordinating Body (*Coordinadora*) of Nicaragua (CSN), made up of the CST and the ATC together with the CAUS, CGTi, FO, CUS, Federation of Health Workers (FETSALUD), the Journalists' Union of Nicaragua (UPN) and ANDEN, the teachers' union. Only the CTN, tied to the Social Christian party, remained— by is own decision—outside the Coordinadora, although soon afterward the CUS left.[13]

The CSN thus represented the first fruit of a movement of broad union conciliation around a class perspective. Pointing to the relation between workers' claims and reconstruction, the Coordinadora's platform issued July 16, 1981, explicitly adopted the FSLN line:

There should be an effort, in the first instance, to resolve any labor conflict or problem without turning to work stoppages. This does not mean renouncing the right to strike, far from it; what we want to affirm is rather that the strike should be the last resort for the workers; that they must exhaust all other measures before taking it up, since any stoppage reduces production and undercuts the fulfillment of the plans and programs of the Government of National Reconstruction and the strategic project of our Sandinista Popular Revolution (*Los Trabajadores*, July 16, 1981).

The CSN Plan of Struggle, of which the above forms part, was a considerably elaborated effort to interweave the positions of the minority union confederations with the strategy of the FSLN. Its objectives included the strengthening and defense of the revolution; the growth of production and productivity, and the fulfillment of the goals of national reconstruction; promotion of greater worker participation in the Sandinista Popular Militias; elaboration of a new salary scale "in accordance with the economic situation of the country"; a raise in real salaries; improvement of working conditions in general and occupational health and safety in particular; opposition to indiscriminate salary increases that are "obstacles to the process of economic reconstruction of the country"; reform of the Labor Code; struggle against bureaucratism, abuses of power, negligence, and waste in the APP enterprises; prevention of capital flight and damage to production in the private enterprises; stimulus of worker initiative; organization of voluntary work; elevation of political education and the technical formation of workers; strengthening of labor discipline both within the APP and the private sector, and promulgation of a "democratic, anti-feudal, anti-oligarchic, and anti-imperialist" agrarian reform.

Sandinista hegemony in the trade union area, as in the revolutionary camp in general, was expressed through the CST and ATC direction of the workers' movement and union struggles. The period beginning in late 1980 was marked by intense mass mobilizations, pushed mostly by the ATC and the CST, against the opposition parties in general and especially against the decapitalization maneuvers of the bourgeoisie. In this sense, the constitution of the CSN implied both an important step in the process of unifying the workers' movement and explicit recognition of the leadership that the Sandinista union organizations exercised in this process.

The CSN Plan of Struggle maintained a certain autonomous right to demands for the worker organizations, and although it relegated strikes and other forms of direct action to measures of last resort, it explicitly recognized their legitimacy in such conditions. Nevertheless, the development of the economic crisis, aggravated by the production retreat of the bourgeoisie, military aggressions, and the inevitable disorder of the social transformation, would make it an ever more marginal form of worker activism by the state, at the same time that the union organizations increased their militancy.

The Base Document of the Second Assembly for Workers Unity,

published at the same time, specified the following principles as a guide:

> The class independence of the proletariat in light of revolutionary doctrine; . . . the consequent practice of proletarian internationalism; the hegemonic role of the working class in our revolutionary process; the unity of the workers' movement, of all the workers and people behind the banners of the struggle for scientific socialism; the unity of the union movement into a Single Workers Confederation around the fundamental principles and historic tasks of the working class; . . . to categorically sustain the revolutionary alliance of the working class with the poor peasants as the motor forces of the Revolution; the determinant role that the popular masses play in all the political, economic and social transformations of our country; . . . to sustain and develop the truly democratic and anti-imperialist alliance of our people for the defense of National Sovereignty and the economic and social development of Nicaragua (*Los Trabajadores*, July 16, 1981).

The document went on to note, however, that "the social contradictions in our country have been exacerbated to such an extent that it is not possible to cover up the antagonisms between classes."

Based on this focus—class struggle, unity, anti-imperialism—the CSN demanded a greater development of worker participation in overall economic management and the direction of each enterprise; effective political control by the state over the capitalists; strengthening of the union movement and rejection of class conciliation; the adoption of a uniform salary policy based on increased production and productivity, together with cost-of-living increases; creation of unions by branch of industrial production; incorporation into the militias and strengthening of defense in all areas; immediate confiscation of decapitalizing enterprises.

It is interesting to note that the whole document takes the government as the explicit or implicit interlocutor of its proposals. The government received these demands in a balanced way. The policies against decapitalization, capital flight, and the like were strengthened considerably; diverse measures were adopted to avoid bosses' reprisals against workers in the militias; the development of unions by branch was stimulated; the Ministry of Labor pushed for the progressive institutionalization of worker participation in management of the enterprises in the collective labor agreements. There was no increase in salaries as a general policy, but rather as a product of union negotiation capacity, and the Law of the Economic and Social

State of Emergency (September 10, 1981) established prison sentences of from one to three years for "those that incite, help or participate in inciting or continuing a strike, stoppage, or takeover of workplaces" and "those that promote or participate in land invasions or takeovers in contravention of the dispositions in the Agrarian Reform Law."

The FSLN confronted the economic crisis by strengthening its control of the state with respect to the antagonistic classes. It seemed evident to the Frente that the strategy of exhortations for a greater labor discipline on the part of the workers had not furnished the hoped-for effects:

> . . . as a conjunctural factor that has had a very serious and important impact on this crisis we have to mention labor indiscipline. In these two years of revolution, because of the labor time lost by the workers the country has lost $150,000,000 as a result of strikes, stoppages and different forms of interruption of work—in a word, as a result of generalized labor indiscipline. $150,000,000 is equal to 30% of all our exports. It is a figure that is too heavy for our country (Carrión 1981: 20).

Finally in December 1981 the Council of State suspended the right to strike. This suspension remained in effect until July 1984.

The reformulation of the role and tasks of the union movement in accord with the necessities and possibilities of the current stage of the revolution has thus mixed persuasion with control. The deepening of the economic crisis, the confrontation between the revolution and the bourgeoisie, and above all, the pressures and aggressions of the U.S. government have framed the greater or lesser weight that each of these elements has acquired at each moment. In the cases in which control was resorted to—including elements of repression—the targets were the leadership cadres of the organizations affected, while political work, persuasion, and political education were emphasized for their bases.

WORKER PARTICIPATION IN ECONOMIC MANAGEMENT

Immediately after the liberation war, it became evident that the key to revitalization of the economy was active worker participation. A large number of industrial and agricultural enterprises were destroyed or seriously damaged; in some regions the insurrection had coincided with the beginning of the agricultural cycle and a good deal of the work had not begun; a large number of farms and businesses had been abandoned by their owners, many of whom left Nicaragua. In these conditions, the workers were put to the urgent task of preserving the existing means of production, repairing as much as possible such equipment as could be saved, taking possession of the abandoned enterprises, advising the inexperienced technicians and administrators of the recently created APP, or getting the bourgeoisie to start up their paralyzed businesses again and reinitiate investment. Particularly in the countryside, these worker initiatives took on a highly insurrectional tone, denoting their class will to assume effective control of the means of production that had come into their hands.

The demand for worker participation, a permanent demand of the union movement, comes from the conviction that nationalizing the economy is not enough to assure the transformation from authoritarian to democratic management; thus "a change in ownership forms is necessary but not sufficient to guarantee more profound transformation of the social economic structure; for that active participation of the workers is necessary in the political, ideological and, of course, economic life of the society" (M. Castillo 1983: 2).

The concept of worker participation is becoming progressively explicit. The Assembly for Trade Union Unity (April 1980), called by the CNI, outlined workers' participation as a two-stage process: participation in production and in the transformation of the state. The first is characterized as increasing production and productivity, watching over the physical installation and machinery of the work centers to avoid sabotage, vigilance over the operations of the enterprises to prevent their decapitalization, struggling to complete the labor legislation and industrial and occupational hygiene measures, strengthening the APP, and preventing production paralysis.

Participation is viewed here as a function of overseeing the owners of the enterprises and as incorporation into tasks that are themselves productive, instead of as an effective incidence of the workers in the economic decisions of the productive establishments. As for wider participation in the state transformation, this was characterized as the election of qualified representatives to follow up implementation of the Economic Reactivation Plan; to combat bureaucratism, squandering, graft, inefficiency, and so on; to promote the technical capacitation and political education of the workers; to suppress worker-boss relations in the APP; to inform the state about de-capitalization practices or violation of the labor laws.

Worker participation, therefore, was fundamentally seen as effective fulfillment of the production goals, political vigilance, and collaboration with state organs in supervising the business conduct of the bourgeoisie and the APP administrators. It did not yet imply incorporating the workers into the elaboration of basic decisions for the enterprises (investments, production goals, costs, organization of the labor process, etc.), but neither was it confined to the limits of each enterprise. Nor was the role of the union reduced to that of a mere information transmission belt between the state organs and the rank and file. The trade union is this, but it is more than this; it is assigned a function of *revolutionary vigilance* over the productive process, a role in the progressive transformation of the relations of production and of the labor process in the APP—a struggle against bureaucratism, elimination of bosses' criteria of labor discipline, and so on—and in raising the technical-cultural and political-ideological level of the workers—in a society that had just emerged from illiteracy. Worker participation is therefore seen as a process oriented to the totality of economy of the state, and not only to one or some specific units of production. It is at the same time a more political than technical-economic participation. Said another way, it is more *macropolitical*—that is, tied to the project of the overall transformation of society—than *micropolitical,* which has to do with production goals of each enterprise, costs, and the like.

Based on more than a year's experience, and in a context in which the economic crisis was becoming more acute, the Second Assembly for Workers Unity (July 1981) tied participation to the advance of economic recovery. In the base document already mentioned, participation in economic management encompasses both overall planning of the national economy and the direct management of the enterprises, in the APP and the private area.

Explicitly raised in the base document was the issue of participation as a dimension of progressive class autonomy of the worker's movement. So too was the question of democratization of union practices. The CSN sought a clean differentiation from the proposals of some opposition unions and even certain sectors of private enterprise in the co-management proposals. Both of the latter saw the possibility of a political opening to attract the FSLN's worker bases.

On the first anniversary of the revolutionary triumph, a group of Conservative party industrialists from the city of Granada took the initiative of implanting a system of profit-sharing for the workers in their businesses. The project was denounced by the FSLN unions as diversionary; according to them these same businessmen had refused to pay the salary increase decreed by the government the previous May 1, and had boycotted the union meeting convoked by the Sandinista organizations.[14] The Sandinista unions also denounced the advice lent to this project by U.S. Embassy personnel.[15] The minority union confederations, especially the CTN, demonstrated enthusiasm for this kind of strategy. Precisely on July 19, 1980, the CTN published in the opposition daily *La Prensa* an extensive *Manifesto* where it advocated independent and classist unionism, and the establishment of the "social property of the workers."[16]

It is obvious that this project went in the opposite direction from the kind of participation postulated by the Union Coordinadora and the Sandinista organizations. In reality another kind of unionism and another kind of society underlay these frustrated initiatives. They reflected an effort to generate an alternative political project that would irritate the bourgeoisie less. Although from a technical and economic perspective it appeared to offer the workers much more than the Sandinista conception of worker participation, these initiatives confined the union organizations to a subordinate position in a system designed to order for the bosses. In this sense, the class orientation they invoked *reduced the class to the union* and to its capacity to get some piece of the pie that would always be cooked in capital's oven.

The Sandinista experience of worker participation in economic management has thus evolved amid tensions and contradictions. While the period since July 1979 is rich with lessons, they cannot be considered definitive; it has been a period of experimentation and search, where the errors are as elucidating as the achievements.

Participation in enterprise management, which began as a series of initially spontaneous worker actions in the last days of the insurrection, was slowly institutionalized, in large part through collective labor agreements, which had a great boom after the revolutionary triumph; beginning with 1981 the law creating the Agrarian Reform enterprises contemplated decrees specifically regarding the participation of the agricultural workers.

Tables 5.2 and 5.3 show the distribution of the collective agreements concerning participation, by area of property, sector of activity, and union central to which the respective unions belong.

From a total of 718 collective agreements 422 (59 percent) incorporated clauses relative to union participation in management. In the APP the proportion of agreements with such a clause is slightly higher than in the private area: 61 percent (122 over 199) and 58 percent (300 over 519), respectively. The most active union in this is the CST, with almost 75 percent of the agreements.

The clauses that refer to union participation are various: labor

Table 5.2
Collective Agreements with Clauses about Participation
by Sector of Activity and Area of Property

Sector of activity	Area of property		Total
	APP	Private area	
Agriculture and mining	16	45	61
Industry, agroindustry, and construction	73	144	217
Commerce	10	53	63
Services	23	54	77
Others	—	4	4
Total	122	300	422

Source: Based on Ministry of Labor figures.

Table 5.3
Collective Agreements with Clauses about Participation
by Sector of Activity and Union Central

Sector of activity	Union Centrals							Total
	CST	ATC	CGTi	CAUS	CTN	CUS	Other	
Agriculture and mining	14	39	2	1	4	—	1	61
Industry, agroindustry, and construction	163	—	10	19	13	8	4	217
Commerce	45	—	—	4	9	4	1	63
Services	64	—	2	—	4	6	1	77
Others	3	—	—	—	1	—	—	4
Total	289	39	14	24	31	18	7	422

Source: Based on Ministry of Labor figures.

discipline, administration of the labor force, evaluation of the productive process, capacitation of the labor force, and so on. In general the unions have achieved participation in the elaboration of the enterprise's internal rules, control over the contracting of new personnel and of promotion, transfer, and firing schemes; access to information and consultative capacity regarding costs and goals; resources for technical and professional capacitation of their members (permissions, scholarships, subsidies, and the like).

Regarding the overseeing of the productive process and participation in the general direction of the enterprise, the Nicaraguan experience has passed through different phases in a process that has not yet ended. The first effort to generalize a participatory form, after the initial stage of insurrectional spontaneity, was constituted through the *Economic Reactivation Assemblies* (AREs). These assemblies included personnel from the enterprise, the union's board, the directors of the enterprise, and eventually the corresponding minister or vice-minister, and in some particularly important enterprises a member of the government or representative of the FSLN participates as well.

The AREs existed throughout 1980. Discussions covered everything from the enterprise's productive process to the country's economy, and the articulation between the two—supply of primary materials and other inputs, scarcity or lack of spare parts, availability of foreign exchange, and so on. The organization of the AREs sought to break with the tradition that tied the workers exclusively to the immediate sphere of labor, and to open their interest and their participation to broader horizons. In this sense they pointed the way toward various objectives: knowledge of the production plan of the enterprise by the workers in all sections and departments; deepening of the tasks of the government economic program that concerned the workers; review of the production process with regard to the plan; evaluation of the plan itself by sectors, brigades, sections; detection of existing problems; maintenance of the means of work; rational use of available resources; proposals for the improvement of productivity; organization of worker incentives; and extension of the AREs to the level of production branches.[17]

The development of the AREs was a way to disseminate the government economic program and the enterprise's production plan, assure discussion of both by the workers, and identify points of coherence or gaps between the two. The AREs encouraged worker participation in broader areas, including factory management and even economic policy-making. Some were more successful than others. The better ones, in terms of worker participation, levels of discussion, and the like, were those that arose through the unions' political work with their bases, such that the bases themselves proposed, at times even belligerently, the necessity of knowing and pursuing issues that until then had been veiled from them. The existence of a strong union, solidly rooted in its bases, was the condition for developing a really participatory process. By contrast, when the AREs were organized vertically from the administration down to the bases, workers were not interested in pushing the process further.

The AREs created a space for intense confrontations between the workers and the enterprises' administrations, due to the unwillingness of many directors to give the union access to information about the functioning of the enterprise, or to the reproduction in the APP of worker-boss relations from the private area, bad resource administration, or whatever. At the same time, ARE practice revealed that, with the cultural and technical levels that still prevailed in the working class, the organization of participation had to start from the workers' immediate arena within the technical division of labor: the section or department. In general the better assemblies were those that originated in those arenas; they permitted the workers better levels of discussion to improve their knowledge of the themes; also at this level the preparation of the AREs had been much more careful than at that of the enterprise as a whole; finally, the workers were much more familiar with the problems of their department or section than with the others and their participation therefore was generally limited to questions directly related to their immediate area of work.

The AREs permitted the workers to see that the enterprise administration was nothing mysterious or distant, and to understand the importance of organized work to realize fixed objectives in their respective field by the revolutionary state. But at the same time they showed the necessity of giving some continuity to the experience, instead of limiting it to one or two moments in the annual production cycle. From this arose the Permanent Production Assemblies, a means by which the various sections of the enterprise constantly evaluated the implementation of goals fixed in the AREs. These assemblies functioned positively regarding production, but again distanced the workers from the framework of administration and separated administration from production.

On the other hand, it often became evident that the workers' expectations regarding levels of participation and their efficacy clashed with the reticence of many administrators, who saw such participation as a reduction of their authority. This generated strong tensions between the workers—who proposed to share in administration functions—and the directors of the enterprise. The initial answer to this was to incorporate some members of the union's board into the administration of the enterprise; the union began then to function as a transmission belt between the workers and the leadership. This permitted an improvement in carrying out the productive process in some centers, but at the same time it gave birth to a bureaucratization process in the union leadership and, consequently, to the desertion of its members. Within a short period this process led to one of two ends: either the union leadership, trying to solve the production problems, progressively loosened its ties with its bases and completely assumed the administration's perspective, or, as a way of maintaining its representiveness, the union leadership abandoned the administration and assumed a belligerent attitude toward it, aggravating the problems that in principle it had tried to solve.

The successes and failures of the AREs led to the search for other forms of participation, beginning with the immediate arena of work—the section or department. Thus the Production Councils were formed, to which each section of the enterprise elected a representative, based not so strongly on political criteria, but on criteria of productivity: the vanguard worker. This group of workers from all sectors or departments, plus administration representatives by section, made up the Production Council of the enterprises.[18]

The Production Councils discussed the production goals of the enterprise, the difficulties emanating from technical problems or as repercussions of the national economic situation, and contemplated ways of dealing with the situation; they elaborated the internal rules of the enterprise; they defined measures to improve the general conditions of work and occupational safety, and so on. Initially they had to counter a certain worker apathy, but the union's fundamental political work was to overcome this attitude. In TEXNICSA (an APP textile factory), for example, the factory union, affiliated to the CST, organized weekly meeting circles to inform the workers about the progress of the factory, the capacity for insertion that the councils made possible, and so on, trying to motivate them to participate actively. In the Benjamín Zeledón sugar refinery (also APP) the union organized weekly meetings with the personnel of each section, with the same goal. The results were generally successful: they got the representatives to attend the council, and other members of the section began to demand that they render accounts of what had happened in the meetings.

The experience of the councils permitted the workers to begin to take charge of issues that until then were the domain of the enterprise's executive, such as labor discipline. To deal with this, Discipline Committees were created in each enterprise, charged with eradicating the attitudes that impaired production and the raising of productivity: absenteeism, negligence, squandering of resources, and the like. The committee is made up of representatives of workers themselves; instead of repressing or fining workers they use persuasion, through political discussion with each worker about the significance of his or her actions, the impact on the course of production, on the work morale of the other workers, all in the context of the revolutionary process. If despite these meetings indiscipline continues, the committee begins to consider it a deliberate effort to step outside class interests and only then applies sanctions.

In general this mode of participation has developed more in the enterprises with unions affiliated to the CST; more in the APP enterprises than the private sector—where still few examples can be found—and within the APP, more in the urban-industrial sector than in agriculture.

The dispersion of the rural labor force, the seasonal nature of some employment there, and the low development of the material productive forces have limited the development of worker participation in this sector. Nonetheless there is a first effort to legally regulate this, unlike in the urban industrial sector. The law that created the Agrarian Reform Enterprises (ERAs) established that each ERA would have a Consultative Council, in which a worker representative would participate. One task of the council, among other things, is to revise and approve the annual technical-economic plans and/or proposals of the enterprise that the director prepares, and to revise and approve any changes introduced into them. Despite its name, however, the council is not merely a consultative body, but also has decision-making faculties.

In addition to the workers' representative—generally an ATC activist—the council includes the ERA director who presides, and functionaries of the enterprise that he deems necessary. This composition gives the worker a minor representation, but in practice decisions are taken by consensus rather than by vote. This has translated into the possibility that the workers' opinions will have a greater weight than their numerical presence would suggest. Nevertheless, few ERAs yet have their Consultative Council, and the experience gathered up to now shows that this is not the level where worker participation has evolved with the greatest intensity. In reality the participatory practice of rural workers has tended, for various reasons, to follow its own channels (M. Ortega 1983).

In the first place, each ERA is composed of various State Production Units (UPEs), equivalent to what in an industrial enterprise would be a department or section. The UPE is made up of a confiscated *finca* or establishment, and together with other UPEs constitutes the ERA. This was the arena in which rural worker participation initially took place. Originally the farms thus administrated were called Sandinista Agrarian Communes; they adopted their current name later in the context of the institutionalization process and the increasingly direct state presence. The new ERA-oriented Consultative Councils took functions away from the UPE, and took decisions about its evolution away from the workers in that unit. For example, the overall technical-economic plan is not divided by UPE, and thus it is complicated for the workers to offer opinions on questions that involve dozens of UPEs, of which they often only have a very rudimentary idea for reasons of distance, lack of communication, or whatever. At the same time, the UPE is the level at which participation is usually the most intense, since workers not only work there, but also regard it as a supply center, and many of them live on or near it. In sum, there is a contradiction, or at least a gap, between formal participation levels and the real forms in which it unfolds.

This has led to giving the UPEs their own consultative council, although at the moment only 20 percent of them have such a body.[19] To confront the dispersion of the UPEs within the same enterprise, some ERAs have begun to create Production Complexes, which group together various UPEs. These complexes are an intermediate body between the UPE and the enterprise directors, which permit some problems to be faced that go beyond the level of the determined production unit: supplies for the workers, fuel, and others.

These forms of participation have been developed almost exclusively in the APP. Recently the ATC has been organizing Zonal Workers' Councils, comprising delegations of workers from both the APP and the private sector, to discuss problems that affect the whole zone, independent of the property arrangement of the farms. The councils also organize workers from private farms into APP production units for voluntary work brigades in cases of emergency (floods, necessity to harvest quickly, etc.) or motivated by dates of political significance. In general these experiences have generated high interest and good participation among the workers.

Recently the ATC has begun to promote general assemblies in which the workers openly discuss suggested issues. They are called above all to discuss the ERA director's report about goals and production evolution, development of specific projects, the perspectives being outlined, and the like. In the sugar agroindustry, for example, assemblies are held before the beginning of the harvest period; the first was in 1982.

Both the ATC and the CST are currently promoting pilot participation projects in selected enterprise groupings to evaluate experiences through systematic follow-up in the course of a year. In the agricultural sector, MIDINRA, with ATC participation, selected ten ERAs based on their level of development (compactness of their UPEs, profitability, union organization), with the goal of developing an experimental management model. The ATC has assumed the task of assuring the organization of unions by enterprise, since up to now they have existed only at the UPE level. In this way they try to establish correspondence between the organization of each ERA and that of the union. In the industrial sector the pilot project comprises eight APP enterprises and is promoted by the CST, with the support of the People's Industrial Corporation (COIP). The experimental character of both projects, and the short time span since their initiation, prevents judgment of their impact on either worker participation and ability to incorporate initiatives from the base into the enterprise's decisions, or their incidence in the evolution of the productive process of the enterprises.[20]

Involving workers in management of the enterprise in which they work is only one facet of worker participation in economic initiatives. The state also sees union participation in various dimensions of its structure, and in the design of their respective policies. Regarding economic policy, the CST and ATC consult on various bodies: the Employment and Standard of Living Commission, commissions on occupational health and safety, consultative commissions on agricultural policy (cotton, coffee, cattle, rice, bananas, sugar, basic grains). The ATC joined the National Committee of the National Food Program and the National Council of the Agrarian Reform; the Union Coordinadora participates with the Ministry of Labor in elaborating and executing the emergency employment plan. The ATC and the CST, as well as the CGTi, CAUS, and CUS, are represented in the Council of State.

Union participation in these different levels is unequal, and receptivity to their initiatives is higher in some aspects of the state than in others. Not all functionaries are inclined to discuss things with the representatives of the organizations, nor do they always plan the most propitious conditions for the discussion to take place—for example, making information available with enough lead time to carefully analyze it, standardizing criteria between the branches of the state, and so on. Other times the paternalism of some agencies or functionaries leads the union representatives to lose their belligerence, or else the technical outline is presented in unnecessarily complicated terms, hampering the effective participation of worker delegates.

WORKER PARTICIPATION, CLASS STRUGGLE, AND THE REVOLUTIONARY STATE

Worker participation is not a gift of the revolutionary state to the workers, but a right they have won, and one that they assert. This does not refer only to their support of the FSLN struggle against Somocismo, or to their character as an exploited class, but to the effective evolution of their participation in the current stage of the revolution. The incorporation of the organized workers in economic management had to be fought for by the unions against the private business owners, and against some APP administrators and state functionaries.

In this struggle the FSLN union organizations have generally made up the vanguard. Through mobilization, internal and public criticism, denunciations, and so on, they have progressively opened the space for workers' participation. Naturally the greatest resistance came from the private sector. In an economy like Nicaragua's, demands for participation rapidly acquired an openly subversive character from the bourgeois perspective. Participation in the administration of the enterprises, development of the union movement, the echo that the workers' demands found in the state apparatus, meant a break with the bourgeois principle of authority in the enterprise, in the same way that the revolution had broken with it in society as a whole. This was particularly visible in the rural sector. If collective labor agreements switched around worker-boss relations in the urban economy, in the countryside they created a total commotion. The farmworkers' unions got to participate in the writing of internal rules for the haciendas, administration over hiring and firing the labor force, and so on.

There was also resistance, though a little less intense, in the public sector and in the APP. At the end of 1980, for example, the Union Coordinadora strongly criticized the technicians of the Ministry of Planning for not taking the workers' opinions into account in elaborating the 1980 Economic Reactivation Plan, despite the fact that a group of unions had requested a meeting with the functionaries.[21] Other times the criticisms refer to the lack of firmness by some state agencies in dealing with the private sector when it obstructs union participation or refuses to recognize the workers' rights. The ATC demanded more vigorous action by the Ministry of Labor against business leaders who violate labor legislation, infringe collective agreements, and impede the exercise of union participation. The ATC denounced the passivity of some functionaries in the face of systematic failure of the bosses to fulfill their obligation to permit union access to the businesses' accounting books. According to the ATC, "There are cases where if we don't provide transport to the inspectors they won't go make an inspection. The inspectors need to identify themselves more with rural work and the agricultural workers, to get better organized so they can guarantee the fulfillment of the labor legislation."[22]

It is clear that the type of participation pushed by the ATC and the CST challenges the bourgeois principle of authority more incisively than do traditional strategies of participation in company benefits, or letting workers be minority capital stockholders. It is because of this that sectors of the bourgeoisie have supported the latter initiatives, and developed a close alliance with the union federations that promote them.

The workers have also had to confront directors and administrators in the APP who tend to reproduce bourgeois worker-boss relationships: authoritarian behavior, refusal to discuss anything with the workers, and the like. In such cases the unions' attitude has been as belligerent as in the private sector. For example, the workers from Plywood—a wood plant of the APP—took advantage of a visit from Cmdte. Víctor Tirado to outline to him, in an improvised assembly, their criticisms of the administration: violation of the collective agreement, failure to know the union's functions, lack of support to the innovative workers, ideological confusionism, fixing of prizes and commissions for management personnel, and so on.[23]

On another occasion the workers from COIP's plastics complex denounced one administrator's excessive expenditures for fuel and repairs for his own vehicles, and the lack of control over primary materials.[24] In early 1983 the workers of the Fabrica de Hilados y Tejidos Nicarao (also of COIP) challenged the manager's administration in an assembly, blaming him for accounting losses.[25]

There are many other examples. In general the workers' demands and criticisms are well received by COIP's leadership. One illustrative case is that of PLASTINIC, the main APP enterprise for plastic products. In August 1982 more than 350 workers and the union leadership outlined to the government a series of problems that had arisen in the factory: inadequate plant maintenance, insufficient spare parts, little incentives for the innovators, excessive commissions for the head of production and the salespeople, a boycott on the part of administration against the union movement and worker participation in management, among others. In October COIP and the union signed an accord in which the administrator of the operation would be changed. However, the change did not take place and the union and workers reinitiated their pressures, although without stopping production. After new mobilizations, at the end of January 1983 they finally got the administrator fired. As on other occasions, the process was fully covered in *Barricada,* the official daily paper of the FSLN.[26]

In summary, the Sandinista triumph has not eliminated the trade union struggle, but has given it wide receptivity in the revolutionary state, as a function of the overall process promoted by the revolution. For the moment, worker participation is more an attribute of the union than of the workers themselves. This is particularly evident in the state institutions (political commissions, councils, etc.), where union representatives are directly designated by the federations, without participation of the bases. In the companies, on the other hand, the union leaders are elected in worker assemblies, as also occurs in general with delegates to the committees.

In many cases, nonetheless, a gap can still be seen between the level of participation and concern in general among the union cadres and that of the bases. The weight of authoritarianism, product of the long dictatorship, has not been totally liquidated; illiteracy has left bad habits that still have not been eliminated: all this joins together to lower the effective levels of worker involvement in management. One element not always taken into account is that participation requires certain minimum qualifications, and a dedication of time and effort; it is an additional task for the worker, which demands training and above all the development of a firm political conviction. Still today an important part of union activity is to motivate the bases to actively join in participation: attend assemblies, participate in discussions, demand reports from their delegates, inquire about the progress of production in their own section or department, and the like. For example, during the Production Assembly celebrated by 600 workers of the Oscar Benavides enterprise (an agrarian reform enterprise), the ATC representatives urged the workers to adopt more belligerent postures regarding management and to raise their participation in their respective workplaces and in the armed defense of the enterprise: "Let's realize once and for all that these companies are ours; for this reason we have the obligation of knowing and directing them, as well as defending them."[27]

The current role of the unions, as a result, is to train the bases to increase their incorporation into the available forms of participation. The task is not simple, because many times the union leadership is not much better off than the workers: they are overworked and lack experienced cadres, among other things.[28]

These elements create the conditions for the development of paternalistic practices and leadership by substitution within some state sectors and within the administration of the APP enterprises. Either the opportunities for participation are obviated so as not to overload the workers or their organizations with additional tasks, or the functionaries have better technical knowledge, or even the union's response is slow—all of these lead to a situation in which decisions are adopted from above and passed down, and the workers' representatives simply put their seal of approval on these decisions.

One issue that always comes up in a discussion of worker participation—but which affects other areas as well—is the type of relations that evolve between the state and union organizations, and in particular the type and level of autonomy that unions can have with respect to a state whose fundamental social bases are the working masses, and how, given this and the project it assumes, a popular state is defined.

As noted, the FSLN generally gives the unions the role of transmission belt between the workers and the administration of the enterprise. Some observers have criticized this practice, noting that in reality it reduces the union organization to a mere instrument without real autonomy, and suggests it may become a mere state apparatus (e.g., H. Weber 1981, Van Eeuwen 1982).

It is undeniable that such tendencies exist in some segments of the state and even of the FSLN; they have been repeatedly denounced by the FSLN National Directorate.[29] Nevertheless, five years of union practice shows there to be effective autonomy with respect to the state, reinforced by adherence to a common political project. Its effective margin is a product of its capacity for action and initiative, the representativeness of its leaders, and the combativity of the bases. This does not mean, however, that there are not tensions between the unions and the state administration, or that one cannot find overlaps or confusions of levels between them. It is not only the worker movement that lacks sufficient and experienced cadres or has a tradition of such problems; the same limitations exist within the state and the FSLN.[30] On the other hand, one must go beyond merely noting the transmission belt character of the unions with respect to the state; it is also necessary to determine the real meaning, in the current stage of the revolutionary process, of this characterization.

The intense worker mobilizations during the first half of 1981 against decapitalization and the emptying out of companies by sectors of the bourgeoisie offer a good opportunity to reflect on this. In March 1980 the government had issued a decree that tried to put a brake on business practices, such as decapitalization, disinvestment, clandestine export of assets, and neglect of the productive process, that were making economic recovery even more difficult. Evaluation of the 1980 Economic Program further revealed that private industry had generally not responded to expectations placed in it, and together with the hardening of the opposition bloc, had increased its recourse to decapitalization.

From the beginning of 1981 denunciations by the CST and ATC grew louder; they organized occupations and takeovers of factories and land, demanding the strengthening of the March 1980 decree and the confiscation of business owners who carried out these practices. The mobilizations found an echo in the FSLN National Directorate; in June, Cmdte. Jaime Wheelock denounced some notorious cases of decapitalization and flight of foreign exchange, adding that "the antipatriotic attitude of some sectors of Nicaraguan private enterprise is endangering the survival of this [mixed] type of economy. If we are going to have an economy here that robs and decapitalizes, we would prefer to close down this type of economy completely."[31] Days later, in the closing of a workers' assembly, Cmdte. Bayardo Arce did the same, denouncing many business owners who were "programmed by imperialism to destabilize the revolution."[32]

In other words, the FSLN National Directorate took the workers' demands and projected them at a national level: it was no longer solely a question of an attempt against the goals of economic programs (the first level of the issue) but became one of maneuvers promoted or inspired by imperialism. It therefore called into question the legitimacy of the mixed economy scheme by virtue of which the bourgeoisie's existence was acceptable in the new stage (second level).

The answer of the worker organizations was not long in coming. The mobilizations increased; land takeovers, factory occupations, and direct production management by the workers themselves became more widespread; to the CST and ATC were added UNAG, the CDSs, AMNLAE, and the youth and student organizations, with the slogan of immediate confiscation against decapitalization. Numerous marches were organized with these demands; the four union organizations of the FSLN—ATC, CST, FETSALUD, and ANDEN—also added the demand that APP technicians and administrators who wasted enterprise resources or were negligent managers be thrown out of their positions.[33] The popular organizations of the departments of Matagalpa and Jinotega sent a "Letter of Justice" to the government, demanding the confiscation of landowners that were decapitalizing, and a similar thing happened in Granada where long lists of companies and ranches that were being decapitalized and abandoned were published by the ATC- and CST-affiliated unions, which in the majority of cases proceeded to take them over.[34] In a joint declaration the ATC and CST laid out that the real choice was "worker control or decapitalization."[35] The Ministry of Justice echoed the popular demands and charged that Nicaraguan business leaders had met with Central and South American business organizations to discuss common strategies to facilitate the decapitalization process.[36] The ATC from the cotton department of León launched a struggle plan demanding the immediate confiscation of those who decapitalized or did not cultivate their lands, adding that "the workers will take the initiative to make them produce."[37]

For its part, the Second Assembly for Workers' Unity demanded that once a specific decapitalization had been denounced, the enterprise be immediately regulated for the duration of the investigation.[38] The CST General Secretary, Lucio Jiménez, addressed a workers' assembly called under the slogan "Against decapitalization, we demand confiscation," saying: "We workers cannot continue on the defensive . . .; we must move immediately to the offensive in a clear struggle, not against any old element or one or two bourgeois administrators or even against one or two bosses, but with a forceful blow to the bourgeoisie as a class."[39] He then denounced the benevolence of some state functionaries toward the problem: "There are state organisms that seem to be accomplices of decapitalization, because they give time to the businessmen to invent financial books."[40]

This rapid escalation of popular mobilization alarmed the bourgeoisie, who denounced it all as a FSLN campaign against the private sector and the mixed economy project.[41] But at a certain point there was a shift on the part of the state; at the end of July 1981 the Ministry of Labor released a communiqué prohibiting stoppages, strikes, and land and factory takeovers motivated by decapitalization. Although the communiqué did not contemplate sanctions against offenders, the CST publicly declared its disagreement with the document.[42] A government communiqúe, however, supported the Ministry of Labor position "categorically."[43]

By then popular agitation had been reinforced by the announcement of the imminent passage of the Agrarian Reform Law, as well as a new law against decapitalization, which would incorporate several of the demands and suggestions of the labor organizations. In August the Council of State finally approved the new law, but while it incorporated the initiatives of the popular organizations it also prohibited "any action tending to modify the relations of production in the enterprises by way of direct acts."[44]

Although the law did not contemplate sanctions for such acts, it provoked open opposition by all union representatives in the Council debates, including those of the CST and ATC, even though it was supported by the FSLN representatives.[45] Denunciations about decapitalization have not ceased since then, but in general have been less intense, and without recourse to direct actions.[46]

I have dealt with this at length because it clearly illustrates how worker mobilization on issues crucial to the advance of the revolution are articulated with the overall orientation of the revolutionary vanguard. From specific demands about concrete points, led against limited bourgeois sectors, they become subsumed within a broader political perspective which is at the same time anti-imperialist and class-based. At a certain point *worker* mobilizations join with the whole of the *popular* organizations, making the fundamental class contradictions more acute. At the same time, these contradictions involve technical and professional sectors in ideological solidarity with the decapitalizing bourgeois fractions. Thus, this widening and deepening of popular mobilization also creates tensions for the mixed economy project and for the alliance with some bourgeois sectors promoted by the FSLN. At this point the state intervenes to limit worker and popular activism at the same time that it institutionalizes the fundamental aspect of their demands.

Other cases could be cited, but all support the point that current reality is too fluid and complex, and the participants in it too active, to draw any definitive conclusions about the relation between the state, the FSLN, and mass organizations.[47] Based on the evidence this dynamic reality offers so far, it seems tendentious to suggest, as some do, the existence of an authoritarian position that prefers to tranquilize the union organizations' capacity for criticism and autonomy. On the contrary, the revolution's advances seem to be based precisely on the popular classes' capacity for mobilization and organized struggle and on their *dynamic dialectic relationship* with a vanguard political organization. This relationship is dynamic in that the FSLN's vanguard character is continually reaffirmed through its development, and dialectic in that it does not exclude the existence of contradictions.

The contradictions are due to two basic factors that have already been noted, but that are worth re-emphasizing briefly. On one side there is the project of national unity and mixed economy with popular hegemony, in which the political vanguard must guarantee that the dynamism of the hegemonic forces does not endanger the alliances on which the project rests. Concretely this means that the activism and the autonomy of the popular classes should not alarm a class as alarmist as the Nicaraguan bourgeoisie, from which the revolutionary project still expects adequate investment behavior. In these conditions the government and even the FSLN position with respect to the worker and popular demands will always be strongly conditioned by the political conjuncture and by the state of the economy. On the other side, this process, always complex and charged with tensions, is much more complicated and difficult in a society such as Nicaragua, which has no democratic tradition, little prior experience in union organization, a working class that less than four years ago was predominantly illiterate, and an extremely backward and depressed economy. Moreover, this society, because it is promoting a revolutionary process in these precarious conditions, must also stand up to economic aggressions, propaganda, military attacks, and the threats of direct invasion by U.S. imperialism. For the moment, therefore, for the revolutionary leadership workers' management means keeping watch so that in the midst of aggressions production is not held back.[48]

DEMOCRATIZATION OF PRODUCTION AND WORKER DISCIPLINE

The development of workers' participation in economic management has meant a democratization of the productive process in broad areas of the economy. In its different modes, this participation introduced profound breaks with the traditional authority principle. It is not a question of a complete break, nor is it equally extensive in all areas; but it has implied an effective challenge to the prevailing patterns in the enterprises. Where directors or administrators have offered resistance, far from inhibiting union initiatives, it has meant an increase in mobilization and political recourse to the intervention of the FSLN.

Before new concepts of authority could be developed, in a temporary vacuum, what is often called a lack of labor discipline has developed, a circumstance which should be properly seen as a manifestation of the workers' struggle to transform the existing relations of production.

It is necessary to remember that each system of production, and in general each kind of society, has its own criteria of labor discipline. In capitalism it is based on the exploitation of the workers, on the disorganization of the labor force, and on the existence of high levels of unemployment and underemployment, above all in dependent capitalism. The high levels of efficiency and productivity that capitalism flaunts are based on these elements: ferocious control of labor power through policing both within and outside the company; the possibility of substituting undisciplined workers through the existence of a mass of people without work. Thus what from the capitalist viewpoint is "productive efficiency" and "labor discipline" from the workers' perspective is exploitation and repression.

When society is transformed by revolution the social organization of production is also transformed as well as the criteria of efficiency and labor discipline. The bourgeois image of discipline as worker submission, as the capacity to exploit the workers, is replaced—sometimes violently—by criteria based on the political-unionist protagonism of the proletariat in its classist responsibility, in its patriotism.

It is a difficult process, full of contradictions. It is inevitable that in the first moments of the revolutionary transformations, popular euphoria and workers' enthusiasm provoke a neglect of efficiency in the labor process. The will to eliminate all vestiges of the old dominant class is sometimes carried out at the cost of maintaining the means of production that have just been appropriated; other times it appears almost like a desire to personally collect the balance due for a long life of exploitation, injustice, and subordination. These are some of the phenomena that can be seen in the first moments of any social revolution: normal reactions in the face of the old order of exploitation and misery. At bottom, it is a kind of testament to the will of the masses to liquidate an unjust social order and make real their own emancipation. Furthermore, demands for greater productivity and efficiency are formulated above all by the bourgeoisie; it is understandable, therefore, that some sectors of the working class consider that preoccupation about labor discipline and labor productivity are "bourgeois vices" that true revolutionaries should overcome.

It is thus common to assert a fall in labor productivity after the

Table 5.4
Evolution of Physical Productivity of Labor
in the Manufacturing Industry, by Size of Enterprise

Period	Large enterprises[a]		Small enterprises[b]		Total	
	Index	Variation (%)	Index	Variation (%)	Index	Variation (%)
Second half 1977	100.0	—	100.0	—	100.0	—
First half 1978	99.8	− 0.2	98.4	− 1.6	96.9	− 3.1
Second half 1978	86.5	− 13.2	97.5	− 0.9	88.7	− 8.4
First half 1979	67.4	− 22.1	69.0	− 29.2	69.7	− 21.4
Second half 1979	87.0	+ 19.0	59.1	− 14.2	85.5	+ 22.6
First half 1980	108.3	+ 24.5	61.9	+ 5.1	102.2	+ 19.5
Second half 1980	103.3	− 4.6	66.9	+ 8.1	98.3	− 3.8
First half 1981	106.9	+ 3.5	61.0	− 8.8	100.3	+ 2.0
Average	—	+ 2.4	—	− 5.9	—	+ 1.0

Source: CETRA (1982).

[a] Enterprises with a productive employment volume of more than 50 workers.
[b] Enterprises with a productive employment volume of up to 50 workers.

triumph of a revolution, and the Sandinista revolution has been no exception. In this case however, the fall has been documented by impressions only: no one has provided systematic information, and impressions all refer to the first moments of the revolution—the end of 1979, beginning of 1980 (Foladori 1982; Colburn 1983). The subsequent period has seen contradictory appraisals by different branches of the revolutionary government.[49]

Available information indicates, however, that labor productivity has recovered after an initial fall. In fact, research by the Labor Ministry on the productivity of labor in the manufacturing industry indicates that after the fall of productivity levels during 1978 and the first half of 1979, during the second half of 1979 and all of 1980 a rapid recovery occurred (CETRA 1982). Table 5.4 shows, however, that the growth of productivity after July 1979 took place in the large factories, while in the small ones the fall has not stopped.[50]

These results are supported by an analysis of industrial surveys: Table 5.5 shows strong growth of labor productivity in the manufacturing industry in the period 1979–81. We saw in the previous chapter, however, that this growth was not uniform throughout the industry. In the first years after the triumph labor productivity was lower and evolved more slowly in the APP enterprises than in the private sector (see Table 4.2).

Although there is no available information about the situation in

Table 5.5
Nicaragua: Evolution of Productivity of Industrial Employment,
1979–1981

Years	(1) Employment[a]	(2) Value added[b]	Productivity[c] (2:1)
1979	33,446	1,843.4	55,117
1980	45,040	3,941.8	87,518
1981	47,472	4,836.7	101,886
Rates of growth (%)			
1980/79	34.7	113.8	58.8
1981/80	5.4	22.7	16.4
1981/79	41.9	162.3	84.8

Source: Based on figures from INEC (1979, 1980, 1981b).
[a] Number of people employed.
[b] Millions of 1980 cordobas.
[c] 1980 cordobas.

the countryside after the initial breakdowns, the evidence presented here obliges caution about conclusions concerning social transformations and labor productivity. Furthermore, the growth of productivity registered by the study of the Ministry of Labor and by the surveys of INEC took place in conditions that it is important to briefly recapitulate: in the first place, the rapid and broad development of unions; second, intense labor and political mobilization; third, profound changes in the ownership system of the enterprises, leadership personnel, and in administration criteria; fourth, an economic crisis that obstructed the normal functioning of the enterprises (lack of inputs, spare parts, reduction of exports); fifth, unchanging technological conditions; sixth, a relatively accelerated inflationary process that provoked the deterioration of real salaries.[51]

The fact that in these conditions productivity has increased suggests that the frequent association between social transformation and labor indiscipline lacks foundation, at least as regards the Sandinista revolution. At the same time, it shows that the concern of the unions about raising the efficiency of the labor process does not remain at the level of mere words, but is evidence of the class responsibility and political commitment of the workers to the revolution.

6

Popular Democracy
and Ideological Struggle:
The Case of Education

As the capitalist state developed, the concept of *citizen*, as the political subject of the state, centered on the notion of ownership of the means of production. In an era in which bourgeois ideology did not engage in circumlocutions, Adam Smith was particularly clear: "Civil government, so far as it is instituted for the security of property, is in reality instituted for the defense of the rich against the poor, or of those who have some property against those who have none at all" (1776: 674).

Therefore only property owners have the right to participate in politics. Thomas Cooper elaborated this view in 1829: "Society was instituted for the protection of property; quarrels about property would naturally give rise to it. What reasonable claim can they have, who have no property of their own, to legislate on the property of others? What common motive and common interest is there between these two prescriptions of inhabitants?" (p. 363).

These lucid representations by a class on the rise are representative of the predominant bourgeois thinking of the epoch (see Witmer 1943; Williamson 1960). Their contrast with the reality of twentieth-century capitalist democracies shows that what today is known as *bourgeois democracy* (universal suffrage, right to free association, shorter working day, etc.) is more the product of workers' struggles to gain recognition of their political and social rights than it is the application of the original class conception (Therborn 1977). However, the result, and at times the objective, of these struggles was participation in a political system that definitively responded to, and expressed, class interests alien to the workers' own. Politics reproduced economics: thus there were *first-class* citizens and *second-class* citizens.

What, then, is the situation in a revolutionary process of constructing a democratic-popular state? Who will make up the political subject of this process, the real profile of the citizen of this new state? The Sandinista revolution offers one answer to these questions; it is not the only answer, but it is an answer remarkable for its originality, and for the multitude of difficulties and aggressions that surround its development.

The previous chapter looked at an important dimension of this process: the democratization of the relations of production through the development of worker participation in economic management. Here we turn to the incorporation of the mass organizations in defining and executing the revolution's educational policy.

There are several reasons for choosing education as a central discussion point. First, it is one of the best-known aspects of the Sandinista revolution. More generally, education is one part of the political-ideological dimension of a social formation, and is also a *product* and a *sphere* of the class struggle. It thus presents its own contradictions at the same time as it serves to process—or condense—contradictions that pertain to other spheres. This latter capacity is important: the intensity of the debate regarding educational transformation in Nicaragua cannot be explained without recognizing that it is a confrontation of distinct political projects, not simply technical-pedagogical differences. Finally, the development of the New Education presents a revealing case of how popular participation is projected in the Sandinista conception of democratic construction.

POPULAR DEMOCRACY AND NEW EDUCATION

Immediately after the triumph, the FSLN was ready to initiate bold transformations in the educational field, drawing the popular classes into it. The National Literacy Crusade (CNA) reduced the national illiteracy rate from 50.4 percent to 12.9 percent in only five months, teaching half a million adults to read. At the same time there was a strong expansion in school matriculation; between 1978 and 1984 enrolment more than doubled, though in some levels particularly ignored by the dictatorship—primarily adult education, but also preschool and special education—the jump was spectacular

(Table 6.1). Such a rapid growth in enrolment at all levels has affected school attendance figures; current levels are still far from ideal, but the advance has been very rapid, above all in primary education: from 65 percent in 1978 to 80 percent in 1980. Coinciding with this, the budget for the educational sector, which in 1978 represented only 1.4 percent of the gross domestic product, rose to 3.4 percent in 1980 and to 5 percent in 1983, 11.5 percent of the total budget (MED 1983b: 147).

The figures in Table 6.1 reveal the magnitude of the growth, but they represent only one part of the New Education; just as important, and relevant, is that the educational system in which this growth took place is considerably different from that which existed before the revolution. The opening up of the educational system has not meant distributing "more of the same," but putting at the disposal of the people, and through their active participation, "more of *something else*."

Indeed, the increase in enrolment would not have been possible without these changes. An increase of almost 300,000 people cannot happen from one year to the next, nor can nearly half a million adults be taught to read in only five months in a country with grave problems of physical integration if the educational system itself does not immediately introduce profound changes.

Educational change is part of a broader process of profound revolutionary transformation. The effective participation of the popular

Table 6.1
Nicaragua: School Enrolment, 1978–84

Education	1978	1979 1980	1980 1981	1982	1983[a]	1984[a]
Preschool	9.0	18.2	30.5	38.5	61.4	66.8
Primary	369.6	431.1	503.5	534.9	579.2	135.6
Junior high	98.8	110.7	139.7	139.9	161.6	186.1
High school	23.7	29.1	34.7	33.8	39.7	41.2
Special	0.3	—	1.4	1.5	1.8	2.8
Adult	—	—	167.8[b]	148.3	167.3	194.8
Totals	501.6	589.3	877.7	897.2	1,005.3	1,127.3

Source: MED (1984).
Figures are thousands of students.
[a] Projected figures.
[b] Second semester.

classes is not possible in the midst of ignorance. Obscurantism and ideological backwardness served to reproduce the social exploitation and political oppression of the masses. The Sandinista revolution, which recognized its motor forces in the peasantry, working class, and working masses of the rural and urban areas, could do nothing other than assume their liberation from ignorance as one of its most urgent priorities. The liquidation of the dictatorship was required for this to become possible; but that in turn could not be consolidated without the emancipation of the people from their cultural backwardness.

Education in the Sandinista revolution is not then a mechanism of reproduction. It is no longer a mechanism of reproducing dependent capitalist society, but on the contrary a dimension of the process of *liberation of the great popular majorities from the material and ideological conditions in which they were reproduced as exploited and oppressed classes.* Nor is it *yet* a mechanism of producing the new society, in that the new society itself is still part of the horizon of revolutionary construction, and within this process there remains much to be overcome and eliminated.

The New Education is conceived as a means for emancipating the popular classes from ignorance, and helping them advance their comprehension of the world in order to transform it. It is consequently presented as a space for confrontation between the motor forces of the revolution and the old bearers of a social order in retreat.

The revolutionary context of the New Education contrasts markedly with other experiences of educational reform in Latin America, where adhesion to the dependent capitalist parameters of the economic and social order has meant that popular demands for social transformations have been shifted to the educational, and in general ideological, plane. There they have been constrained by a limited response capability and by a few educational reforms with no support in the material base of society or in the state. Educational reforms within modernization projects thus appear as a strategy to present a nondisruptive alternative to the tensions generated by dissatisfaction and popular struggles. Where such reforms in fact express an alternative class project, the resulting tensions provoke mediation by the state to guarantee the reproduction of the popular classes as economically exploited and politically subordinated.

Moreover, the quick leap from elite education to mass education, from an education for the reproduction of an unjust and oppressive social order to one for the creation of a liberating social order, is qualitative not only because of the opposing objectives but because of the organizational, methodological, and other conditions that must be satisfied by all of society so that the new vision can be reached. The participation of the mass organizations in the educational transformation is thus a key question.

In the traditional scheme the educational process is basically composed of two agents only, the teacher and the student, though the nature of their relationship may vary. At most the presence of the student's parents is accepted in the sphere of basic education. However, apart from being more symbolic than effective, parental participation is fundamentally reduced to disciplinary questions and definitely obeys the conception of child-student as the private property of the parents, and to the student's own incapacity—for reasons of age, "rebelliousness," scant development, "immaturity," and so on—to take certain kinds of decisions: *study hard and behave yourself.* Undeniably, the issue of the relation between the school and the community has been raised on occasion, but most of the time this tends to appear as an external reference to the educational process and in an eminently passive role.

The New Education is breaking with this scheme by opening the way for the participation of the mass organizations, both in formal and informal education. They are involved in the implementation of educational policy as well as in the definition of the policy, progressively carrying the totality of the educational process to the heart of the popular classes. The dichotomy between the state as definer and population as executor of educational policy, however progressive, does not adequately express the reality of revolutionary Nicaragua. Here it is the people, enrolled in their own organizations, who orient the fundamental definitions and forms of the educational process.

The *community,* as an abstract and external entity of the educational process, gives way to the "people" as a concrete entity, which designs the new education based on its material conditions of life and its effective participation in the revolutionary process. This goes beyond the usual reforms—delegating the execution of some aspects of educational policy to get around the lack of state resources or the complaints of some sectors—in that all dimensions of the educational process are opened up to the full participation of all the popular classes. Along with other arenas of the revolutionary process, education is experiencing a movement that we could call "socialization," insofar as the mass organizations effectively participate in its different aspects. The whole society becomes the active subject of the educational process, and to the extent that it is a process oriented by the popular classes themselves, education is progressively converted into a gigantic process of self-education.

Perhaps the National Literacy Crusade and Popular Adult Education program provide the best evidence of growing mass participation in a new kind of educational process. Of an approximate total of 80,000 literacy crusade workers, only some 7,000 were professional teachers; the rest consisted of high school and university students (55,000), public workers, housewives from popular barrios, workers, and so on (MED/DEI 1981; Miller 1982). Popular Adult Education presents a similar picture: of a total of 17,000 teachers in mid-1981, 70 percent were illiterate before July 19, 1979. In other words, for each ten teachers, seven were *recently taught to read and write,* and therefore belong to the most exploited and oppressed sectors of society.

Another characteristic of these "popular teachers" is that they do not develop teaching tasks professionally outside of the other dimensions of their daily life, but rather integrated into them.[1] In the same sense, by mid-1981, of a total of 14,175 functioning Popular Education Collectives (CEP), more than 84 percent were located in rural zones, where there is also 81 percent of the enrolment in Popular Adult Education.

It seems clear that an educational process promoted by the masses themselves is a process of a new kind. This is so not only because it exchanges the image of the professional teacher for that of a popular teacher who is part of the reality in which this new education operates, or because the educational process is carried out outside of the traditional teaching institution. It is because for this to be possible, it is necessary to carry out equally important transformations in methods, content, and the physical teaching environment. For the masses to experience the educational process as their own, it is necessary to overcome the break between it and the concrete mode of their daily lives—their insertion into the activities of production, defense, political-ideological debate, and so on. This is not only a scholastic issue: *education does not automatically become popular education by becoming de-schooled*. It is a question of designing a system in which the popular classes are the active and direct subject of the educational process. The experience of Nicaragua, with its successes and limitations, shows that this is possible only in the context of a revolutionary process promoted by the popular classes themselves.

THE NATIONAL EDUCATION CONSULTATION

At the beginning of 1981 the Ministry of Education consulted all the mass organizations, political parties, parents associations, unions, and business groups about the goals and objectives of the New Education, the educational forms that should be promoted, their content, the characteristics that the so-called new man and the new society should assume. In the midst of an intense ideological struggle, rejection by the bourgeois organizations, and counter-revolutionary attacks, more than 50,000 people, in thirty mass organizations, political parties, unions, and other revolutionary organizations, participated all across the country for two weeks in an intense collective discussion about such issues.[2]

The National Consultation represented an extraordinary experience in self-education for the participating organizations. For the large majority it was the first time that they had ever had the opportunity of freely discussing questions traditionally considered "technical" and therefore beyond the opinion of the majority of the population. The richness of the information collected, and the bases of the criticisms and recommendations, demonstrate the prejudicial character of those traditional considerations and show that there are no issues that cannot be handled by those who lack formal training if they have the right conditions. In this sense the Consultation can be considered a singularly important chapter in the process of democratizing Nicaraguan society, and as evidence and product of the popular essence of this process.

An important proportion of the responses related to the role that the mass organizations played, and should play, in the educational process. This is particularly true regarding demands outlined by the participants in the Consultation; they demanded greater participation of their organizations in the tasks of the New Education, criticized their operational deficiencies or the refusal of some cadres to participate more fully, demanded the consolidation of the organizations, and suggested new educational methods and modes of action that directly involved these organizations.

These responses produced an image of an educational process in which the popular organizations have a broad field of action, a process that is closely linked to the organized participation of the people. Like the rich experiences gathered by the Literacy Crusade, they derive from the creative and systematic involvement of the mass organizations. Faced with the traditional concept of the educational relation (teacher-student, or at best teacher-student-parents), and further separated from real society, a new educational process was defined in which the organizations of the people would assume a leading role.

This leading role of organized people in education is really an aspect of a broader social reality in which the people in struggle appear as its central and permanent element. This is seen clearly in the three basic principles of the revolution. *Popular democracy* is conceptualized above all as organized participation of the people in the government and in the tasks of the revolution; as construction and practice of popular power.[3] *Nationalism* is seen as the defense of national sovereignty, the interest of the majority, and the right of self-determination of peoples. *Anti-imperialism* is characterized mainly as a rejection of all foreign domination, a struggle against neo-colonialism, and solidarity among peoples struggling for their liberation.

The educational recommendations all emphasized popular participation and the tying of education to the reality of the popular classes and the tasks of the revolution. The people clearly requested more schools (technical, agricultural, industrial, urban, and rural), and more preschool and adult education centers. But equally they demanded the development of new study programs in tune with national and local reality and with the necessities of the revolutionary process, incorporating the values of the popular culture. The methods and teaching forms should systematically incorporate the joint participation of teachers and the students, the link between theory and practice and between study and work, and should develop the creative and investigative capacity of students and their scientific vision of the world.

As the conclusions to the *Preliminary Report* of the Ministry of Education pointed out: the organizations that participated in the

National Consultation demanded new education that ties study to work and theory to practice; one that is open to the new currents of thought and that will stimulate the creativity and the scientific spirit of teachers and students; one that is innovative in its methods and forms, and that is linked to the organizations of the people. The new education should be one that accompanies and promotes the revolutionary process, that eliminates individualism and opportunism, and that contributes to forming a new human being and a new society (MED 1981: 139).

TWO ANTAGONISTIC PROJECTS

It is evident that these transformations cannot be carried out without contradictions.

In the first place, there is the contradiction between the New Education, liberator and producer within its own sphere of a new kind of society; and elitist education, reproducer of the old social order, which in some sectors of society still persists as the only possible form. The antagonism between the revolution and the counter-revolution is also prosecuted in the educational sphere. It could not be any other way, when the educational system was one of the arenas where the power of the bourgeois class was protected and when the New Education cannot be implanted immediately and simultaneously in all its aspects. This is even more the case in a stage of the revolution characterized by political pluralism and based on a mixed economy, in which the continuation of some sectors of the old dominant classes is accepted. Political control of its material bases of reproduction (regulation and taxation of economic activity through nationalization of the financial and foreign commerce systems, development of the APP, strengthening of the unions, labor legislation, control of exchange, etc.), consolidation and development of the mass organizations, and progressive strengthening of the revolutionary state all define these bourgeois fractions as subordinated. But this does not mean that they are going to be passive, resigned to a revolution based on the popular classes, supported by the organized force of the people in arms. If one thing is clear to these groups of the bourgeoisie, it is that this is *not their revolution.*

Through the newspaper *La Prensa,* the radio stations that remain in private hands, their presence in some spheres of private education, and their relationship to sectors of the Catholic church hierarchy, the bourgeoisie has tried to impede the advance of the New Education, although with limited results. In the period between November 1980 and March-April 1981 especially, education was one of the arenas in which the ideological class struggle was presented most intensely. But the clumsy character of the bourgeois campaign, its retreat as a class on all fronts, and the intense and effective involvement of the masses in the revolutionary tasks—not only the tasks of the New Education—condemned the bourgeois campaign to failure.

To be successful, bourgeois ideology must be able to penetrate deep into the population and mobilize it against the revolutionary state. This is managed via a double process of *reduction* and *articulation:* the first, appealing to the *public*—in itself, a concept of bourgeois manufacture—in its character as *parents* and *Christians;* the second, through the articulation of this image of Christian parent to the most authoritarian aspects of bourgeois ideology. Thus the New Education was characterized as *totalitarian* and *atheist,* aimed at cracking the family, undermining parental authority, and denying the people's religious beliefs: a 1981 article by UPAFEC, the parents' Christian education association, began by stating: "The participation of civil society and the state in educational affairs should be subordinated to the principles and values of the parents, since it only complements the tasks of the family," and "it is considered an established fact that we are moving toward a 'popular democracy'; any half-enlightened person knows that this is the name with which Marxist-Leninist dictatorships fool the world." The president of the association went on to specify the proper goals of education:

> To educate is to end by giving form to—forming—the man begun by God. To educate is not to finish the works of men. To educate is to finish the work of God. . . . To educate is to end by giving man the forms that God has conceived. The model to follow is God's plan about men. Those who form children and youth through models that are not those of God betray God. Man that is the end result of the children and youth entrusted to us is not a man conceived by one philosophy or another, it is not the man thought of by Rousseau, Freud, Marx or Lenin, but is the man of God.
>
> And because we (the parents) are the ones in charge, we are the ones who must direct that which is related to the education of our children. The responsibility is ours, and no one else's. No one has the right to interfere by directing for us what the education of our children should be.

And what is the fundamental contribution of the state in education? To take it upon itself to direct everything related to education so that parents have no responsibility left? To take it upon itself to educate directly through state-controlled schools? The captain of the soccer team is not supposed to throw the other ten players off the field and remain playing alone. The captain of the team is to coordinate the game of the others and try to assure that each plays his own position well. The state is not supposed to throw the parents off the field of education. The state's obligation is precisely the opposite: to assure that the parents have the role that belongs to them, to assure that parents can in fact educate their children well; to assure that parents can in fact decide about the education of their children with absolute freedom. True ministers of education should be ministers at the service of families. This is how it would be if the plan of God were respected.

. . .We ask God that someday we may have such an order here in Nicaragua. It would be the Nicaragua of God (Zavala Cuadra 1982).

Even in Central America, one seldom finds a bourgeoisie like Nicaragua's, one which at the end of the twentieth century must still be shown that universal, secular, and free education is not a communist stunt. But by adopting this viewpoint, the bourgeoisie showed itself once again to be a victim of its own prejudices and condemned itself to failure. The *parent* the Nicaraguan bourgeoisie is thinking about is also the owner of his children, a domestic projection of the bourgeois image of authority in business and in the state, and the *family* is the arena in which this parent/owner/entrepreneur exercises his authority. And the *Christian* that the bourgeoisie has in mind is an isolated being, tied through individual and passive faith to a severe and dictatorial God, author of a static social order as reflection and evidence of the immutable character of the *heavenly* order.[4]

Only historic blindness and the decadent character of its class interests can explain the faith and hope—though not charity—that the bourgeoisie and its intellectual representatives place in these symbols. The parent/owner and the Christian-mystic can have no meaning for the popular classes in a society like Nicaragua's, where at least since 1977 the younger generations massively joined the FSLN struggle, where their participation in the insurrection meant months of absence from their homes (homes very different from those of the bourgeois image), and where the political practice of the children often politicized and civically matured the parents. This is a society that after the triumph saw its children go up into the mountains again and mix with the peasantry, the working class, the semiproletariat, to teach the masses to read and write, living among them and learning from them the brutal face of hunger, misery, early death, and destroyed lives. This is a society in which the great majority of the popular classes found out what education is only because there was a revolution.

At the same time it is a revolution in which Christians actively participated, in a questioning Christianity oriented toward the masses, contributing militants, heroes, and martyrs to the Sandinista struggle (Molina 1981; Cabestrero 1983). It is a revolution that guarantees the exercise of Christian faith and proclaims that "one can be a believer and at the same time a serious revolutionary and that there is no insurmountable contradiction between the two. . . . Many Christians are militants of the FSLN and as long as there are Christian revolutionaries in Nicaragua, there will be Christians within the Frente Sandinista" (FSLN 1980b).[5]

This contradiction arises in the context of making explicit the political aspect of any educational project, its relationship to how society is organized, and finally, to a class perspective. In a stable capitalist society, this political component masquerades as apolitical, as the only possible mode of organization, and consequently the normal and obvious order of things. The interests of the bourgeoisie are thus elevated to constants of a history whose own nature is also diluted. The political element, as a specific form of class leadership of society, is experienced as ideology: it permeates all dimensions and structures of individual and collective life, it gives daily life shape, and for that reason it is experienced *without being felt* and even *without being known*. The content—not to mention the methods—transmitted by the educational system is joined to a structure of concepts and applications that are the product of a capitalist organization of social life and that only make sense within it.

The sharpening of the political-ideological class struggle forced political explicitness in all spheres of society, among them, obviously, education. The identification of a given social order with the interests of a class and the reduction of the nation to the measure of a dominant class linked to imperialism, are challenged by the masses, the state, the practice of the revolution, and the concomitant new political discourse. The *de*construction of bourgeois political discourse takes away its power as an ideology and unmasks it as lies. To the degree that it is made visible, it loses conviction.

It is clear, therefore, that the contradiction between the old capitalist education and the New Education *is not* a contradiction between an apolitical educational project and one that is politicized—as the old dominant classes suggest. The real contradiction is in terms of the *type of political focus* they contain. The New Education does not introduce "politics" where before there were none, but replaces one perspective, that of an unjust, repressive political order, with another, that of a popular and anti-imperialist order. A distinctive feature of the Nicaraguan New Education is its political *explicitness,* in contrast to bourgeois education that sells its product without advertising it.

From this perspective, class conflict is a battle over who defines the meaning of concepts. Thus there is a bourgeois meaning of the concept *patria* and a popular-revolutionary meaning, a bourgeois meaning of *nation,* and a popular-revolutionary meaning; it is the same in every case. The educational system consequently becomes one of the key settings of the ideological class struggle and the confrontation of their political projects.

INTERNAL TENSIONS

There are also tensions and conflicts within the New Education, largely concerning its effective reach, how it should advance, the unequal pace of change in different aspects, and so on. These issues do not seriously question the development of the process, but rather the concrete modes by which it is unfolding.

To begin with, there is the tension between formal and non-formal, or non-school, education. The most spectacular successes of the New Education are found in the non-school sphere: the National Literacy Crusade and Popular Education for Adults. But after nearly three years of popular education, the complex question arises about how this sphere should relate to the formal system. The answer is difficult, since both developed almost entirely separately, with their own methods and their own networks of recruitment of students and teachers. They also have different ideological symbols and profiles: literacy and popular adult education as prolongations of the insurrectional struggle; formal education as a prolongation, in a new context, of traditional school education.

Nonetheless the fact that changes in the sphere of formal education have been slower or less spectacular does not mean that none have existed. Without question, they are more difficult than in non-school education, not as regards technical issues, but political-ideological ones. Non-school education, as massive popular education of adults, is a field created by the political practice of the revolution itself, in an environment where the FSLN has long been consolidated as vanguard. Something different is happening in the sphere of formal education, the traditional preserve of the old dominant classes and of broad sectors of the petty bourgeoisie that saw it as a mechanism of social mobility. Four years of revolution have not been enough to completely eliminate this. Furthermore, the struggle for the New Education in this formal sphere expresses in some measure the dynamic of this "educated" and educationist petty bourgeoisie to maintain its own position in the revolutionary society (Castilla Urbina 1982b, 1983).[6] In the same way, the reduction of *popular education* to the sphere of *non-formal and adult education,* and its consequent "critique" of school education, is largely a product of middle-class radicalism rather than an objective reflection of reality.

Closely linked to this is the issue of developing human resources for the New Education, and adapting existing personnel to a new political context and a new academic and pedagogical focus. There is still a marked separation between the academic-pedagogical dimension of training and its political-ideological dimension. The greatest efforts seem to be oriented to the first of these, reinforcing the image of the absence of politics in pedagogy. The notion of *educational quality* has become an absolute, existing outside of, and even in contradiction to, the political-ideological development of educational cadres.

This separation between what is "properly educational" (pedagogical) and what is political definitely affects the persistence of old conceptions of education as something technical and outside class struggle. This position contrasts markedly with a revolutionary society that is politicized in all spheres and in which the political-ideological conflict has become intense. As a result, the level of political-ideological development of the student population is generally much more advanced and solid than that of its teachers, generating a contradiction that has immediate repercussions in the quality of the professor's "technical" performance. His or her pedagogical practice becomes routine, tedious, not effectively related to real life; the output of the student drops, absenteeism increases, and the conventional manifestations of student "indiscipline" become generalized.[7]

The revolution has not only introduced changes in the educational sphere, but at the same time has altered the conventional *limits* of the educational system. Traditionally, education is reduced to pedagogy, limited to the institutional sphere of the school. As such it is separated from the sphere of production ("economy"), from reproduction ("family"), and from political practice. The revolution has broken this fictitious compartmentalization and has converted all dimensions of social practice into educational ones. This goes beyond the issue of non-school education: all tasks of the revolution are transformed into tasks of preparation and of training of the popular masses. The successive Popular Health Campaigns, community development and environmental sanitation campaigns, the physical reconstruction of zones affected by natural disasters, voluntary work in agriculture and defense, have all facilitated the training and preparation of tens of thousands of people, and shaped a gigantic and multifaceted process of apprenticeship in which the Nicaraguan people have participated enthusiastically and massively (e.g., MINSA 1982; Donahue 1983).

It is no longer the school, nor even the popular education collectives (CEPs), that make up the physical environment of the New Education, but all of society, the revolution in all its aspects, requiring new methods and techniques of teaching-learning that are adequate to this educational practice. The barrio, the factory, the market, the cotton field—these are the places where the educational process is taking shape, at the same time as the productive or reproductive practices of these environments themselves are developing. The character of the teaching-learning process in turn changes its content. Learning and doing are no longer separated, the first occurring in the school or university and the second in the factory, street, or countryside. Now it is, or is becoming, a dialectic unity located in a single place, where theory gets worked out in practice, and practice is decoded theoretically. The new pedagogy becomes a dimension of production, defense, and reconstruction, in the same way and at the same time as relations of production, tasks of reconstruction, and the practice of defense are transformed into spheres of pedagogical reflection and political growth.

The demands that this progressive reshaping of "education" puts on human resources are enormous. The health brigadista, the social promoter, the popular teacher, who all come from their own communities and continue to work closely in these with the participants of the new educational process, are some of the answers that the revolution is generating in the search for new cadres and the transformation of education.

As noted, all these changes have been directly linked to creative and critical participation of the mass organizations. It is not possible, however, to ignore the resulting pressures on these organizations, nor the existence of competing notions of how their participation should be carried out.

First, the tasks of educational change have been added to all the other activities that the mass organizations have been fulfilling in the revolutionary process. If indeed the balance is positive, it is clear that the combination of tasks creates intense pressures on the capability for action and on the resources of the organization, particularly in that, with the exception of the teachers' union, these organizations are relatively young and undeveloped.

Though temporary, these limitations are no less objective. Frequently one can note a certain tendency to delegate to the state's technical cadres tasks that the state administration expects of the organizations. Whether because of too much work, internal operational problems, or the insufficient development of some cadres compared to the urgent nature of the tasks they have to face, the fact is that at times the participation of the mass organizations is merely formal, reduced to validating with their political prestige and moral authority the policies pushed by the administration. For the majority of the mass organizations, participation in the definition and administration of educational policy means penetrating an area with which they are not yet familiar, and this has a decisive influence. Experience up to now shows that this is not an easy process, but that the mass organizations are moving forward, opening a new path between technical complexities and administrative obstacle courses. On the other hand, it must be recognized that this is also a new process for the technicians and administrators themselves; for them too the course between sympathy for active popular participation and its effective practice requires a long and difficult apprenticeship.

At times, state institutions favor these limitations. The danger of bureaucratism has been denounced time and again by the FSLN National Directorate and by the mass organizations themselves; but in some spheres bureaucratism tends to be identified with—and reduced to—the slowness of procedures, paperwork, and unjustified delays, rather than to the separation of the state apparatuses from their social bases. The former is an administrative issue; the latter is a political problem. Other times a lack of continuity can be noted between the organization's demands and the state's response; the lack of efficient state follow-up to investment of scarce resources demanded from the organizations; or the lack of sufficient information given to the organizations in general.

In reality, this issue is part of the larger problem of the relation between the state and the mass organizations outlined in the previous chapter, and to which we will return in the next.

7

A Society
in Revolution

This chapter returns to the four basic issues of any process of social revolution and national liberation outlined at the beginning of the book. Here we will evaluate them in terms of the analysis in previous chapters: the nature of the agroexport model developed under the influence of imperialist domination; the class structure and social profile of the popular bases of the revolution; the strategy of national unity and mixed economy; the modes of popular participation and their relationship to the new state; and the alliances and tensions on which the revolution relies.

These themes are taken up now as *problematics,* as interrelated dimensions of the revolutionary process that call for treatment and resolution. They are regarded as open to various interpretations and solutions, and therefore open to both search and confrontation.

ACCUMULATION AND DISTRIBUTION

Although the Sandinista revolution triumphed in the midst of great economic disorder provoked by the war and the flight of capital, and a regional crisis that has since become even more aggravated (Torres Rivas 1982), the capacity of recovery under revolutionary direction has been notable in comparison to the recession throughout the rest of the isthmus. Table 7.1 shows that between 1980 and 1983 Nicaragua had the highest average growth rate in the region—in fact, it was the only GDP that experienced real overall and per capita growth during the period. International cooperation undoubtedly was a factor, but the determinant factor has been the capacity of the young state to direct the development of the economy, the responsibility with which it assumed its international financial commitments—including almost all those contracted by the dictatorship—and the confidence that it was able to inspire in Europe, Canada, and Latin America.[1]

This merits highlighting, because one of the most urgent necessities of any successful revolution consists in generating a capacity to direct the national economy and, in particular, to control the market. This is particularly important in a mixed economy oriented toward wide-ranging social change. In this situation, in which the public sector is not in the majority, the market is still the arena of bourgeois power, while the APP represents, at least potentially, the hegemony of the popular project (Ramírez 1980). The relation between the state and the market therefore expresses the confrontation of the two class projects in the economic realm.

The struggle over direction of the economy concerns the internal conditions of production and circulation as well as the external

Table 7.1
Central America: Real Growth of Gross Domestic Product
and Per Capita Gross Domestic Product, 1979–83
(in percentages)

Countries	1979	1980	1981	1982	1983[a]	1980–83
		Annual GDP Growth				
Nicaragua	−25.5	10.0	8.5	−1.2	5.3	5.6
Costa Rica	4.9	0.8	−2.3	−9.1	0.8	−2.4
El Salvador	−1.5	−9.6	−9.5	−6.4	—	−6.7
Guatemala	4.3	3.7	0.9	−3.7	−2.7	−0.4
Honduras	6.8	2.9	0.1	−1.0	−0.3	−0.4
Central America	0.1	0.6	−1.2	−4.7	−0.4	−1.4
	Annual Per Capita GDP Growth					
Nicaragua	−27.8	6.5	5.0	−3.9	2.6	2.5
Costa Rica	2.1	−2.3	−4.8	−11.8	−1.6	−5.1
El Salvador	−4.3	−11.5	−11.1	−7.3	−0.6	−7.6
Guatemala	1.2	1.0	−1.5	−5.8	−5.2	−2.9
Honduras	2.9	−0.6	−3.4	−4.7	−3.6	−3.0
Central America	−3.0	−2.4	−3.8	−7.1	−2.5	−3.9

Source: CEPAL.
[a] Preliminary figures.

sector. Capitalism in Nicaragua was characterized by a strong dependence on the international market and foreign financing; during the 1970s it practically lived on credit. The political submission of the dictatorship to the United States absolutely guaranteed increasing indebtedness. This political submission ended with the revolutionary triumph; and with it ended the dollars. Furthermore, the terms of exchange maintained the negative tendency that appeared in 1978; the general disorder of the economy due to the war, the economic retreat of the bourgeoisie, the impact of the ownership changes in the large enterprises, and the regional recession all reduced exports.

The first years saw reliance on foreign financial assistance; approximately U.S. $1.6 million in financing and close to U.S. $260 million in grants entered Nicaragua. But despite the "soft" terms of the former, the foreign debt has increased by an average annual rate of 24 percent between 1980 and 1982. As a result, foreign debt service, which represented something less than 16 percent of exports in 1980, grew to 43 percent in 1981 and to 57 percent in 1982, and reached between 70 percent and 90 percent in 1983.

It is undeniable that the effective rates of growth of the domestic product were more modest than originally programmed. Goals were overestimated, in large part due to an exaggerated vision of the economic presence of Somocismo in the productive sector. The potential of the APP was especially overestimated (MIDINRA 1982b: 7).[2] In any case, four years after the revolution the Nicaraguan economy has yet to reach 1977 levels of activity, with the exception of the agricultural sector. Taking 1977 as the base year, the only categories where production has not gone up are those with the greatest number of large agrarian owners—and in the case of bananas, foreign owners.[3]

In fact, the deceleration of economic growth since mid-1981 and the drop in 1982 are due not only to exogenous variables, but also to internal factors. Despite exchange and price incentives accorded them in January 1982, the large cotton bourgeoisie sowed 16 percent less land in the 1982-83 cycle than before the incentives (which they nonetheless accepted), maintaining that same level in the 1983 cycle (see Table 4.6); the behavior of the large coffee and cattle bourgeoisie was no different. Notwithstanding the transfer of surplus in their favor, large producers for the external market did not respond adequately; Nicaragua's exports were less in 1983 than in 1981 (Table

7.2). Insofar as these groups still realize a high proportion of agricultural export production, their responsibility in these results is beyond doubt.

Another element that has served to diminish export income is the persistence of an overvalued cordoba with respect to the dollar, despite continual changes in exchange rates. For their part, the disorganization of many APP enterprises, their obsolescence and the lack of administrative technicians, also retarded their recovery (Nolff 1982).

Analyses of Nicaraguan capitalism and its external dependence have emphasized agroexports: international market specialization is considered the principal cause of subordination to imperialism and the backwardness and general disarticulation of the economy, although in reality this is true of all third-world countries. On this basis a discussion was opened just after the revolutionary triumph about the survival of the agroexport scheme and about the necessity and/or possibility of relating to the international market in an entirely new way, including reorienting the whole process of accumulation to the internal market. There is even an occasional tendency to identify industry with revolution and agriculture with reaction, which extends to the simplistic focus of the worker-peasant alliance problematic, discussed in the next section.

Nicaragua has not been outside this debate, but here it has lacked the intensity, prolongation, and certain foolishness that other processes have experienced. The conviction seems to have quickly prevailed that the roots of dependence lie less in agroexports themselves than in the mode in which the agroexport sector is organized,

Table 7.2
Nicaragua: Evolution of the External Sector 1980–83

	1980	1981	1982	1983
F.o.b. exports	451	500	408	411
C.i.f. imports	803	922	723	760
Commercial balance	− 352	− 422	− 315	− 349
Balance of current account	− 512	− 585	− 520	− 521
Terms of exchange[a]	− 1.8	− 5.5	− 9.6	− 11.9
Balance of foreign debt	1,579	2,163	2,797	3,385

Source: CEPAL.

Figures are millions of U.S. dollars.

[a] Variation with respect to previous year (in percentages).

the type of relations of production and circulation that characterize it, and in the form in which it is tied to the rest of the local and international economy; in other words, not so much in the production of use values, as *in the way in which these are converted into exchange values.* As a consequence, the revolution has sought to eliminate the productive backwardness of the sector and integrate it with agroindustrial processing, seeking a more advantageous position in the international division of labor. At the same time a vigorous program of investments in the whole of the agricultural sector has been promoted. Assigning 1978 the base value 100, the coefficient of agricultural investment reached the level 274 in 1981, and 400 in 1982. This is an investment effort unparalleled in Central America or possibly in the rest of Latin America. In Costa Rica, for example, the coefficient of agricultural investment was reduced from 100 to 27 between 1978 and 1982, and in Guatemala it fell from 100 to 43 in the same span (*Barricada,* May 9, 1983).

One aspect of accumulation problematic in a revolutionary process refers to the balance it tries to establish between accumulation and distribution, that is, to the economy's capacity to rapidly satisfy the population's demands for better living conditions—a fundamental dimension of the motivations that propel a revolutionary process. Experience shows this balance to be an elusive one, however. All social revolutions have had to take charge of the mess left by the old dominant classes, with economies in profound crisis or completely in shambles; in such situations the general improvement of living conditions *above certain basic levels* has had to be postponed until the transformation of the economic structure could be considerably advanced. Furthermore, the imperialist and counter-revolutionary aggressions that all revolutions have to confront force them to reorient a good part of their efforts to defense, delaying attention to popular well-being even more. For these reasons, a revolution cannot promise the masses an immediate solution to all their social problems; but it does assure them the possibility of constructing the conditions to make this possible. This indicates once again that the vanguard character of a class or fraction in a revolutionary process depends on the project that the revolution promotes, more than the immediate benefits that it generates.

The Sandinista revolution tried to respond first to the most urgent necessities of the population, particularly to the victims of the war and related destruction. The Ministry of Social Welfare was created to channel foreign funds to this sector and to execute a broad program of social assistance. Minimum wage levels were fixed for workers and the historically postponed demand of the popular classes was satisfied—partially—by way of nonmonetary incomes, rather than through higher wages. The general expansion of economic activity made possible a rapid expansion of basic consumption, which grew almost 30 percent between 1979 and 1980 (Table 7.3) and reached the 1977 level in real values. But beginning in 1981 the deceleration of growth, greater external restrictions, and the debt burden (and its impact on inflation) forced a reduction and change in social spending. Between 1981 and 1982 per capita social spending was reduced more than 9 percent in real values, and was oriented fundamentally toward basic education and primary health care (JGRN 1983). The health achievements of the Sandinista revolution have been particularly notable—including a drastic reduction of infant mortality, elimination of endemic diseases such as malaria and dengue fever, total prevention of poliomyelitis, and near total eradication of measles—as have those in education (MINSA 1982).

Table 7.3 shows the changes in consumption in the periods immediately prior to and after the revolution. In a general context of contraction, public consumption has behaved much more dynam-

Table 7.3
Nicaragua: Evolution of Consumption 1977–83

Type of consumption	1977	1978	1979	1980	1981	1982	1983[a]
Total	109.7	109.1	82.5	100	94.6	90.6	88.9
Public	62.7	76.6	84.3	100	109.8	130.4	153.0
Private	120.7	116.7	82.0	100	91.4	81.4	73.6
Basic	98.3	94.3	70.1	100	103.0	98.1	103.1
Nonbasic	154.5	150.5	100.1	100	73.1	56.1	27.2
Composition (in percentages)							
Total	100	100	100	100	100	100	100
Public	11	13	19	19	22	27	33
Private	89	87	81	81	78	73	67
Private	100	100	100	100	100	100	100
Basic	49	49	51	60	53	73	86
Nonbasic	51	51	49	40	47	27	14

Source: INEC, MIPLAN, author's estimations.
Figures are based on 1980 cordobas; 1980 = 100.
[a] Estimated.

ically than private, although the latter continues to be the majority component of the category. Within private consumption, basic consumption has maintained this real historic level, while 1983 nonbasic consumption represents a third of its 1980 level, and less than one-fifth of that of 1977.

To the extent that different types of consumption are related to distinct social groups, these figures suggest a rapid deterioration of consumption by sectors with the highest income levels—bourgeoisie, middle classes—and a precarious maintenance of traditional levels by the popular classes. Nonetheless, the situation is more complex, since the problematic of accumulation and distribution is directly tied to that of inflation; indeed, the latter is one way in which the former is expressed.

Reliable estimates indicate that between 1980 and July 1983 the general consumer price index grew more than 90 percent, and almost 120 percent in the "food, drinks, and tobacco" category; indices also show that during the first half of 1980 the growth of prices with respect to the same period of 1982 was a third higher for groups with incomes less than 2,000 cordobas per month (around 53 percent of the active urban population) than for higher income levels. This would provoke a growing polarization of real incomes, above all in the urban arena. An investigation of family income in Managua showed that the difference grew between 7 percent and 20 percent, depending on the measure of polarization employed (CETRA 1983b).

These figures call attention to the efficacy of policies that try to defend the standard of living of the popular classes. Subsidies of basic food prices are an example: other factors held constant, the impact of the cost of living increases should be greater at the higher family income levels than at the lower ones, but the data show that this has not been the situation to date.

It is probable that, among other aspects, the issue has to do with the different sources of supply in different income strata. Notwithstanding the growing network of popular stores pertaining to the Ministry of Interior Commerce (MICOIN), the greater part of family consumption is purchased from markets and small merchants, where overpricing is usually very high.[4] A study of food distribution and consumption in families with monthly incomes of between 1,000 and 5,000 cordobas in Managua shows that of a list of twenty basic products, the popular stores are the most frequent sources of supply for only four, while the *pulperias* (small stores) and merchants figure first in eleven categories, and street vendors first in the other five. Popular stores appear as a second option for only two products among nineteen (CIERA 1983b: 36; CETRA 1983b). The difficulty of exercising adequate price controls in this swarm of small distribution units, the minimum efficacy in these aspects shown up to now by the mass organizations, and the necessity of the small merchant to compensate a small volume of operations with high utility margins by product sold, translate into price rises beyond regulatory controls. These mainly affect low-income consumers and those with fixed incomes (principally salaries), which comprise the bulk of demand for these distribution channels.[5] According to a MICOIN investigation, the difference between official prices and market prices can be considerable in some products of the basic market basket: 99 percent in the case of corn, 62 percent in beans, 12 percent in rice, 16 percent in beef, 25 percent in chicken, and 23 percent in vegetable oil.[6] The result of all this is an appreciable decline in real family income. The cost of the basic food basket for a family of six was calculated in 1980 at 2,000 cordobas; in 1981 it had increased to 2,600 cordobas, and in 1982 to 3,300 cordobas. This means that in this last year almost 40 percent of the families in Managua could manage only to partially satisfy their basic food needs (CETRA 1983b). A recent investigation by the ATC showed that the food supply situation for agricultural workers is even worse than for the rest of the population. According to this study, field workers spend less for food and other basic goods than urban workers, but not because food is cheaper in the countryside, or because of different eating habits; rather, agricultural workers have neither physical nor monetary access to a good part of the basic products.

The nonsalaried sectors, particularly the informal sector, are better able to confront inflation in the short run, in the sense that they receive incomes through prices, and control over these has not been effective to date. By contrast, workers with fixed salaries experience the full weight of price rises. Furthermore, as pointed out in Chapter 5, the growth of physical labor productivity that took place in the industrial sector during the first two years after the triumph went hand in hand with a deterioration of real salaries. In these conditions it is easy to see a transfer of surplus from salaried workers toward nonsalaried, and from productive workers toward nonproductive (CETRA 1983a). Notwithstanding the advances experienced through the organization of the working class, those sectors tied to small and medium urban commerce do better in appropriating the monetary benefits of the market.

The inherited economic reality has been stronger than many of the revolutionary policies designed to modify it, and these diverse sectors have taken full advantage. With the same enthusiasm that four years earlier they joined the insurrection, today they participate in price rises "come what may" and join with ardor in practices of speculation, frequent contraband, and foreign exchange trafficking. For them there does not seem to be a particularly concrete contradiction between ideological adhesion to the revolution, including participation in some of its tasks, and tax evasion, overcharging, and hoarding of basic goods. Some elements of this multifaceted urban spectrum continue picking a difficult path between legality and crime, closer to roguery than alienation. But it is a path nourished by broad contingents of the *active* population, including elements of the proletariat, who channel important amounts of money capital and appropriate a good part of it, and who, through this redistribution of surplus to the detriment of the mass of salaried and productive workers, have the capacity to diminish the impact of various policies—food supply, prices, and incomes—by simply operating through the market mechanisms.

Unarguably small commerce, services, and the like assure the distribution of generally accessible goods and services that are not included in the basic consumption basket. But it is also clear that this is done at a price that reinforces inflationary tensions, distorts the market, and introduces obvious inequalities for different classes, reinforcing existing ones. Up to now, however, the problem has been handled through the mass organizations—especially CDS and AMNLAE; the government does not envision nationalization of this sector (Wheelock 1983: 101–2).

The growing boom in this intermediate sector is not the only source of inflationary tensions, however (although it illustrates the capacity of certain groups in the sphere of circulation to appropriate surplus generated in spheres in which they do not directly participate). Some aspects of the state's financial policy also generate inflationary pressures, to the detriment of lesser income groups, especially salaried workers. A Ministry of Labor study noted that the foreign exchange and tax incentives to the agroexport sector implied an additional deterioration of 14 percent in minimum salaries in 1982. Similarly, agricultural producer price increases for the export harvest of 1983/84 implied a growth in money supply not correlated to material production, adding to the already high fiscal deficit: 12.4 percent of the GDP in 1980, 13.2 percent in 1981, 21 percent in 1982 (Medal 1982).

The tax structure puts the most pressure on the lesser income sectors; almost three-fourths of taxes comes from indirect taxes (MIPLAN 1981: 139; Medal 1982), a situation similar to that prior to the revolution. Finally, the relationship between the formal and informal sectors—especially with the production of inputs and final products in the APP, the limitations of official distribution channels and their relative inflexibility compared with private and informal channels—favors the development of a surplus transfer from the APP to the private sector that fundamentally benefits large and medium-sized capital (Vargas 1981). The existence of price controls in the APP with absolute freedom of prices in the private sector operates as a state subsidy to private commercial capital.

One effect of these clashes over appropriation of the surplus is the rapid growth of the amount of money in circulation as well as in the rate of circulation. The first grew 23 percent between 1980 and 1982 (in prices) and the second more than 16 percent (INEC 1983). The deceleration of production, political subordination of the bourgeoisie, and the situation of class coexistence without social conciliation tend to displace the class struggle to the sphere of circulation.

In these conditions the situation of the trade unions that support the revolution is particularly difficult. The limitations of the anti-inflationary policy cannot contain the deterioration of real salaries; the distortions in food supply and the necessity of maintaining the mixed-economy scheme means that a massive salary increase only reinforces inflation—not only through higher labor costs, but also through the lack of a corresponding elasticity on the supply side. The answer of the organizations has consequently been the exercise of pressures on the APP administration and private sector bosses: incorporating specific demands in collective agreements, promoting accords for salary levels, and so on. When a union is sufficiently strong, workers have been compensated for the rise in living costs, but this in turn undermines the union centrals, which depend on the ability to present a united front. It also leads to the appearance of what one union leader called *salary anarchy*.[7].

This anarchy can be interpreted as proof of labor indiscipline or worker impatience; but it can also be considered a result of the government policy of salary containment, in acute contrast with incentives for the agroexport bourgeoisie and of tolerance toward the intermediate sectors. So-called union anarchy is, from this perspective, one of the responses of the workers' movement to an increasingly grave situation. Another response is the gradual shift of the labor force from salaried productive occupations toward simple mercantile production, small intermediary functions, and the so-called informal sector in general.

Finally, this accumulation and distribution problematic raises a question about the fate of this mass of surplus appropriated in the sphere of circulation. Until September 1981 it was evident that the existence of a free foreign exchange market permitted the exit of much of it from the country. But the issue became more complicated after the 1981 exchange measures, reinforced in May 1983. The black market in dollars has not disappeared; the experience of other revolutions shows the difficulty of controlling and reducing it slowly, and not eliminating it with one fell swoop, above all when the national currency is overvalued. Everything indicates that part of the surplus is channeled toward the exterior in this way: either situating it outside, or using it for nonpriority imports for which Central Bank channels will not grant foreign exchange at the official rate, or for imports greater than the amounts authorized at the official rate. At the same time, local commercial capital is recycling some of its surplus. The investments that the APP is making in this sector— hotels, tourism, commercialization of different products, and so on—suggest that the revolutionary state is disposed to recover at least part of this surplus in the same terrain in which it circulates, to reorient it toward productive ends.

"PEOPLE," CLASS, NATION

The national unity project promoted by the Sandinista revolution is supported by a number of contradictory alliances, resulting in what I have called *class coexistence without class conciliation,* expressing the hegemony of the popular camp and the *political* subordination of the bourgeoisie.

The dynamic pole of the alliance is characterized in terms of *"the people"* more than *class,* encompassing not only the working class and the peasantry, but also the urban and rural poor, small- and medium-sized business owners, artisans, slum dwellers, students, technical and professional sectors, salaried petty bourgeoisie, and so on—all committed to the revolutionary process.

The category "people" has a class reference, but it is not exhausted by it, in that its linkages are more political-ideological than structural-economic. It embraces sectors that are not defined by their insertion into relations of production, but whose practice relates to a historic perspective that is clearly a class one: the women's movement, the student movement, national defense organizations, are all examples. The popular camp, as a political grouping, permits the incorporation of groups and fractions that are integrated into the tasks of the revolution or support them, notwithstanding their different insertion into relations of production and circulation in class terms. In the same way, elements that oppose the revolutionary process despite their structural situation can be located outside this camp, such as in the case of union organizations that have joined the opposition bourgeois bloc.

The "people" is therefore a sociologically heterogeneous and contradictory force, unified politically by the dynamics of the revolution. The existence of these contradictions is not unknown, but their development is subordinated and the attempt is made to orient them in favor of the goals of national unity: economic recovery and national defense: "The contradictions are less important than the solutions [this unity] contributes in the struggle against the common enemy" (Wheelock 1981: 68–69).

The working classes have developed rapidly in this framework. Agrarian reform has provided an answer to peasant and medium-sized producers' demands for land, credit, and technical assistance, articulating the small individual producer and cooperative sectors with large state agricultural enterprises, medium-sized rural bourgeoisie, and remnants of the large landowners. The current agrarian structure shows the rapid retreat of the large bourgeoisie, the strengthening of medium-sized production, and the advance of small producers and the APP. Integration into the Sandinista Popular Militias, Popular Education Collectives, and mass organizations testifies to the peasantry's active commitment to the revolution. The living and working conditions of the agricultural proletariat have improved noticeably through the guarantee of minimum salaries, the extension of basic services, social security, and nonmonetary incomes (health, education, consumer subsidies, child care, improvements in the distribution system, etc.). In the cities, working conditions and the organization of salaried workers in general have experienced noticeable improvements; the state and the unions oversee enforcement of labor legislation, and the collective bargaining system has resulted in a wide gamut of workplace benefits—training, transport, food, and sports.

The worker-peasant alliance is a central issue in the problematic of constructing hegemony within the popular camp. At times there has been a tendency to see this alliance as the economic and political subordination of the peasantry to the proletariat, pushing collectivization and proletarization (especially large state farms). In this vision, the peasants' role would be to generate growing volumes of surplus to feed the working class—fundamentally the urban working class—and to liberate ever larger margins for productive investment.

This simplistic focus is supported in an erroneous interpretation of the scheme of relations between "department I" (production of the means of production) and "department II" (production of the means of consumption) in economies such as Nicaragua's. The first is seen as urban and proletariat, and the second as eminently agrarian, peasant, and, at bottom, precapitalist. This view also reflects Marx's analysis of French small-holders in *The Eighteenth Brumaire of Luis Bonaparte* (1852): by extension, if the nineteenth-century French peasantry was petty bourgeois, conservative, and reactionary, so therefore must be the Central American peasantry of the twentieth century.

The issue, of course, is infinitely more complex; not only because the peasant "conservative temperament" stereotype does justice neither to Marx nor to the peasants (see, e.g., Vanden 1982), but also because in Nicaragua's dependent capitalism, the scheme of relations between "department I" and "department II," and between the city and the countryside, have their own characteristics, as analyzed in Chapter 2. There we saw that the agrarian structure showed a marked differentiation between agriculture for export and for the internal market, with better land and technology concentrated in the former; as a consequence, production for local consumption remained backward, and local food supply depended in large measure on imports. Proletarianization was more widespread in the rural than urban areas; only a relatively small proportion of the active urban population is proletarian, while two-thirds of it is found *outside the productive sectors*.[8] As a result, the worker-peasant alliance in Nicaragua is mainly a rural phenomenon.

The Nicaraguan economy requires decisive state intervention to promote the transformation of the dominant relations of production and circulation, stimulate the development of the productive forces, and design new labor processes. But this is not a process that is easy or free of contradictions.

The promotion of the peasantry in the current stage contrasts with the attention paid to the demands of the workers' movement: the provision of lands, credits, and inputs, the condoning of the agrarian debt, and the reduction of taxes stand out in the face of the acute fall of real salaries.

Table 7.4 compares the evolution of real prices for producers of corn and beans (typical peasant crops) and real salary for cotton and coffee pickers: it is evident that producers' incomes have been maintained, while those of the agricultural worker have deteriorated

Table 7.4
Nicaragua: Prices (by hundredweight) and Salaries in Agriculture
1979–83

	Agricultural year			
	1979–80	*1980–81*	*1981–82*	*1982–83*
Price of corn to producer				
Current	60	80	100	130
1980*	89.45	80	77.5	78
1980 (index)	111.8	100	96.8	97.5
Price of beans to producer				
Current	180	220	320	350
1980*	368.3	220	248	210.1
1980 (index)	121.9	100	112.7	95.5
Minimum salary for cotton pickers				
Current	20	29	30	35
1980*	30	29	23.2	21
1980 (index)	102.7	100	80.2	72.4
Minimum salary for coffee pickers				
Current	3	3.85	4	4
1980*	4.5	3.85	3.1	2.4
1980 (index)	116.9	100	80.5	62.3

Source: Figures compiled from the Ministry of Labor, Minister of Interior Commerce, and INEC.

*Deflator: consumer price index in the category: "food, drinks and tobacco."

Table 7.5
Nicaragua: Real Urban Salaries, 1977–83

Salary	1977	1978	1979	1980	1981	1982	1983
1980 cordobas*							
Average salary	2,829	2,752	2,370	2,001	1,859	1,782	1,628
Minimum industrial							
salary	1,276	1,293	1,103	973	879	725	586
Indices							
Average salary	140.5	136.8	80.9	117.8	100	92.4	88.5
Minimum industrial							
salary	131.0	132.8	60.1	113.3	100	90.3	74.4

*Deflator: Consumer price index.
Source: Figures from INSSBI and INEC.

substantially.[9] The bottom of the table shows the relation between the peasants' income and that of the agricultural workers. With the base in 1980–81, guaranteed minimum income for peasants in the agricultural year 1982–83 is almost a third higher than the salaries of cottonpickers, and more than 50 percent higher than those of coffee pickers.

Beside being a production incentive, the agricultural price and salary policy has acted to return to the land poor peasants who previously sold their labor power in the agroexport harvests. The agrarian reform, plus the fall in real salary in the harvests, created disincentives for the seasonal salarization of this labor force. The rationale for this policy seems to be that the price incentives to produce basic grains will increase their supply, improving distribution to the working class and, other factors remaining constant, reducing its cost of reproduction. This, of course, is a medium-range objective; meanwhile, the policy of subsidizing basic consumption and extending state commercialization networks, added to the general improvement of working conditions, tries to compensate for the real salary drop or reduce its impact.[10] At the same time, the agricultural policy reduces agroexport labor costs and, combined with foreign exchange incentives, generates an increase in the surplus appropriated by the large producers.[11]

Table 7.5 indicates that a fall in real wages similar to that in rural areas took place in the cities, above all in the minimum industrial wage. Due to the rise in consumer prices and the policy of containing nominal wages, the average salary deteriorated 25 percent from 1980 to 1983, while the minimum salary reduction was almost double: 40 percent.

In recent years a movement of the labor force toward the non-salaried and nonproductive salaried sectors has been developing, the effect of which is the reduction of the productive proletariat. In one year the urban proletariat shrank by between 5,000 and 9,000 people, according to the way the category is defined.

The growth of the nonsalaried and particularly the informal sector is evident in the cities. If in 1980 the Planning Ministry estimated this sector at more than a third of the nonagricultural labor force (MIPLAN 1981: 93), by mid-1982 it represented around 43 percent (INEC 1982). Evidence suggests that when factories cut back or close because of the external crisis—lack of foreign exchange, shortage of imported inputs, reduction of exports—productive workers prefer to move to petty commerce, artisanal activities, repair work and the like, rather than accept emergency productive employment.[12] At the same time, the existence of a broad and growing informal sector reduces worker pressures for salary increases, in that it appears as a more profitable alternative—at least in the short run—in contrast to a sector of formal employment in which real salaries rapidly deteriorate through inflation.[13] The nonproductive sectors,

Table 7.6
Nicaragua: Urban Proletariat, 1981–82

EAP	1981		1982		
	1,000s	*(%)*	*1,000s*	*(%)*	*Difference (%)*
Total	422.0	100.0	454.2	100.0	+7.6
Workers and day workers	146.6	34.7	141.5	31.1	−3.5
Employees	125.0	29.6	139.3	30.7	+11.4
All others (Bosses, self-employed workers, nonremunerated family workers, others)	150.4	35.7	173.4	38.2	+15.3
Nonagricultural workers, machine and transport vehicle operators and assimilated workers	159.0	37.7	150.6	33.0	−5.6

Source: INEC 1981c, 1982.

which at the end of the 1970s represented almost two-thirds of the nonagricultural EAP, have continued growing in the early 1980s.

The question arises: If this movement of the labor force toward the nonsalaried and particularly the so-called informal sector continues, what will be the nature of the urban working class in the future? We must ask: What is this sector's capacity to absorb the shift, and finally, what are its limits?

In these conditions, the proletarianist approach which encompasses the whole of the working and popular masses under the headline *proletarian,* has given way to the identification of differentiations and contradictions within the popular camp. The Rural Workers' Association (ATC), which at the beginning grouped together both agricultural workers and peasants, in April 1981 shifted to organizing only the former: UNAG was created as a specific organization of the peasants and medium-sized agricultural producers. In the non-agricultural arena small and medium producers do not have a similar organization, either to push their demands or to be sure they are included in the policies of the state.

In addition, the ardor of the peasantry in pressing their demands, and the attention and coverage this receives, contrasts with the measuredness of the workers' movement in laying out its demands.[14] The current stage of the revolution undoubtedly provides the peasantry a greater capacity to incorporate its demands into the political direction of the process than it does the workers' movement. I suggest that, other considerations aside, this is basically due to the existence of the mixed economy scheme. While economic incentives to the peasantry tend to directly affect production levels, and the nationalization of some elements of the commercial sector determines that the surplus is distributed between the direct producer and the state as an expression of the popular project, something else happens in industry and agroindustry. Here the impact of economic incentives to direct producers is mediated by the drop-out behavior of the bourgeoisie, which still controls a major proportion of the product; the surplus generated by the workers contributes significantly, therefore, to the coffers of capital—hardly interested in reactivating the economy. In a stage in which reactivation is a priority goal, the "return" of economic incentives to the direct producer appears more secure in the peasantry than in the proletariat. At the same time, the necessity of maintaining the national unity strategy does not permit the elimination of capitalist mediation. In this sense the promotion of worker participation in economic management is oriented toward introducing worker responsibility over the mechanisms of the business economy which, under the control of the bourgeoisie or inefficient administrations, retard the conversion of those incentives into greater production.

Nevertheless this distribution of immediate costs and benefits is not sufficient to identify a peasant hegemony in the current stage of the revolution—first, because hegemony is direction, a political issue that in principle has little to do with the portion of surplus appropriated by whoever exercises it; second, because the Sandinista revolution still finds itself in a period in which its motor forces are in search of a relatively defined, but not necessarily permanent, correlation within the popular camp. Therefore, by its tasks as well as the national and international context in which they are promoted, the political direction of the revolution by the FSLN in this stage expresses the hegemony of the *whole* "people" in the national unity—within which there is relative independence of distribution of immediate economic benefits.

The unequal distribution of benefits and economic incentives to the agroexport bourgeoisie, the peasantry, and the working class is registered not only in the economic arena. The bourgeois fractions that still remain in the country, controlling important positions in export production and, therefore, in the generation of foreign exchange, constitute a strategic group both for the revolution and for the counter-revolution. Through economic incentives as well as, more generally, the transfer of surplus, the government seeks to counterbalance the ideological thrust of the counter-revolution. The creation of an attractive, reliable economic climate is related to the political interest of the revolution in maintaining these elements within the national-democratic camp, even as internal opposition. Above all, it is a question of consolidating national unity with the broadest possible spectrum of social forces, including the *non-counter-revolutionary* fractions of the bourgeoisie. From this perspective, the mass of surplus transferred toward them by the incentive policies is the price paid to maintain the national unity. But as we have pointed out, this price is borne unequally within the national camp.

The bourgeoisie, then, finds itself drawn to opposing magnets, supported by various governments in the region in the name of a *pluralist* democracy. Up to now its response has consisted in the strategy that has brought such good results in the past: take the incentives offered, occupy the space granted, demand new concessions, but prolong its foot-dragging economic behavior, reinforce its international ties, rely on the idea that continuation of the international crisis will oblige the FSLN to be ever more flexible, and, at bottom, hold on to the conviction that "before" was better.

The capacity of the revolution to get the bourgeoisie to accept that its subordinate political position is compatible with the function expected of it in the sphere of production remains for now an open hypothesis. In the meantime, the financing of this hypothesis by salary containment, fiscal deficit, and the inflationary process promises growing tensions between the development strategy based on a mixed economy and national unity on the one hand, and the characterization of the working class as one of the motor forces of the revolution on the other. This is not the issue of hegemony within the popular camp, but the problem, confronted by any national liberation revolution, of articulating the fundamental contradiction, which is one of class, with the national contradiction.

The FSLN has opted to confront the external crisis and the growing international pressures by stressing the level of political-ideological commitment of the masses and intense mobilizations, to concede economic benefits to the bourgeoisie, and to appeal to the tolerance of the workers on behalf of the survival of the revolutionary project. From the outset, this strategy has relied on its acceptance by the mass organizations. But within the national arena, it has also permitted these fractions of capital to reproduce and grow, together with their eventual capacity to impose their viewpoint in managing the instruments of economic policy in some areas of the state.

In any case, in the face of renewed external aggressions, there has been a slow shift away from the themes that constituted an important part of the dominant revolutionary discourse in the first years after the triumph. Efforts to emphasize the class character of the national unity project, with the APP as the strategic axis of the development strategy, and publicly recriminate the bourgeoisie for its puny response to the incentives directed its way, have given way to an emphasis on the *national* theme more than on its class projections, and to an interest in negotiating with the *noncounter-revolutionary* fractions of the bourgeoisie.

THE SANDINISTA CONCEPTION OF DEMOCRACY

The struggle of the FSLN against the Somocista dictatorship was characterized by high levels of popular participation. The last two years saw a true mass struggle; the popular insurrection was the fruition of a long process of incorporating broad sectors of the population into the revolutionary struggle. Numerous organizations were promoted to channel and strengthen the integration of the people. The formation of the United Popular Movement (MPU) in 1978 was the first organic formulation of Sandinista hegemony in the popular unity project; later the constitution of the Nicaraguan Popular Front (FPN) projected this hegemony to all the democratic and anti-imperialist forces.

Popular participation constituted the central axis of two decades of Sandinista struggle, and is today the essential element of the Sandinista concept of democracy. In the words of the FSLN:

> For the Frente Sandinista democracy is not measured only in the political terrain and is not reduced to the participation of the people in elections. Democracy . . . means participation of the people in political, economic, social, and cultural affairs. The more people who take part in this, the more democratic we will be. . . . Democracy is initiated in the economic order, when social inequalities begin to weaken, when the workers and peasants begin to improve their standard of living. . . .
>
> Once these objectives are achieved, we will immediately move into other areas: the government camp will be broadened; when the people have influence over their government, when the people determine their government, whomever they prefer.
>
> . . . in a more advanced phase, democracy will mean participation of the workers in directing factories, farms, cooperatives, and cultural centers. In synthesis, democracy is the intervention of the masses in all aspects of social life (FSLN 1980a).

This is a more complex concept than electoral democracy. The slogan "The people already made their election," launched by the FSLN at the beginning of 1980, expressed in part the commitment of the popular majorities, endorsed by enormous sacrifices, to a struggle and a project of social transformation. At the same time, it was a judgment against the pre-1979 electoral practice, which served only as a sop to the contradictions within the dominant class, and in which the permanence of the Somocista regime was a given.

Democracy for the FSLN is thus one in which:

—the economic regime assures men and women their basic necessities in food, work, housing, education, and food;
—the governmental institutions are designed to improve the flow of
communication between the apparatus of power and the popular majorities;
—the government rests the defense of Popular Power on the armed
population;
—it counts on organized popular participation for the realization of
economic, political, and social plans;
—there exists the political will, the legislation and the mechanisms to
effect and guarantee the political, social and cultural rights of the
majority;
—power is held by the working masses (C. Núñez 1983).

The practice of four years of revolution evidences the development
of this process in the different spheres of society. Some aspects are
more obvious than others; some are more advanced; others have
experienced serious difficulties. But as a whole, they have contributed to the design of organized popular participation in the process
of transforming social reality, in the betterment of their living conditions, and in the construction of a new political order.

The Sandinista Popular Militias (MPS) make possible the voluntary integration of students, poor peasants, rural and urban workers,
professionals, and technicians into the defense of the revolution; a
very important part of confronting the counter-revolutionary forces,
and the defense of the production centers, is handled by the MPS.
The Popular Health Brigades incorporate the people into improving
hygiene and environmental health, eradication of endemic diseases,
prevention of epidemics, and so on. The progressive institutionalization of the revolutionary state includes a broad participation of the
popular organizations in numerous structures and at many levels:
the Council of State, the National Council of Agrarian Reform, the
National Popular Council for Health, the Anti-Somocista Popular
Tribunals, the Defense Headquarters, the National Advisory Council for Education, beside the instances indicated in Chapter 5. Areas
of society usually considered as technical and thus reserved for
specialists are opened to direct intervention of the population
through the mass organizations.

The practice of Sandinista democracy outlines general questions of political theory that are worth at least a mention, even though they are outside the reach of this book.

The political subject of Sandinista popular democracy is no longer the *citizen* as conceptualized in liberal-bourgeois political theory. In that conception the citizen is an isolated individual—the institutional corollary of the *free* producer/owner—in the exercise and defense of a kind of micro-sovereignty, reaffirming individuality in the face of the state. For the Sandinista revolution, what converts the *individual* into a *citizen* is precisely the break with this reciprocal isolation and the voluntary integration into mass organizations, so that insofar as this integration takes place, the *practice* of their new political, social, economic, and cultural rights has real life.

Does this mean *mediating* the concerns and interests of the people through these new structures? At bottom, the bourgeois criticism of the mass organizations has centered on this point: from this perspective, the mass organizations are forms that manipulate the people and constrain their freedom and independence of judgment. In particular, these criticisms have centered on the CDSs, whose participation covers a wide range of activities—defense, supply, environmental health, and so on.

Notwithstanding the disorder, errors, and even arbitrariness into which they have at times ventured, and the inevitable limitations derived from the lack of experience and scarcity of resources, the focus of the mass organization as a mediator of a relation that should be direct reveals the presence of elements of bourgeois democratic ideology that we noted above.[15] But the state-mass organizations-population relationship could also be thought of in a different way, in which the organizations make viable the development of popular participation in new areas.

This issue has at least two related dimensions. On the one hand are the traditional rights of the person, individual and personal, limited only by exceptional situations such as war (rights, although enunciated in all constitutional and legal texts, which never existed for the mass of people); and on the other hand, are *new rights*—also recognized for all the population, but with a class reference; as the product of the revolutionary popular triumph, the *exercise of these rights* requires the integration of their holders into collective structures. To the degree that the state is constructed through the exercise of these new rights of *collective practice,* the individual is transformed into a citizen by joining the structures that make these practices possible.

Sandinista democracy so far is more developed in the socioeconomic than the political-institutional sphere. The FSLN characterization of popular democracy—as popular participation that begins in the socioeconomic sphere and progressively advances into political-institutional terrain—expresses the current stage of development of this process. It underscores the necessity of the revolution to bring the popular classes into a situation to effectively exercise the practice of democracy, while at the same time, the process of creating the conditions for a fuller democracy is in itself a dimension of the process of constituting popular power. This affects the interests of the old dominant classes—materially as well as symbolically, although in an unequal way, as we have seen—and feeds its confrontation with this conception of democracy.

With the triumph of the revolution the issue of democracy has changed its content; it is no longer a question of liquidating the power of the dictatorship or assaulting the oppressor state, but one of constructing a new political power, with a popular content. Different stages of the struggle against the dictatorship involved distinct alignments of forces, alliances, and antagonisms, but the Sandinista strategy always had as a goal the realization of profound social transformation. The struggle itself ignited the enthusiasm and the consensus of practically all civil society, but as social transformation and the constitution of a new power advances, the revolution's basis of legitimacy becomes reformulated; support is withdrawn by those social sectors that see that the post-triumph revolution is not developing in their interests, while sectors that for various reasons did not participate decisively in the antidictatorial struggle can play a very important role in the stage of social transformations.

The treatment of the opposition is one of the most debated issues in the analyses of the revolution, although generally the focus has tended to reduce the opposition to that of the nonparticipating bourgeoisie, ignoring what we could call the left opposition. If for the former any revolutionary advance is excessive, for the latter it is always too little.

The experience of these four years shows the progressive drift of the opposition bourgeoisie into the ranks of the counter-revolution, despite the dialogue that the FSLN has continually tried to maintain, despite the economic incentives (at the cost of postponing the satisfaction of popular demand), and despite the care taken to differentiate the opposition as such from the counter-revolution. The unfolding of the revolutionary process, and in particular its political discourse, cannot impede this movement. The position of the revolution in this regard is well known: that they limit themselves to exploiting their means of production and use these means to survive, not as instruments of power, of imposition (Wheelock 1983: 35).

Up to now, however, the bourgeoisie has demonstrated little desire, or little aptitude, to face this demand. But at the same time state controls over its behavior, and the effective monopoly of political power in the hands of the revolutionary camp, orient their opposition strategy into the realm of ideology—apart from the battles that have been seen in the sphere of circulation. Religion, education, questions of civil guarantees, and traditional political rights become privileged arenas of the class confrontation.

The international use of liberal-bourgeois ideology has meant the discussion about the political power that the Sandinista revolution is constructing centers on themes such as elections, media policies, and the like. What is wrong—in the best of cases—with this discussion is not the issues themselves, but the way they are broached. The debate about the elections has been carried out, both by the bourgeoisie and by their international allies and friends, without a serious consideration of the concrete conditions in which Nicaragua is carrying out its revolution. In the whole history of the country there is no precedent that could serve as a reference point; the prior experience, on the contrary, fed the lack of confidence, or the contempt that broad sectors of the population have toward such proceedings. One thing that was evident to any close observer but which foreign observers did not seem to perceive was that elections did not attract the attention of the majority of the people. In the previous chapter we noted that in the National Consultation on Education only one organization (of construction companies) listed elections as an attribute of democracy; people were concerned rather about basic provisions, the high cost of living, defense, participation in the mass organizations, and so on. Nor did those demanding elections analyze issues that do stir up popular concern, even though they have a strong impact on the country's very ability to carry out elections: the military attacks from Honduras, the millions going to finance the counter-revolution, the blockade against financial assistance by international lending agencies, the destruction of roads, bridges, oil storage deposits, the kidnapping of peasants, the massacre of entire communities. Was this the most propitious set of conditions for carrying out an electoral campaign? What candidate who was not a revolutionary militant would be attracted to venture into the areas that border on Honduras?

Finally, it is very difficult to avoid noting that however genuine, the concern about elections was seen by many as a counter-revolutionary demand, or at least a confrontation with the revolution. In fact the only ones who demanded elections were the opposition groups, because they saw in them the possibility of acceding to an elusive power.

Opposition pressures regarding elections undoubtedly were directed beyond the elections themselves. In August 1980 the FSLN committed itself to hold elections in 1985, and since mid-1982 the revolutionary government adopted diverse measures toward this end. Consequently, the insistence of the opposition parties, the U.S. government, and other foreign elements could only be explained as maneuvers to put in doubt the political honesty of the Sandinista revolution, presenting the electoral call as the result of its own pressures, rather than as the compliance with a revolutionary commitment.

The opposition "of the left" that existed in the first moments of the revolutionary triumph could not sustain the confrontations that developed in that period. Currently the political and union organizations that occupy this span of the ideological spectrum support the FSLN; as such they are the spokespeople for working-class positions at the same time that they accept the priorities and strategies defined by the FSLN.[16] Questioning of the political line of the FSLN and efforts to dispute its hegemony in the revolutionary camp have disappeared from their documents and public pronouncements. Yet they explicitly maintain their stress on the deeply felt demands of the working masses—especially the salary claims—and on the necessity of increasing political and economic pressure on the large bourgeoisie; positions that have virtually disappeared from the statements of the Sandinista unions since mid-1981.

The constitution of a popular democratic power is not reduced to the question of the political opposition, however. It has already been pointed out that the process of constructing a popular democracy is also the process of constituting a *political subject* distinct from that of the liberal-bourgeois democracies. If the latter is constituted by its confrontation with the state, the political subject of a popular democracy is constituted through the effective participation that the revolution puts within its reach and on which its own advance depends. From this perspective, the crucial issue is that of the relations between the revolutionary state and the mass organizations that make possible the exercise of popular participation. In particular: What is the character of that participation? Is there really a progressive de-statization of the social policy of the revolution—in the sense of a greater arena for autonomous participation of the mass organizations? Or should the participation of the mass organizations be characterized as their slow *conversion into apparatuses* of the state? Is the participation of the mass organizations *political* or does it obey *technical* or *operational* criteria? Is the lack of sufficient resources solely the result of confusion, Somocista pillage, and external aggressions?

In a revolution begun so recently, in which not only the mass organizations but the state itself are in a process of seeking their own identity, the nature of their reciprocal relations is also still in flux. It is therefore impossible at this stage to offer a definitive answer. But the exposition developed throughout this book allows a few suggestions.

It seems beyond doubt that the rapid results in the field of education, sanitation, defense, and so on would not have been possible without the participation of the people through the mass organizations, given the limitations of resources. But this participation was not simply technical, nor limited to the operational plane. It is, in the fullest sense of the word, *political* participation, in that it implies within itself a project of organization and direction of the society; in short, a class project. The state donates the material resources as far as possible, but it does not supplant, or even subordinate, the organizations. On the other hand, as has already been mentioned, institutional arenas of participation have been created within the state itself in which the mass organizations outline their points of view and discuss their positions regarding issues of policy. As decisions are generally taken by consensus, the numerical inferiority of the organizations does not necessarily mean the lack of real weight.

The National Consultation on Education presents a particularly clear case of the way in which the suggestions of the organizations are received by the state and converted into policy; the objectives of the new Nicaraguan education adopted on March 1, 1983, reproduce almost textually the majority recommendations of the participants in the Consultation (MED 1983b). There are similar, though less well-known cases: the incorporation of women into military service, the housing law, family legislation, the political parties law, and the decapitalization law are, among others, evidence of the effective capacity of mass organizations to determine objectives and political lines, to criticize and express dissent.[17]

Furthermore, given that the discussion is about a state in the process of constituting itself, to speak of *de-statization* is premature. These activities have never been part of the state; the revolution is creating them, in a direct way, as spheres of popular participation.

Finally, discussion about the relations between the mass organizations and the state must take as a starting point the fact that both are the product of the same revolutionary political project—a fact that is *not* always taken into consideration in academic discussions of this subject (H. Weber 1981; Petras 1981). This does not mean overlooking the problems, or the fact that narrow notions of efficiency, technocratism, and excess concern with apparatus are part of the internal dynamic of any social revolution, especially in a society without any tradition of popular organization or participation, and above all when it must confront armed aggressions and mounting external pressures. In these conditions, the optimal process of trial and error is at times subordinated to efficiency and performability criteria favoring a tighter relationship between the mass organizations and the revolutionary state.

The process of constructing a popular democracy in Nicaragua is taking place in a totally different context from that which surrounds the efforts of the popular classes of other countries of the continent to articulate their perspectives in the political system. In those countries the popular struggles for democracy take place in the environment of a preexisting state and thus with an already defined class domain. In Nicaragua, by contrast, the democratic project of the masses goes hand in hand with the process of constituting a revolutionary and popular state and, even more, with the introduction of profound modifications to the socioeconomic structure. This therefore implies *creating* a new state, not merely imposing a new character on an already existing one.

The Sandinista revolution must take charge of creating the state not only as the state of a popular and anti-imperialist political project, but in the most basic sense of a *modern* state: from a national army to an efficient communications service; from a judicial power to an educational system; from the institutionalization of the citizenry to the ordering of urban transit; from the physical integration of the territory to the creation of a moderately efficient bureaucracy.

It would be naive to suggest that the process of developing democracy in Nicaragua could be carried out without setbacks or difficulties, or that these are due only to the pressures of imperialism. At various points we have noted the lack of a democratic tradition, of legal and political institutions in the country; all this translates into a lack of experience. This makes it wrong to focus only on the limitations of Sandinista democracy, or stress only the errors. It is not a question of closing one's eyes to reality: the errors of revolutionaries are more harmful to the revolutionary process than are the attacks of their enemies. But the *denunciation* of errors from outside the revolutionary process is irrelevant to their correction. In a work of this type, then, it is a question of *understanding* the limitations of a popular democratic process in a society such as Nicaragua, in the midst of enormous pressures, and without a prior democratic practice to serve as a reference point.

Observers of the Sandinista revolution are often tempted to judge the process of popular democracy in Nicaragua by comparison with other societies of the region (Venezuela? Costa Rica?) or with an ideal model of popular democracy (H. Weber 1981). Yet this overlooks the fact that none of these societies has Nicaragua's history: in none of them has illiteracy imprisoned more than half the adult population until a scant three years ago, for example. Nor are the limitations of this history incorporated into their concepts of what *should be a true revolutionary democracy*.

Naturally, we observers are not the ones that Sandinista democracy has to satisfy; the people of Nicaragua are. The experience of four years confirms the active commitment of the people of Nicaragua and their disposition to fight and die for their revolution.

THE STRUGGLE FOR SURVIVAL

The current challenge facing the FSLN is the rupture of foreign dependency. As Cmdte. Bayardo Arce put it:

> We have defined the Sandinista struggle as anti-imperialist, anti-oligarchic, and anti-dictatorial. For us the fundamental enemy has been U.S. imperialism and the principal enemy the dictatorship. We have now eliminated the principal enemy, but we still have not freed our-

selves from the fundamental one, which is imperialist domination. To break this dependency is now the strategic task of the revolution (1980b: 10)

Economic subordination to imperialism in Nicaragua has occurred more through the international financial sector and commercialization than through direct production; direct foreign investment has not been significant. Moreover, the imperialist presence was always more marked in political, military, and diplomatic than in economic terms. Consequently, the stage that opened with the revolutionary triumph does not entail vast nationalization, as was the case with the Cuban revolution, for example (Valdez Paz 1980). With the exception of the financial interests and the gold and silver mines, the APP was constituted mainly on the basis of properties recovered from Somocismo.

In an effort to avoid the same confrontational situations of other revolutionary processes, the Sandinista revolution adopted a cautious policy regarding the nationalized foreign firms and those that have remained in the country.[18] The withdrawal of Standard Fruit in 1982 was a unilateral decision of the company in violation of previously signed agreements with the government of Nicaragua.[19] In the industrial sector the foreign companies have enjoyed tax facilities similar to those of nationals and in certain cases have received subsidies (Nolff 1982). In general, the government has tended to make some fiscal sacrifices if they could avoid political confrontations in areas central to the economy, or refute the Reagan administration's rhetoric against the revolution.

In this way, without great uproar but with firmness, the Sandinista revolution has initiated steps to improve the position of the national economy in the international division of labor and to free it from subordination to the United States. This is unquestionably a long and difficult process.

Table 7.7 shows the diversification of foreign commerce between 1978 and 1982. The United States is still Nicaragua's principal buyer and seller, although its proportional importance has been reduced. Commerce with the socialist countries has expanded rapidly, especially in the area of imports, but the link is still far from comparable in relative terms from that which Argentina and Brazil, for example, maintain with the Soviet Union (Sizonenko 1981; J. A. López 1983). The capitalist industrial countries (Canada, Europe,

Table 7.7
Nicaragua: Foreign Trade, 1978–82

Countries and regions	Imports				Exports			
	1978		1982		1978		1982	
	millions U.S.$	*%*	*millions U.S.$*	*%*	*millions U.S.$*	*%*	*millions U.S.$*	*%*
United States	186.1	31	147.4	19	150.8	23	96.5	24
Rest of industrialized capitalist world	146.3	25	172.8	22	245.8	38	175.9	43
Socialist countries	3.6	1	89.1	11	1.1	0	31.3	7
Third-world countries	257.9	43	366.2	47	248.4	39	104.1	26
Total	593.9	100	775.5	100	646.1	100	407.8	100

Source: Ministry of Foreign Trade.

Table 7.8
Source of Loans and Grants to Nicaragua, 1979–81
(in percentages)

Countries	Bilateral loans	Multilateral loans	Donations	Total
Third world	44	71	49	49
Western capitalist	28	29	26	32
Socialist	28	0	25	19
Total	100	100	100	100

Source: JGRN (1982: 13).

and Japan) have increased their participation in foreign sales, while commerce with the third world shows opposite behavior in each category. The growth of imports pertains fundamentally to the growth in the oil bill, while the fall of exports basically expresses the generalized economic retraction of the Central American economy, the principal destiny for Nicaraguan exports.

Sources of loans and grants between 1979 and 1981 are similarly diversified (see Table 7.8).

These figures show that concerns about a shift of the Nicaraguan economy toward the "Soviet orbit" are unfounded. Certainly commercial and financial relations have increased, but prior to 1979 Nicaragua lacked any kind of link with the socialist economies; naturally, if the comparison is made with this previous situation, the change is very large, but if the comparison is with other economies of the continent—Venezuela, Mexico, Argentina, Colombia, or Brazil, for example—the opening of foreign commerce and technical cooperation appears relatively small.

At the same time, diversification of international commerce has not yet been able to eliminate the strong ties with the U.S. market, suggesting continuing vulnerability for the Nicaraguan economy. The U.S. government has taken advantage of this situation to reinforce its pressures on the revolution, blocking the supply of parts and spare parts, making the request procedures ever more difficult, putting hobbles on transport. In 1983 the Reagan administration surprisingly decided to eliminate Nicaragua's sugar quota in the U.S. market, and shortly afterward closed all but one of Nicaragua's commercial and consular offices in the country (in reprisal for the revelation that U.S. diplomats were engaging in espionage activities and in plots against leaders of the revolution).

These commercial pressures have been added to the blockade of funds in international lending agencies and the suspension of credit assistance and food programs approved by previous administrations. Although many of these decisions were adopted in the last days of the Carter presidency, Ronald Reagan's entry into the White House implied a very rapid hardening of the U.S. position toward the Sandinista revolution, and the shift to direct as well as indirect destabilization measures.

In February 1981 the United States suspended the disbursement of $15 million of a $75 million loan negotiated during the Carter administration. The following month it suspended a $10 million loan for the purchase of wheat under the PL-480 program. In April 1981 the U.S. government announced the indefinite suspension of all future bilateral aid under the pretext of supposed arms traffic from Nicaragua to El Salvador; it thus suspended a loan of $11.4 million for programs of rural development, education, and health. During the first year of the revolution, the $8.9 million in credit that the Export-Import Bank conceded to Somoza in its last year was reduced to $40,000. This bank suspended guarantees to finance imports from Nicaragua, a decision that above all affected the supply of spare parts. In December 1981 the U.S. representative in the Inter-American Development Bank vetoed a project of $500,000 for the development of rural cooperatives. In early February 1982 the United States pressured the World Bank to unilaterally suspend its loan program to Nicaragua and demand a program of economic stabilization, rejected by the Nicaraguan government.[20]

During fiscal year 1982–83 alone, by contrast, the U.S. government spent almost $50 million in covert assistance to the counter-revolutionary groups.[21] Huge contingents of former Somocista guardsmen were trained in the United States and later in Honduras with U.S. advisers, equipment, and financing; the U.S. president and administration lavished praise on the counter-revolutionary troops that daily penetrated Nicaraguan territory from sanctuaries in Honduras and Costa Rica. The participation of U.S. army officials and the training and support of these activities has been repeatedly verified and denounced by the Nicaraguan delegation to the U.N. Security Council and the General Assembly, the Organization of American States, the World Court, and other international forums.

The impact of this openly sponsored counter-revolutionary activity on the Nicaraguan economy has been very serious. In just one year (May 1982 to May 1983), an incomplete government estimate figured the economic loss at $612 million from destruction of equipment, damages to production, and lost earnings. Attacks on oil storage depots forced the government to restrict the consumption of hydrocarbons. More than 1,000 people have been assassinated, kidnapped, or wounded by the counter-revolutionary forces from Honduras and to a lesser degree Costa Rica; 380 of those assassinated were peasants—mainly beneficiaries of the agrarian reform; and another 218 peasants were kidnapped and taken into Honduran territory. More than 32,000 people had to be relocated to new settlements to avoid artillery and troop attacks from Honduras.

It is evident that in such conditions the course of production and life in general of any country would be far from *normal*. Without having completed the tasks of national reconstruction, Nicaragua must now confront military attacks, financial pressures, and an intense U.S. propaganda campaign. Without being able to fully respond to the demands of the working population, the revolution must channel increasing efforts to defense, simply as a question of survival.

The accusations of a Sandinista military build-up do not consider the effect of these attacks and threats against a backward, economically vulnerable country that is trying to take the first steps toward developing its productive forces, democratize all spheres of social life, and make national sovereignty really effective.[22] Such accusations, which protest the incorporation of people into the militias or the army build-up while keeping silent about an ongoing war against Nicaragua, amount to agreement with the goals of the U.S. government and the counter-revolutionary groups.[23] Disarming the revolution would mean nothing short of surrender of the Nicaraguan people.

Once more, as in the times of José Dolores Estrada, of Benjamín Zeledón, of Augusto Sandino, Nicaragua must confront the aggressions of the United States. The present struggle of the Sandinista revolution is related to the clearest anti-imperialist traditions of the Nicaraguan people and testifies to the continuity of their struggle for full national sovereignty and affirmation of their national identity.

Final Considerations

The process of revolutionary change in Nicaragua is new, making it impossible to draw definitive conclusions; to do so would risk giving a static image to what is still dizzying motion, "closing" a process that is actually quite "open." This risk is even greater given that the international situation weighs so heavily now on the Sandinista revolution. The exposition that follows, therefore, is simply a brief recapitulation of the preceding analysis.

1. In the past three decades Nicaragua experienced rapid capitalist development, above all in agroexports. Unlike in the other countries of the isthmus, where foreign capital assumed a very important role, Nicaraguan agrarian capitalism was characterized by the dominance of a local, medium-sized rural bourgeoisie, subordinated both to large local and foreign capital and to the Somocista state in the spheres of commercialization, financing, and agroindustrial processing. The proletarianization of the labor force was greater in the countryside than in the city. Class structure in the former shows a mass of agricultural workers and semiproletarianized minifundista peasants, above all in the Pacific region, together with a medium-sized peasantry located principally in the interior of the country, both exploited by a dominant bloc of rural landlords and large agroindustrial bourgeoisie. Industrial capitalism, developed in the 1960s in the framework of the Central American Common Market, did not fundamentally alter the pattern of development or the position of the economy vis à vis the international market; the proletarianization process of the urban work force that it created was greater in terms of impoverishment and elimination of artisan and nonsalaried workers than it was in generating industrial employment.

263

2. The Sandinista National Liberation Front historically developed in the same direction as did proletarianization: it was initiated in the mountains in the interior, supporting itself fundamentally among the poor and middle peasantry, continued among the agricultural proletariat and the semiproletarianized peasants of the Pacific, and culminated in the cities, where its revolutionary call was directed toward students, industrial workers, the working masses, and the petty bourgeoisie. The historic social basis of the FSLN is without a doubt the peasantry, but the social subject of the popular insurrection in which two decades of Sandinista struggle culminated had a predominately urban profile, and was more popular in the broad sense than proletarian in its strict meaning. In this process the bourgeoisie that opposed Somoza came along behind, trying to define an alternative to the revolutionary strategy of the FSLN, and thus to obtain the political support of the United States.

3. The economic transformations begun after July 19, 1979, were *more anti-oligarchic than anticapitalist*. The creation of the area of people's property (APP) has taken place on properties confiscated from the Somocista regime; its aim is national recovery rather than state planning. The agrarian reform guarantees efficiently managed large property—with criteria that are not excessively rigid—affecting only idle, abandoned, or badly exploited lands, or those on which peasant labor is exploited through rent—monetary, labor, or in kind. The agrarian reform is peasant oriented, favoring cooperative forms of production, but accepting the maintenance of individual property, whether small, medium, or large. The outrage of the Nicaraguan bourgeoisie, therefore, cannot be explained by the threat that the revolution poses to their basis of accumulation or by the imperative to modernize and continue productivity. The real nature of the bourgeoisie—the presence within it of typically oligarchic elements, its anti-worker attitude, its profound cultural alienation, its ideological backwardness and lack of political expressions that it can call its own, its dependence on the perspectives of the U.S. government—marginalizes it from a process which, in principle, does not challenge its material bases (at least to the extent that they are employed as capital, not as sources of rent). The symbolic practice of the revolution—the content of the dominant political discourse, the level of class confrontation implicit in the slogans, the Marxist resonance of the revolutionary language—has been more aggressive than the economic practice, and it is to the symbolic practice that the bourgeoisie

has responded, underlining the relevance of the political-ideological arena in the process of social transformation.

4. The attention given to the satisfaction of peasant demands—land, financing, prices, technical assistance, infrastructure—and their high level of mobilization and organization, contrasts with the less aggressive behavior of the salaried, and particularly urban, proletariat. The period following the revolutionary triumph is characterized by a rapid growth of union organizing both in the countryside and in the city, the improvement of working conditions, and the development of varied forms of participation by workers in the administration of the enterprises. But at the same time, working-class income has deteriorated, despite subsidies and other political measures destined to compensate for, or reduce, the effect of the fall of real salaries. The union organizations—above all the Sandinista organizations, which predominate—seem still to be in search of their own identity as well as of a relationship with the state that unites the current socioeconomic initiative with the historic project of the revolution (which defines the proletariat as one of its motor forces).

5. The liquidation of the Somocista state has given way to a process of constituting a state of a new type, characterized by the organized participation of the masses in all spheres of society—defense, public health, education, social welfare, working conditions, environmental protection, legislation, and administration of justice. The arming of the people and voluntary military training in the Sandinista Popular Militias verifies the legitimacy of the revolutionary process, while intense popular mobilization is evidence of the people's active commitment to tasks of transforming the society.

The creation of a popular state, and more generally, of a political system, is not an easy task. Nicaragua lacks such a tradition; the Somocista state was the instrument of a palace clique that ended by isolating itself even from the bourgeoisie. Politics, as the practice of conducting society and therefore of generating hegemony and active consensus, was almost completely absent from the Somocista state. Politics thus played virtually no role in relations with other capitalist fractions, operating only insofar as did not undermine the longings for enrichment—if not always accumulation—of the governing clique. At the same time, the Somocista state institutionalized the subordination of the economy and government to the domination of U.S. imperialism. Lack of experience thus complicated by economic restrictions and external aggressions has slowed the process of constituting a modern state and a popular democracy. To suggest that Nicaragua could have implanted and fully institutionalized a democratic political system in barely four years implies, at the very least, ingenuousness.

6. The unfolding of the Sandinista revolution in the economic field contrasts neatly with the situation operating in the rest of Central America, including the present deceleration of growth that is making itself felt. International assistance has undoubtedly played a role, but the direction imposed on the economic process has generated the positive leap. In the almost five years after the revolutionary triumph Nicaragua has not had to confront the profound shortages and even starvation that other revolutions have known in similar stages. It is worth noting that international solidarity itself reflects Sandinista handling of international relations, so far managing to impede the political and economic isolation that imperialism seeks to impose on all experiences of social transformation. Nonetheless it is evident that the stage of "easy reactivation" of the economy has ended and that in the last couple of years Nicaragua has been confronting difficulties in meeting its international commitments, guaranteeing a sustained expansion of its productive forces, and assuring the real income of the workers. The restrictions on the economic process unquestionably reflect both the hardening of the international situation—reduction of foreign financing, ever "harder" loan conditions, economic and military aggressions by imperialism and the counter-revolution—and the way the mixed economy scheme works in practice. The foreign crisis is added to the economic withdrawal of the large bourgeoisie, whose level of productive investments has dropped dramatically despite financial, exchange, taxation, and other incentives. Up to now the Nicaraguan bourgeoisie has limited itself to taking the profits transferred to it by these means, demanding more, and maintaining a drop-out attitude in the sphere of production: not enough to be accused of abandonment, but enough to undermine any serious reactivation. Thus economic growth is basically the result of the effort and political commitment of the workers—laborers and peasants—but with marked inequalities in the benefits received by each. Furthermore, the incentives conceded to the medium-sized and large bourgeoisie, tolerance toward the intermediaries, and promotion of the peasant economy contrast with the reluctance to agree to salary demands by the workers, and with the fall of their real incomes.

7. The mixed economy scheme, together with the policies of the state, has resulted in transfer of public-sector surpluses to the private sector, from productive activities to nonproductive ones, and from the salaried sectors to the nonsalaried; government efforts to put a brake on this process have up to now been fruitless. If in the countryside the most notable aspect of the current stage is the attention given to the peasantry, in the cities the dizzying growth of intermediaries, especially small and medium merchants, is striking. Rigidities experienced in the sphere of production, the containment of salaried incomes—above all, of productive salaried workers—the lack of effective control, and the existence of objective mechanisms of transference of surplus from production to circulation, translate into high margins of net earnings and thus attract a growing portion of the active population into the circulation sector. Undoubtedly in the short run this sector will present a better income alternative, given the persistent deterioration of the real salary level and the drop in employment in some sectors of production; at the same time, however, it drains the labor force toward nonproductive activities, pushes the inflationary process, and feeds the growth of a mass of capital that moves outside the economic and financial policy of the revolution.

8. The revolutionary process develops amid external aggressions of growing intensity, forcing the diversion of all kinds of resources to national defense and the survival of the popular process. The Sandinista revolution, in this sense, is the highest form of affirmation of the Nicaraguan people's national identity, and is therefore related to their most authentic historic tradition. The nature of imperialist domination has given anti-imperialism a special character in Nicaragua: U.S. domination was always more a question of international relations than of production relations; a problem of diplomacy and geopolitics more than of economy; and, within this, more relevant in the sphere of circulation than in that of production. As a result anti-imperialism today primarily takes the form of affirmation of national independence, insistence on a nonaligned foreign policy, diversification of international commercial, diplomatic, and cultural relations, and technical assistance and cooperation. Nationalization of foreign assets has also taken place, however, contributing to the creation of the APP and placing the basic resources of the economy under state control.

9. The growth of intermediary capital and the state stimulants to

productive capital call attention to the issue of the reproduction of capital within the revolutionary process and, in the broadest sense, to the character of the revolution in its current stage. Rather than a *transition to socialism,* the Sandinista revolution is entangled in a difficult *transition to development.* This is not a politically neutral process: the organization of the economy always expresses an option with respect to the social system. But analysis of the Nicaraguan revolutionary process does not yet indicate any option other than the expansion and consolidation of small and medium-sized property, linked to an area of social property that seems, practically speaking, to have reached the limits of its expansion. If *socialism* implies a *proletarian* project—in the sense of the broad socialization of the means of production, of orienting the principal part of the accumulation process, and of economic incentives and benefits to the state/worker pole—it seems undeniable that this project still belongs to the possible long-term goals of the revolution. Nicaragua today continues to be an agroexport capitalist society.

Things clearly are not as they were before: large private property has been seriously reduced; the strategic axes of accumulation are now the public sector of the economy and small and medium production—above all, cooperative agricultural production. But these are not the beginnings of a confrontation with productive capital, so long as the latter accepts the economic and political lines of the revolution: to produce according to its possibilities and not play the counter-revolutionary game. The creation of popular power, the development of the mass organizations, the experiences of worker participation in the management of the economy, and so on, function more as checks on capitalist domination than as a political negation of the capitalists' right to reproduce themselves in the new Nicaragua. Its predominant social bases, its political orientations, and the general sense of its development renders the Sandinista revolution currently a *popular, agrarian, and national liberation revolution,* more than a proletarian or socialist one. The contradiction leading the process as a whole is clearly the *national* contradiction; the anti-imperialist struggle, understood by the FSLN as defense of the national society in the face of counter-revolutionary attacks and the economic and political aggressions of the United States, assumes the direction of the revolutionary process, and the focus of the broadest possible spectrum of forces that can be put together. National unity, which subordinates the resolution of class contradictions in favor of the struggle against imperialism, thus appears as the current project of the Sandinista revolution. The class struggle does not disappear from the national camp, but the revolutionary process tries to subordinate it to the development of the anti-imperialist contradiction, redirecting class contradictions into the sphere of circulation as well as onto the ideological terrain—religion and education, the social definition of such concepts as nation, patriotism, and democracy, and the organization of the family.

Notes

1. The quotation marks reflect the fact that these are forms of production that predate capitalism, but they have their own dynamic and are therefore *reproduced* by capitalism rather than displaced by it.
2. However this is not peculiar to peripheral capitalism, but true of the initial stages of industrial capitalism. In Europe:

   Artisanal production persisted until well into the 19th century, even in those manufacturing branches such as metals and textiles, in which factories had been established from the beginning. In fact the expansion of factory production revitalized and even created artisanal branches of production, such as the clothing industry or those of construction and machine maintenance. The vitality of artisanal production is not surprising, since it frequently complemented factory production, by permitting the owner of the factory to save capital and increase its flexibility through the system of giving outside work. Furthermore, the level of technological complexity was not yet enough to give the large scale operations and their corresponding economies of scale an overbearing advantage, regarding costs, over those of small scale (Roberts 1980: 36–37).

3. Given the subordination of the production systems of which artisans, the "traditional" peasantry, and so on are a product, the antagonistic axis will tend to be between the bourgeoisie and the proletariat. But articulated to the fundamental class interests of each camp will be the interests of subordinated or secondary modes and forms of production, or the arenas of nonproductive activity.
4. This is not a peculiarity of peripheral capitalism: in his study of the making of the English working class, E. P. Thompson points out that

   the making of the working class is a fact of political and cultural, as well as of economic, history. It was not the spontaneous generation of the factory-system. Nor should we think of an external force—the "industrial revolution"—working

271

upon some nondescript undifferentiated raw material of humanity, and turning it out at the other end as a "fresh race of beings". . . . The working class made itself as much as it was made (1963: 194; see also H. Duncker 1980; W. Abendroth 1975).

As Rosa Luxemburg pointed out: "There are not two distinct struggles of the working class, one economic and the other political; there exists only one *single struggle* which simultaneously tends to limit capitalist exploitation within bourgeois society and to eliminate capitalist exploitation and bourgeois society at the same time" (1978, 1: 364).

5. The composition of the popular uprisings of the end of the eighteenth century in England were similar: "In Witney we find reports against cloth cutters, a tailor, the woman of an alcoholic drink vendor and a butler; in Saffron-Walden (Essex) accusations against two halter makers, a shoemaker, a mason, a carpenter, a sawmill worker, a yarn worker, and nine farmhands; in various towns of Devonshire . . . a spinner, two cutters, a wool carder, a shoemaker, an embroiderer and ten laborers were accused; . . . a carpenter, a stonecutter, a sawmill worker and seven farmhands" (Thompson 1979: 112). According to one investigation, the greatest Bolshevik organizational success before World War I took place in the artisanal sector of the economy and not in the large industrial plants with a large quantity of workers (Bonnell 1975).

6. Insufficient attention to the political-ideological elements that constituted these fractions and groups—especially the role of ideology in their political definitions—led to political errors with grave consequences. Typical was the hypothesis accepted by broad sectors of the left and the European worker movement in the 1920s, according to which capitalist concentration led, on one side, to the progressive ruin of the middle sectors (small merchants, artisans, small landlords) whose economic instability inevitably ended in proleterianization; on the other side, to the disintegration of bourgeois privileges enjoyed by the white-collar fraction of salaried workers projecting these into the proletarian camp. In both cases, impoverishment and the proletarianization of the urban petty bourgeoisie had to provoke not only the "economic" polarization of these fractions around the working class, but also their political polarization. The result would be an alliance between the proletariat and the middle groups and fractions. Against all the social democratic and communist predictions (with few and isolated exceptions) the crisis of these intermediary fractions shifted in the political and ideological displacement of the masses of the petty bourgeoisie toward fascism and Nazism. The economic factors that pushed these petty-bourgeois masses to the proletariat was not sufficient to impede this shift (see Colarizi 1976).

7. In Central American countries such as Nicaragua and Guatemala, the national question is also endowed with ethnic components; the issue of class, for its part, arises with different characteristics in each society of the region; see ORPA (1982); EGP (1982); PGT (1982); EGP-FAR-ORPA-PGT (1982); CIERA (1981); Ortega Hegg (1982).

8. Hou Yuon specified that (1) if the internal conflict is correctly resolved in the framework of conscious national unity, the anti-imperialist Front will be stronger; (2) if the internal conflict is not thus resolved, the front's unity will be weak, and its capacity to struggle less (Hou Yuon 1964). Hou Yuon is one of the Kampuchean revolutionary leaders eliminated in the 1970s by the Pol Pot group.

9. See the program of the assault on the Moncada barracks in Castro (1981).

10. The MLD program contemplated measures such as the call for a Constituent Assembly, abolition of the "anti-democratic legislation of the tyranny," agrarian reform "that guarantees the peasantry the possession of the land," free organization of the working class and the peasantry, mass literacy, social security, development and protection of national industry, statization of all properties of the dictatorship, tax reform, promotion of the internal market and the purchasing power of the masses, health and housing for the people, respect and peaceful coexistence especially with the other countries of Central America and the Caribbean. See MLD (Movimiento de Liberacion Dominicana) 1959.

11. Maurice Bishop echoed this. The political program of the New Jewel Movement (1976) outlined: "(1) Popular participation, popular politics, popular democracy; (2) popular cooperatives for the development of the people; (3) attention to health in accord with necessities; (4) full development of the talents, aptitudes, and culture of the people; full popular control of natural resources; (6) employment for all; (7) decent standard of living for all families; (8) freedom of expression and of religion; (9) liberation of all oppressed peoples of the world; (10) a united people . . . a new society . . . a just society" (Bishop 1982: 37ff).

12. The issue was raised again at the turn of the century, coinciding with a rise of populism and the development of liberal tendencies within it. But then Lenin (1974a, 1974b) demonstrated the abstract character of the debate: by then the rural commune was totally degraded and capitalism had been consolidated as the dominant mode of production in Russia. The issue of "short cuts" therefore lacked practical political interest.

13. See Godio (1983: 91), for whom the Cuban July 26th Movement as well as the FSLN "can be included by their characteristics into the category of 'populisms.'"

14. Orlando Núñez (1982b) uses the figure of the executor, who takes care of the inheritance until the inheritor can exercise his rights by himself. The vanguard "will administer" the interests of the proletariat class

until the latter, having overcome its ideological backwardness, disorganization, and "mixture" with nonproletarian elements of the labor force, can assume direction of the process. The image is also present in the declarations of Comandante Henry Ruiz collected in *El Nuevo Diario* (Managua), March 21, 1983. The situation has a particular relevance in the revolutions of Africa and Asia. Referring to the case of Angola one author points out:

> Without doubt, the MPLA was at the beginning the work of petty bourgeois intellectuals, the majority of whom were Kimbundo *mixtures* and *assimilated* people from Luanda—nothing peculiar to this organization in this respect. In fact, beside its petty bourgeois character, both UNITA and the FNLA had a regional and racial base. Furthermore, all the movements prior to these were organized along the same lines. . . . What is important is that the MPLA transcended both racial and regional barriers. . . . It is necessary to distinguish the situation of social class and skin pigmentation or the region of origin, from the political position in the struggle for national liberation. To do anything else is to assume that color or ethnicity or social origin necessarily determine political position. Nothing can be more fallacious than this. In fact, both the FNLA and UNITA are led by people of modest origins, all of them pure blood Africans as are their followers. Nonetheless their political position is reactionary and anti-popular, to say the least (Makidi-Ku-Ntima 1983).

15. See Rodríguez (1979); Piñeiro Losada (1982); also some concrete experiences in Rodríguez García (1979); Valdez Paz (1980); Houtart and Lemercinier (1981).

16. Portrayed in the gross irony of then president F. D. Roosevelt: "Somoza is a son of a bitch, but he's *our* son of a bitch!"

17. See testimonies of the strong presence of General Sandino's struggle in the political memory of the peasants of the north of Nicaragua, in Cabezas (1982); Morales (1981).

18. See the anthological collection made recently by the Institute for the Study of Sandinismo (IES 1982a).

CHAPTER 2:   THE ECONOMIC AND SOCIAL STRUCTURE OF PERIPHERAL CAPITALISM

1. The cultural yields grew from 14 hundredweight per manzana at the beginning of the 1950s to 25 hw at the end of the same decade and to 41 hw in 1964–65, placing it among the highest in the world for unirrigated cotton. Belli points out that "cotton planting is benefited by the intensive use of insecticides, machinery and fertilizers. Furthermore, its products—seed and fiber—have many uses that stimulate the growth of native industries. Thus, in 1952 approximately 25 percent of the total

consumption of insecticides was mixed in Nicaragua; by 1955 the proportion had climbed to 40 percent and by 1959 it was 98 percent (Belli 1975).

2. According to De Franco and Hurtado de Vijil (1978), in 1972 the idle capacity of the manufacturing industry reached 65 percent for the sector as a whole.

3. See the declarations of Comandante Henry Ruiz, Minister of Planning and member of the FSLN, National Directorate, *Barricada,* June 5, 1983.

4. In 1970 the availability of foodstuffs (production + inventories + imports) represented in milk products 36 percent of national consumption; 73 percent in meat and fish; 88 percent in beans; 21 percent in vegetables; 61 percent in eggs, and so on. In that same decade 54 percent of Nicaraguans were underfed, and 90 percent suffered from parasites: see O. Núñez (1980a); Álvarez Montalván (1960).

5. Figures for the period following the revolution are 63 percent and 51 percent respectively.

6. In reality the *permanent employment* of these workers is rather a labor rotation through diverse farms, with periods of employment of no more than two or three weeks in each farm.

7. In a previous work (Vilas 1982b) however, we passively reproduced the estimates of Deere and Marchetti, without making the criticism outlined in the preceding pages.

8. According to an investigation carried out by the Tutoring Center for Minors of the Nicaraguan Social Security and Welfare Institute (INSSBI) about working minors in the streets of Managua, 39 percent of the minors investigated (1,279 of a total of 3,263 cases) were children of workers; almost 22 percent children of service workers, 10 percent children of white-collar workers; 9 percent children of drivers or chauffeurs (CTM/INSSBI 1983).

9. A family farm is considered as one that is exploited without turning to the employment of a labor force outside the family of the producer—who also lives on the farm. A medium-sized multifamily farm employs up to 12 persons outside the producer's family, but he and his family participate in the work. A large multifamily farm is one that employs more than 12 nonfamily workers per year, regardless of whether or not the family participates in the agricultural work.

10. The dispersion of the size of the establishments is double that of productivity: 1.25 if the personnel/establishment relationship is taken as the indicator of size, and 1.23 if the value added/establishment relationship is used, compared to a productivity dispersion (value added/personnel) of 0.65. The dispersion of the organic composition of capital would be 0.76 and that of the rate of surplus 1.01 (Vilas 1982b).

11. A small industry is considered as one that employs less than 30 workers.

Therefore it includes establishments with less than five workers, which on the other hand is excluded from Table 2.15. See Ministry of Industry (1980).

12. See for example, Coronel Kautz (1961): "Although it seems easy to be a cattle rancher, certain indispensable qualities are required. One needs a moderated attitude toward life, a great common sentiment, a small quantity of technical knowledge, or know were to find it, a great love for animals and, added to all this, to be successful, to live on the hacienda all the time. This last is truly indispensable, all the rest are acquired if this requirement is filled. In Nicaragua, I would venture to say that less than 5% of the hacienda owners live on them." It is clear that this way of seeing things and of seeing oneself has to enter into contradiction with the practice of the large landowners, absenteeists and owners of idle lands.

13. The policy of giving credit to producers that had a certain minimum yield (25 hw/manzana) discriminated against the small cotton growers and condemned them to a vicious circle of growing marginalization: they did not receive bank credit because of their low yields, and the lack of credit impeded them from making the necessary investments to raise their yields. On the other hand, the fixing of prices for cotton seeds defined in practice a subsidy for the industrialized oil plants, to the detriment of the agricultural producer. In the agricultural cycle 1973–74, futures sales to Japan yielded a price that was almost $10 per hundredweight less than that reached in the international market when the product was handed in. The cotton growers mobilized to get from the state a reformulation of the accord that would permit them to benefit from the bonanza; however, the decree of March 9, 1974, obliged them to hand over immediately the 70 percent of the cotton contracted as futures at the prices agreed on in the respective contracts, leaving free only 30 percent of production. The loss that this occasioned the Nicaraguan cotton growers has been estimated at around $40 million. See an account of the contradictions between the distinct fractions of cotton producers and the Somocista state in Navas Mendoza et al. (1983).

14. This method of land preparation has been described in detail by Levy (1976: 385–87); its effects on the ecology are generally very negative.

15. See Morales (1981: 24–25); Ramírez (1983a and b).

16. In 1951 50 percent of the credit financing of the National Bank of Nicaragua went to cotton production (Navas Mendoza et al. 1983).

17. The greatest growth of U.S. assistance to the Somocista regime took place at the beginning of the Alliance for Progress program, especially in military assistance. In 1962 half-year economic assistance doubled, but military assistance grew sevenfold (Booth 1982a: 75).

18. A Conservative party spokesperson offered the following opinion about the Labor Code: "In reality it is not a written code that we most need in

Nicaragua, but the diffusion between bosses and workers of healthy concepts of duty, which are incumbent on each sector, in the area of production and of national life, and it is a defect of the modern codes that have a firmer footing in rights than in duties, which has broken the Christian compact of yore when no other code to regulate our mutual relations was known than the Catechism of the Christian religion, in which all learned the Decalog whose commands are contained in two: Love God above all other things and our neighbor as we love ourselves, and whoever loves his neighbor will do no wrong. From there the social peace that only the law of Christ believed and practiced can spread to the world." Quoted in Gutiérrez Mayorga (1978).

19. Max Weber early on (1947, 354ff.) warned that "only certain kinds of capitalism"—plantations and other colonial, commercial enterprises—are compatible with the type of patrimonial domination, but not the "real kind of enterprise with large investments in fixed capital and a rational organization of a free labor force, oriented toward a market of private consumers." This kind of enterprise is "too sensitive to any kind of irrationalities in the administration of justice, in other forms of administrative practice and in questions of taxation."

CHAPTER 3:
ECONOMY AND POLITICS IN THE POPULAR INSURRECTION

1. Figures for the city of Managua compiled by the Central Bank of Nicaragua.
2. See similar conclusions from a different theoretical perspective in Booth (1982b).
3. Testimony collected by Maier (1980: 31–32). International aid, estimated at U.S $250 million, was to stop at the pockets of Somoza, his relatives, and closest collaborators (Black 1981: 58ff).
4. Some studies suggest that, rather than low incomes, the central element for these urban sectors is the *insecurity* of incomes, which in turn is a product of job instability. "In certain aspects, the economy of marginalized people in the city can be compared to that of bands of hunters and gatherers, who face the problem of survival with no other resources than their skills, their cunning, and social solidarity" (Lomnitz 1975: 96). According to this investigation, qualified workers (called "masters") who lack stable occupations should not be excluded from this situation: "These 'masters' earn more than the minimum salary, *as long as they have work:* but in reality their salary can be deceptive, and the most relevant factor for the definition of marginality is *economic insecurity.* There are schoolteachers that earn less than a construction foreman and

are nonetheless not as marginalized" (Lomnitz 1975: 96; emphases in original). Although I do not share the characterization of these sectors as *marginal,* I believe that Lomintz's study does address the central issue.

5. See *El Nuevo Diario,* February 4, 1983. The commercial house where the employees worked closed; with the value of unemployment security loans they will install a new commercial establishment.

6. Speech by business leader Enrique Dreyfus, president of the Nicaraguan Development Institute (INDE), in *La Prensa,* March 14, 1982.

7. Ibid., in *La Prensa,* March 18, 1983. But if the workers are seen as entrepreneurs, in compensation the entrepreneurs are seen as workers: "In Masaya the *labor leader* and well-known intellectual don . . . , *owner* of the typography shop 'El Heraldo' passed away." *La Prensa,* July 18, 1983 (author's emphasis).

8. "In their small businesses they are boss and employee at the same time, feeling themselves now bosses, now workers, depending on the economic situation in the country, without ever being one or the other, save disappearing like petty bourgeoisie. If the situation is insurrection they will be in more of a hurry than those actually insurrecting; if the situation is one of calm (albeit the calm of a cemetery) they will be jealous guardians of the public order, of fine customs, the laws and good habits" (J. López et al. 1979: 110). See also O. Núñez (1980b) and, for a more general discussion, Mayer (1975).

9. What is understood here by *social subject* is the real participant in the insurrection, as a synthesis of socioeconomic determinations—such as class, occupation, family, and so on—and ideological ones. The concept is based on these elements in their concrete manifestation; therefore it has a class referent, but the subject is *not reduced* to class.

10. This refers to the "Heroes and Martyrs" Program of the Nicaraguan Institute for Social Security and Welfare (INSSBI). The program has a registry of 6,000 cases. Each file comprises a collection of documents; reports; declarations of relatives, neighbors, and in general people who knew the combatant in different periods; reports by INSSBI social workers about the living conditions of the combatant's family; testimonies or accreditations of the respective CDS (Sandinista Defense Committee); birth certificates of the combatant and of the petitioners, and in general whatever documentation verifies family ties and the participation of the fallen combatant in the struggle against the dictatorship. Each dossier also contains the official FSLN acknowledgment that the combatant was in fact a member of that organization— although I personally feel that in this aspect the FSLN adopted a very broad criterion. The analysis carried out in this chapter is based on a simple random sample of 640 cases, extracted from a table of random numbers.

11. This also can be seen in the commemorative plaques placed throughout Managua and other cities; the immense majority of them refer to male combatants. See Maier (1980: ch. 2) for a discussion of the different modes of participation of men and women during the insurrection.

12. Information about the civil status of the parents comes from the birth registries of the combatants. This sample was much smaller (n = 98), possibly owing to the nonexistence of population registries in the rural areas and in the majority of the small towns, and to the fact that certainly the registry of births seems to be an infrequent practice in broad sectors of the population. Information about the type of family was taken from 388 cases.

13. A large number of families from which information was obtained have more than six children each.

14. The case of Luisa Amanda Espinoza is illustrative:

"On August 19, 1948, in Managua, doña Antonia Espinoza gave birth to Luisa Antonia, known as Luisa Amanda. Luisa Amanda grew up in the Barrio El Calvario, Managua, in conditions of economic and social marginalizion. Her mother, a humble woman, took in washing and ironing to help with the survival of the family, obtaining small pay for this hard work. When she was seven years old, she was sent to Granada, to the house of Nicolás Gutiérrez, a maternal uncle, owner of a bakery, who was in a better economic situation. There Luisa Amanda went to primary school and worked selling bread in the streets. At twelve, she returned to Managua, to the Barrio San Luis where her mother lived. She began her studies in commerce in the Instituto Centroamericano. . . . When the Espinoza family moved to Reparto Amanda, kilometer 8.5 on the Northern Highway, Luisa Amanda, in order not to leave her studies, stayed living in the Barrio San Luis, in the house of doña Carmen, who sold food in the barrio and collaborated with the FSLN. . . . Luisa Amanda made ties with the Sandinista National Liberation Front in this house, which was visited by Chief of the Revolution Comandante Carlos Fonseca, José Benito Escobar, Julio Buitrago, and other leaders of the Vanguard. Her first work was as a "runner," carrying correspondence to the clandestine compañeros and she was the contact between the safe houses in Managua (Department of Propaganda and Political Education of the FSLN 1981: 3–4).

Luisa Amanda Espinoza was one of the first women actively incorporated into the FSLN; a respected militant, she died in combat against the National Guard in León, on April 3, 1970, when she was not yet twenty-two years old.

15. This is not a peculiarity of the Sandinista revolution. Moore (1978) has noted the presence of defensive elements in the incorporation of people into the struggle against the established order in the European revolutions of the 1840s, in the Russian revolution of 1917, and in the German revolution of 1918.

16. It should be underscored that 37 percent of the cases that figure as students are in reality workers that study at night (ninety-two cases).

These participants were placed in the corresponding occupational category, leaving as students only those who did not work, or about whose work no information existed (156 cases).

17. Although *parents* refers to father and mother, information about the latter is more difficult to discern. In almost 65 percent of the cases for which there is data, the mother is listed as carrying out *domestic activities,* a denomination that comprises activities that could be re-numerated or not—washing and ironing clothes, for example—depending on whether they are carried out for the family home or for someone else, but without this distinction being noted in the registries.

18. The text, directed to students in the university, is dated 1977. See also Comandante of the Revolution Ruiz (1980a): "Our dominant origin was petty bourgeois, student origin . . . ." See also Cabezas (1982), chs. 1 to 6.

19. Cmdte. Bayardo Arce stated:

Unfortunately our country has historically suffered the scourge of unemployment, and we remember how easily a worker or a peasant offered his house to hide clandestine Sandinista combatants, or lent himself to transport arms, to participate in risky actions, and how he steadfastly refused to become an agitator in his factory and his union, fearful of losing his job. There is a practical logic that one can learn only by living directly with the masses. We could synthesize a conversation with a worker compañero who tells us: "If they discover me in this work with the FSLN I will go into hiding. If I go into hiding, I will not see my woman and my children, and in all probability they will die of hunger, but I won't see it. And if they run me out of my job: how will I be able to bear everybody's demand for food, rent, being in the house all day?" This does not appear in any books. Generally the particularities of revolutions do not come out in books. Hence the participation of workers in our country developed more in clandestine or semiclandestine organizational forms; it was tied more to the confrontation against the dictatorship and its repressive apparatus than to the economistic struggle in which many wanted to portray the participation of the fundamental classes of the society (Arce 1980a: 25–26).

20. This was commented on by Carlos Fonseca: "The way things are happening in Nicaragua, the Frente Sandinista is being converted into a vanguard detachment but also into something more than that, to also fulfilling at times the people's post, in other words, a national movement. Perhaps it would be appropriate to qualify our detachment as pro-letarian-popular" (Fonseca 1981: 309).

21. An investigation carried out in the mid-1970s allows a glimpse of this gap between workers and union leaders in the textile industry. If the bases appear with a much more economistic viewpoint than the leaders—in the sense that they see the union above all as the instrument for getting salary, occupational, and educational improvements—the politicization of the leadership ends up being much more abstract, less tied

to the data of the real society. All leaders answered that their objective was to live "in a society without class differentiations," compared to 11 percent of the workers; at the same time 50 percent of the leaders pointed to the capitalist system as responsible for the bad situation of the workers, compared to only 3 percent of the base. But 39 percent of the workers responded that to reach a better society it was necessary to change the government, compared to 17 percent of the leaders. Fifty-nine percent of the workers answered that the rich had a lot of money "because they exploited the poor," and another 18 percent "because they have robbed"—that is to say, 77 percent in total—while among the leaders both answers only added up to 25 percent, but another 33 percent responded that they owed their wealth to "working-hard." Finally, to the question "What party do you think is going to win the popularity of the people in the next years?" 37 percent of the workers answered "FSLN," making it the "most voted for" organization, while half of the leaders suggested the necessity of creating a classist party "of the workers," and none mentioned the FSLN (Pasos 1977).

22. I am referring to various interventions in the Fourteenth Latin American Sociology Congress, San Juan, Puerto Rico, October 1981, and in the Eleventh International Congress of the Latin American Studies Association (LASA), Mexico City, September 1983.

23. Various testimonies collected by the author in Matagalpa in September 1980 and in Managua, suggest that many youths threw themselves into the struggle in September 1978 and in June–July 1979, claiming themselves to be part of the FSLN but without really having any organic tie with the Frente and even without knowing members of the Frente; their first contact with the FSLN took place in the heat of combat. This leads us to think that for these people the FSLN was synonymous with the struggle against Somocismo.

24. A seldom related anecdote serves to illustrate the complex relation between spontaneity and organization that characterized the first insurrectional experiences. As soon as the insurrection in Monimbó was known, the FSLN dispatched various of its cadres to support and consolidate the movement. These cadres succeeded in breaking through the circle that the National Guard had set up around the barrio, but they were detected by the people's self-defense patrols and taken prisoner. According to their own account, this was due to the fact that they were not known by the people of Monimbó, and that they were armed and carrying money—all of which caused the people to think that it was an effort by the Guard to infiltrate. After intense interrogation, the FSLN cadres were set free to join the struggle, once the people became convinced of their political affiliation. Decisive in this outcome was the intervention of an old and important FSLN collaborator, who had been active in organizing the insurrection, but who had lost close contact

with the Frente when his superior had fallen in the effort to take the Masaya National Guard barracks in 1977. (See IES 1982a, 1982b).

25. The person in charge of this task was Cristian Pérez, one of the best strategists of the FSLN's urban insurrectional war. Cristian Pérez, however, could not see the crowning of his work: he died in combat with the National Guard in May 1979, days before the launching of the insurrection in Managua.

26. In this regard Cmdte. Humberto Ortega pointed out:

> The Palace action moved the national and international political context in such a way that it even led to partial, spontaneous insurrections, such as in Matagalpa; and this in turn motivated them even more, which practically carried them to a natural overflow; given this situation we said: if we leave the movement alone, without conduction, the enemy is going to massacre it and it will be difficult later to recuperate the enthusiasm, the morale for struggle further on, it is necessary now to take the lead in this decision, and conduct it and gain better positions than we have today (1980: 30–31).

CHAPTER 4: NATIONAL UNITY AND MIXED ECONOMY

1. See the transcription of the deliberations and proposals in *La Prensa,* March 1 and 2, 1974.

2. For a characterization of these organizations see Booth (1982a), ch. 6.

3. The following organizations constituted the MPU: Workers' Struggle Committee (CLT), Trade Union Action and Unity Central (CAUS), Union Movement of Laboring People (MSPT), National Employees Union (UNE), Revolutionary Student Front (FER), Revolutionary Student Front Marxist-Leninist (FER-ML), Secondary School Student Movement (MES), Students Center of the National University (CUUN), Association of Secondary Students (AES), Association of Women Confronting the National Problematic (AMPRONAC), Federation of Youth Movements of Managua (FMJM), Nicaraguan Revolutionary Youth (JRN), Revolutionary Workers Movement (MORE), and Communist Party of Nicaragua (PC de N).

4. In his report about the insurrection in Managua, Cmdte. Carlos Núñez registered some of the reactions of the subordinated bourgeois groups faced with the struggle: "Unlike barrio Riguero, one could not help but feel a sense of repulsion on observing the timorous, hostile, and hypocritical character of the petty bourgeoisie: some extolling us because they lacked any other remedy, others hidden in their houses, sticking their heads out in evident fear, and a minority that graciously offered their homes to the combatants. . . . The population of El Dorado, due to its same class characteristics, tended to remain enclosed in their houses

and offer no kind of collaboration; in fact some offered lodging to snipers (C. Núñez 1980b: 36,38).

5. "Carlos [Fonseca] sustained that Somoza was like a precious piece of jewelry on which was stuck all the contradictions of our people, on which national liberation and liberation from the dictatorship could become a little confused, on which were concentrated the economic contradictions with the bourgeois sector of our country; in synthesis, the profile of dictatorship and class oppression were both well defined in Somoza." (Ruiz 1980a).

6. After the revolution COSIP came to be called COSEP (Superior Council of Private Enterprise).

7. See the analysis of Burbach and Draimin (1980), and Gorman (1981). The latter work starts from the supposition that the Twelve represented interests of the bourgeoisie; for this reason one of its central arguments refers to the surprising radicalization of some members of the group.

8. The Chilean army in 1973 and the Argentine army in 1976 both offer examples of this articulation between the political function of the armed forces and their apolitical nature in terms of *party*. As Argentine General Alcides López Aufranc specifies: "The Armed Forces are at the service of national sovereignty and the maintenance of private property."

9. The Patriotic Front of the Revolution was created on July 23, 1980, by the FSLN, the PSN, PPSC, and the PLI. Its "Programmatic Bases" outlined as aims and objectives: "(a) to back the democratic policy that the Government of National Reconstruction carries forward; and (b) to defend, consolidate, and promote the Nicaraguan revolution, with the goal of assuring socioeconomic transformations with democratic popular bases and with the object of National Independence."

10. For example:

    A brake has been put on industrial reactivation by the prevailing political uncertainty and labor problems that include even the takeover of business by the unions. . . . In practice National Unity has been destroyed, as a consequence of the intention of the FSLN to implement National Unity around itself, submitting the rest of the political, economic, and social organizations to its dictates. This is very far from National Unity in freedom, without the submission of one or the other, that gave rise to the Program of Government and carried us to triumph over the dictatorship. . . . The armed forces of the nation have been converted into the armed forces of the FSLN party" (COSEP 1980: 17, 24); see also INDE (1981: 45–54).

11. Consider for example the intervention of the Democratic Conservative party representative in a session of the Council of State. According to the daily *La Prensa* (October 22, 1983), the PCD representative said that "the violation of the principles established in the Original Program of Government on the part of the FSLN, the lack of fulfillment of this plan

and of the commitments of the Sandinista government, were *one of the preponderant causes making the counter-revolution cause concerns and cause acts of sabotage. . . .* We are against warism, against terrorism, and against any act of violence, but we are also against attitudes of the government *that provoke these situations"* (author's emphases).

12. According to the program of the Government of National Reconstruction, the Council of State would include thirty-three members designated by the following political organizations and socioeconomic groups of the country: (1) FSLN; (2) FPN (MPU, PLI, Group of the Twelve, PPSC, CTN, FO, Union of Radio Journalists); (3) FAO (PCD, PSC, MDN, MLC, PSN, CGTi, CUS); (4) COSEP (INDE, Chamber of Industries of Nicaragua-CADIN, Confederation of Chambers of Commerce of Nicaragua, UPANIC, Nicaraguan Chamber of Construction, Confederation of Professional Associations of Nicaragua); (5) National Autonomous University of Nicaragua; (6) National Association of Clergy (ACLEN). See analysis of the confrontation around the composition of the Council of State in Black (1981), Gilbert (1983).

13. The Council was finally set up as follows: FSLN (6 members), PLI (1), PSN (1), PPSC (1), MDN (1), PCD (1), PSC (1), CDS (9), Sandinista Youth "19th of July" (1), AMNLAE (1), CST (1), ATC (1), CGTi (1), CTN (1), CAUS (1), CUS (1), FETSALUD (1), Armed Forces (1), ACLEN (1), National Council of Higher Education (1), National Association of Educators of Nicaragua (ANDEN) (1), Union of Journalists of Nicaragua (UPN) (1), Association of Miskitos, Sumus, and Ramas (MISURASATA) (1), INDE (1), CADIN (1), Confederation of Chambers of Commerce (1), Chamber of Construction (1), UPANIC (1). See *La Gaceta,* April 22, 1980. Later the composition of the Council was increased to incorporate representatives of the National Union of Agriculturalists and Cattle Ranchers (UNAG) and the Ecumenical Axis MEC-CELADEC (reform churches).

14. See Ramírez (1982) for an analysis of the crisis of May 1980. The fact that the COSEP organizations stayed in the Council of State was achieved by the government sanctioning a law forbidding arbitrary or unlawful confiscations.

15. See Dreyfus (1980). The participation of the Catholic church hierarchy in the opposition to the revolutionary government is analyzed by diverse forces in Serra et al. (1981), Serra (1982), Girardi (1983), and others.

16. Arturo Cruz would soon follow the same path. Designated Nicaragua's ambassador to the United States after the restructuring of the government in 1981, he would resign this position months later, joining the counter-revolutionary groups in the United States in 1982, after abandoning Nicaragua.

17. *Barricada,* June 25, July 7 and August 3, 1982.

18. Created by the FSLN to keep channels of dialogue open with the opposition, the forum incorporated, along with the political and mass organizations, two left-opposition political organizations: the Popular Action Movement (MAP) and the Communist party of Nicaragua.
19. *Barricada,* October 22, 1981.
20. *Barricada,* September 9, 1982; *El Nuevo Diario,* September 10, 1982.
21. These measures were announced by Cmdte. Daniel Ortega at the mass rally for the second anniversary of the revolution (see *Barricada,* July 20, 1981). Subsequently, various companies entered the APP when the tie between their owners and counter-revolutionary activities was proved; one of the most famous cases was that of the Coca Cola bottling company. Companies of Alfonso Robelo and Donald Lacayo Núñez (former director of the PCD) were also incorporated into the APP when the two joined the counter-revolution: *Barricada,* August 31, 1983.
22. The figure in parentheses corresponds to the Uniform International Industrial Classification (CIIU).
23. This seems to have been the case with various members of the financial groups BANIC and BANAMERICA.
24. *El Nuevo Diario,* August 6, 1981.
25. *Barricada,* February 1, 1982.
26. *Barricada,* February 9, and November 15, 1982; *El Nuevo Diario,* March 21, 1982.
27. It is worth underscoring in this regard that many functionaries who participated in the definition of the economic policy at the outset have been abandoning the state, the revolution, and the country in recent years.
28. See INDE (1981: 52–53, 68–69); and Herdocia (1982). Nonetheless on various occasions the Supreme Court of Justice ordered the restitution of properties confiscated without legal cause: see *La Prensa,* July 8 and September 8, 1982; *El Nuevo Diario,* October 25, 1982.
29. To mitigate these doubts, part of the political discourse of the counter-revolution is an attempt to differentiate it from the former National Guard, to present itself as a "third way," more reasonable and civilized than that of the veteran Somocistas. This seems to be the role of Arturo Cruz (see for example, the *New York Times,* June 28, 1983) and of some free lance intellectuals and academics.
30. See declarations of Cmdte. J. Wheelock, Minister of MIDINRA, in ATC (1979: 38–39); *Barricada,* April 25 and June 20, 1982; *El Nuevo Diario,* August 15, 1983.
31. *Barricada,* June 28, 1982.
32. *El Nuevo Diario,* December 26, 1982.
33. See, for example, *Barricada,* May 3 and August 3, 1982.
34. "El campesino frente a la agresion," *Barricada,* June 6, 1983.

35. *Barricada,* June 3 and 6, 1983.
36. Statements of the president of a production and defense cooperative to *Barricada,* June 3, 1983.
37. *Barricada,* July 4 and 20, 1983; *El Nuevo Diario,* July 27, 1983; *La Prensa,* July 29, 1983.
38. It should be noted that the figures of Table 4.5 differ from those of Table 2.14. This could be due to the fact that the criteria to define what is understood by *small production* in each case are not homogeneous, or else that the registered growth in recent years is in reality a tendency toward a return to preceding levels (a hypothesis I do not consider valid).
39. See an analysis of incomes in *Barricada,* May 4, 1982.
40. Point 2 of the Declaration of Principles approved by the Constituent National Assembly of the Small and Medium Agricultural Producers of Nicaragua. Managua, April 25–26, 1981.
41. See Ministry of Social Welfare (1981); decree 382 of April 9, 1980 (*La Gaceta,* April 29, 1980); *Barricada,* October 17, 1983.

CHAPTER 5: THE WORKING CLASS IN THE POPULAR REVOLUTION

1. The estimate of 6 percent is taken from *Barricada,* March 16, 1980; the figure is reproduced without questioning by Pérez-Stable (1982). The estimate of 7 percent was given to the author in an interview with Ronald Membreño, of the CST's National Executive on May 12, 1981. The text that follows is based on figures published by the Office of Statistics and Labor Information of the Ministry of Labor.
2. "In this Second Assembly we will discuss unions by branch as a prior step in the struggle for a Unified Central. We also expect to be able to advance toward unity gaining all sectors for the Single Workers' Central, and defeating the pro-bourgeois currents." Base document of the Second Assembly for Workers' Unity, Managua, July 4–5, 1981, point 3.7.
3. These are: General Work Central (independent) (CGTi), created in 1963 and linked to the PSN; Trade Union Action and Unity Central (CAUS), formed in 1973 and tied to the PC de N; Nicaraguan Workers' Central (CTN), Social Christian, created in 1972 (although its forerunner, the Autonomous Union Movement of Nicaragua [MOSAN], existed since 1962); the Confederation of Trade Union Unification (CUS) created in 1972; and the Workers' Front (tied to the Popular Action Movement).
4. For example, according to the Ministry of Labor the CTN has 40 unions and 3,511 affiliates (June 1982); but according to the directors of the central, the affiliation would be some 65,000 workers. Currently the CTN has only nineteen organizations: *Barricada,* June 6, 1983.

5. *El Nuevo Diario,* June 20, 1981.
6. Author's interview with Denis Chavarría, of the ATC's National Executive on September 20, 1983. In total the sugar industry has around 18,000 workers. The respective unions are affiliated currently to the CST, after fierce struggles with the CTN, CAUS, and the Workers' Front.
7. In this respect there is a constant throughout these last four years. See, for example, the document of the Inter-Trade Union Commission published in *Barricada,* April 14, 1980; Cmdte. Luis Carrión (1981); and Cmdte. Víctor Tirado in *Barricada,* September 21, 1983.
8. In 1979 the GDP was reduced by almost 25 percent with respect to the previous year, and the consumer price index grew 70.3 percent.
9. In the case of CAUS, some demands were for 100 percent salary increases.
10. *Barricada,* July 2, 1981.
11. Speech by Cmdte. Víctor Tirado at the inauguration of the First Assembly for Workers' Unity, Managua, November 15, 1980.
12. Speech by Cmdte. Jaime Wheelock on November 19, 1980; *Barricada,* November 20, 1980.
13. *Barricada,* December 3, 1980.
14. *Barricada,* July 11, 1980.
15. *La Prensa,* July 2, 1980.
16. See also *La Prensa,* June 7, 1981.
17. See an evaluation of the experience in *Nueva Economía* 8 (supplement of *Barricada,* December 29, 1980).
18. It is a general description that admits variation. In the San Antonio refinery the council had two representatives from the administration, two from the Directive Junta of the Union, and two from the Ministry of Labor; see *Barricada,* February 9, 1981. In some enterprises the council took different names: Technical-Administrative Council, Enterprise Committee, and so on.
19. *Barricada,* July 11, 1983.
20. See on this Vilas (1983), and *Barricada,* June 29, 1982.
21. *Barricada,* December 10, 1980.
22. *Barricada,* July 27, 1983.
23. *Barricada,* July 9, 1982.
24. *Barricada,* July 24, 1982.
25. *Barricada,* February 16, 1983.
26. *Barricada,* September 2, 1982; January 26 and 27, 1983.
27. *Barricada,* September 7, 1983.
28. See for example *Barricada,* October 1, 1982.
29. For example: "We run up against the fact that at times there is a desire to use the masses as buffers when there are conflicts, and as static instruments when there aren't" (C. Núñez 1980c: 16); see also Cmdte.

Tomas Borge's speech on the occasion of the Second Anniversary of July 19, in *Barricada,* July 20, 1981).

30. A frequent issue is the movement of cadres between the mass organizations, the state, and the FSLN. For example Iván García, first general secretary of the CST, was later made the national head of the Sandinista Popular Militias; Natán Sevilla, experienced leader of the teachers' union, went from the vice-ministry of social welfare to the Department of International Relations of the FSLN; later he was sent to the CST and at the end of 1981 he was designated, by an assembly of associates, as general secretary of the teacher's union.

31. *El Nuevo Diario,* June 13, 1981.

32. *Barricada,* June 16, 1981.

33. *Barricada,* June 25, 1981.

34. *Barricada,* June 27, 1981; July 9, 1981; and see also July 1 and 2, 1981.

35. *Barricada,* June 26, 1981.

36. *Barricada,* June 22 and July 2, 1981.

37. *Barricada,* July 2, 1981.

38. *Los Trabajadores,* July 16, 1981.

39. *Barricada,* July 2, 1981.

40. *Barricada,* July 16, 1981.

41. *La Prensa,* June 27 and 28, and July 1, 1981.

42. *El Nuevo Diario,*July 27, 1981. The communiqué was signed by the then vice-minister, Lic. Edgar Macías, at that time president of the Popular Social Christian party. Later Macís would come into contradiction with the revolution; he moved out of the vice-ministry through the decision of the government, and he would later be separated from the presidency of the PPSC, to finally abandon the country. See also *Barricada,* July 31, 1981.

43. *Barricada,* July 28, 1981.

44. *La Gaceta,* 199 (October 3, 1981).

45. *El Nuevo Diario,* July 31, 1981.

46. See for example *El Nuevo Diario,* August 26, 1982; *Barricada,* July 11 and September 9, 1982, and September 15, 1983.

47. An example was the polemic between ANDEN and the Ministry of Education around the quality of education and school attendance. Both the general secretary of ANDEN and the minister of education are members of the FSLN, which did not hinder the frankness of the polemic or the broad publicity accorded it (see *El Nuevo Diario,* August 4 and 5, 1983; *Barricada,* August 4, 5, and 6, 1983). Later, AMNLAE strongly and publicly criticized the law project that established the Patriotic Military Service prepared by the Ministry of Defense—headed by Cmdte. Humberto Ortega. AMNLAE objected to the fact that the project limited incorporation into active service to men. After mobiliza-

tions and debates AMNLAE saw to it that the text approved by the Council of State would accept the incorporation of women into active service, although in a voluntary character. These and other examples point out the effective existence of autonomy between the mass organizations and the state, and the practice of criticism.

48. Víctor Tirado, in *Barricada,* October 23, 1983.

49. Compare, for example, the declarations of opposing views in *Barricada,* November 8, 1982, and *El Nuevo Diario,* February 9, 1983.

50. According to CETRA, the recovery of labor productivity can be explained by the reactivation of the economy beginning in the second half of 1979, fundamentally as the effect of the dynamizing role of the public sector.

51. The growth of the consumer price index between 1979 and 1981 was almost 60 percent. This theme will be taken up again in Chapter 7.

CHAPTER 6: POPULAR DEMOCRACY AND IDEOLOGICAL STRUGGLE: THE CASE OF EDUCATION

1. "Popular teachers come from the classes that emerge and through their education (which is self-education) they appropriate reality and transform it. It is through the class origin of the popular teachers and through the characteristics and nature of their educational practice within the Collectives of Popular Education, that educational content that has nothing to do with their daily social practices is aborted, discarded, and thrown into the dump with other sterile and useless things" (Castilla Urbina 1982a: 246–47).

2. Each association organized its members into groups of 10 people, to discuss a list of 55 questions, primarily open ones. The answers were not individual but collective. A coordinator designated by the group wrote the conclusions of the debate for each question. Most discussion groups functioned at a municipal level, although some, such as the Nicaraguan Chamber of Construction, and the Nicaraguan Bishops Conference, lacking municipal structures, responded directly through their directive bodies. Coordinators of municipal groups then elaborated *municipal syntheses,* which were then coordinated to form the *departmental synthesis* and, finally a *national synthesis.* Responsibility for the process within each organization was left entirely to the respective organizations.

3. Only one organization (the Nicaraguan Chamber of Construction), the single business organization that accepted the invitation to participate, mentioned the elections as an attribute of democracy. See MED (1981).

4. See O. Silva (1982). It is important to point out that in his trip to Central America at the beginning of 1983, Pope John II chose Nicaragua to make his speech about education (IEPALA 1983: 291–95).
5. This document was confirmed two years later by another communiqué of the FSLN; *Barricada*, August 19, 1982.
6. See Chapter 5, note 47.
7. The issue is all the more important since participation in the Literacy Crusade provoked a process of political radicalization in the students who worked in it, especially among the brigadistas who taught in the countryside and the mountains (Flora, McFadden, and Warner 1983), increasing the gap between them and their teachers.

CHAPTER 7: A SOCIETY IN REVOLUTION

1. The only obligations not recognized were those derived from the purchase of arms.
2. The GDP had to grow 22 percent in 1980 and 18.5 percent in 1981, guaranteeing full recovery in no more than two years. These overestimates meant that the actual rates, while good, were received without much enthusiasm; they have since been used by opposition groups to create an image of economic catastrophe and administrative incompetence.
3. Taking as a base = 100 for the year 1977, the level of activity was 79 for the manufacturing industry and 72 for the global GDP in 1982.
4. The network of state food stores went from 331 establishments before the triumph to almost 3,000 in 1982; CIERA (1983a: 10).
5. In Managua alone there are more than 37,000 retailers in the markets and neighborhoods (CIERA 1983a: 10). In 1982 the "merchants and vendors" represented 16.2 percent of the occupied population; 69 percent of them were self-employed workers. In the informal sector, which reports 90 percent of those occupied in this activity, the self-employed workers constitute almost 76 percent of the occupied population and 98.8 percent of the total of self-employed workers in the "merchants and vendors" category. Elaboration of INEC figures (1982).
6. See MICOIN (1983). According to one study at the end of January 1983 the overpricing of a number of vegetables and fruits sold by tradespeople ranged between 54 percent and 300 percent with respect to the prices used in the supermarkets of the People's Commercial Corporation (CORCOP). *El Nuevo Diario* (*Defense of the Consumer* supplement), January 26, 1983. And see the denunciations about speculation in cloth, in *Barricada*, December 28, 1982, January 4, and August 30, 1983.

7. See for example the declarations of the CST General Secretary in *Barricada,* July 6 and August 12, 1983.

8. In reality this is not a peculiarity of Nicaragua. In Costa Rica (1973) 72 percent of the urban EAP was found in nonproductive sectors; in El Salvador (1975) 68 percent; in Guatemala (1973) 63 percent, and in Honduras (1974) 64 percent.

9. The basic basket on which the price index is calculated collects information exclusively from the urban area. Everything indicates that in Nicaragua the profile of family spending is different in the rural areas, but there is not yet a definition of the rural market basket.

10. On commercialization of basic products in the countryside see Ruben (1983).

11. The minimum salary of workers in the agricultural sector was reduced in real terms by 40 percent between 1980 and 1983.

12. The emergency employment program was created at the end of 1982 to confront the fall of industrial employment resulting from the reduced level of activity. Administered by the Ministry of Labor and the Union Coordinadora, it guarantees jobs in agriculture and construction for displaced workers, paying them the minimum industrial salary. Only a small number of workers opted for the program.

13. See the declarations of the Minister of Labor and the CST General Secretary in *Barricada,* December 1, 1982. According to my preliminary estimates based on a nonsystematic sample taken in November 1982 in two Managua barrios, the monthly income of small merchants in food and drinks (soft drinks and natural juices) can be between three and four times higher than the minimum industrial salary.

14. Compare for example the space dedicated by *Barricada* to the demand to condone the bank debt of the peasants with that assigned the salary issue; at the same time, compare the abysmal difference that exists in the levels of mobilization of the respective organizations around the two sets of demands.

15. See however, in *Envio* 17 (November 1982) the letter of Comandante Bayardo Arce to the CDS coordinators, calling their attention to the need to put an end to transgressions on the part of some CDSs. See also the declarations of a member of the CDS National Executive in *El Nuevo Diario,* January 16, 1983.

16. See, for example, the report of the Workers' Front representative in the Union Coordinadora of Nicaragua, in *Prensa Proletaria* 6 (October 1983), and the communiqué of the Workers' Front regarding the salary question in *Prensa Proletaria* 5 (September 1983); See also the report of the General Secretary and the General Subsecretary of CAUS, in *Avance* 65 (October 1983).

17. See, for example, the CDS criticisms of different aspects of government

management, *Barricada,* September 8, 1982, and January 24, 1983; *El Nuevo Diario,* February 16, 1983.

18. See the compensation agreement with one of the nationalized mining companies, *La Prensa,* December 10, 1982.
19. See *Barricada,* October 27, 1982.
20. See declaration by Cmdte.Henry Ruiz, minister of planning, in *El Nuevo Diario,* December 3, 1982; also *Barricada,* May 23, 1983.
21. According to analysts of the U.S. Congress, cited by the *Wall Street Journal;* see *Barricada,* August 30, 1983.
22. The following quote from a Nicaraguan economist located outside the country illustrates this abstract but *politically oriented* focus:

> In Central America there are at least two relevant cases of militarism as an overall conception of the leadership and control of society: Guatemala and El Salvador, on one side, and Nicaragua on the other. The two models have developed in a diverse way, but they have common features. In Guatemala and El Salvador, to different degrees, the military has advanced from its role as indispensable intermediary between power groups to that of a definitely indispensable element for absolute power and control of civil society, overcoming, from that point, its partially administrative or leadership function in affairs of State. In Nicaragua, on the other hand, the commanders are the only ones that have the power of decision in politics, diplomacy, the economy, the universities, as well as in practically the totality of the means of communication. It could be said that to be military in Central America today, is sufficient to achieve capacity in any area of knowledge. A military person is just as apt to direct a prison camp as a Central Bank or a Ministry of Culture. The important thing is to be trustworthy and to have the vision of power in the long run (D. Castillo 1983: 17–18).

23. Furthermore, this focus forgets that the principle of a *nation in arms* formed part of the oldest military tradition *of the West* right up to the appearance of the Pentagon doctrines of national security and elite troops, isolated from the people in order to better repress them. In the case of Nicaragua, the principle of incorporating people into defense as part of the process of constituting *citizenry* was announced by General Sandino himself with reference to the Army in Defense of National Sovereignty: "We are not military; we are armed citizens" (quoted in Ramírez 1981).

Bibliography

Abendroth, W. 1975. *Historia social del movimiento obrero europeo.* Barcelona: Editorial Laia.

Agnoli, J. 1978. *Lo Stato del capitale.* Milan: Feltrinelli.

Alonso, J. A. 1973. "Elites gobernantes y 'familismo' en Nicaragua." *Estudios Centroamericanos* 296 (June): 331–44.

Altvater, E. 1977. "Notas sobre algunos problemas del intervencionismo de Estado." In *El Estado en el capitalismo contemporaneo,* edited by H. R. Sonntag and H. Valecillos, pp. 88–133. Mexico: Siglo XXI.

Álvarez, Montalván, E. 1960. "Requerimientos y deficiencias de la dieta popular en Nicaragua." *Revista Conservadora* 2 (October): 19–24.

Amnesty International. 1976. "Reporte sobre la República de Nicaragua; incluyendo los resultados de una misión, 10–15 de mayo." *Revista del Pensamiento Centroamericano* 157 (October–December 1977): 111–51.

Arce, B. 1980a. *El papel de las fuerzas motrices antes y despues del triunfo.* Managua: Secretaría Nacional de Propaganda y Educación Política del FSLN.

———. 1980b. *Romper la dependencia, tarea estratégica de la revolución.* Managua: Secretaría Nacional de Propaganda y Educación Politica del FSLN.

Arellano, J. E. 1969. "El estudiante y la revolución." *Revista Conservadora del Pensamiento Centroamericano* 105 (June): 7–14.

Argüello S. J., A. 1979. "Posturas de los cristianos frente al proceso revolucionario nicaragüense." In *Fe Cristiana y Revolución Sandinista.* Managua: Instituto Histórico Centroamericano.

ATC (Asociación de Trabajadores del Campo). 1979. *Memorias de la Asamblea Nacional Constitutiva.* Managua: ATC.

Báez, G. 1981. "Sobre la reforma agraria." In CIERA, *Testimonios sobre la Reforma Agraria,* pp. 1–21. Managua: CIERA.

Báez Sacasa, W. 1970. "Cuánto daría Ud. para hacer una Revolución?"

Revista Conservadora del Pensamiento Centroamericano 123 (December): 45–47.

Baumeister, E. 1982. *Notas para la discusión del problema agrario en Nicaragua.* Documento presentado en el III Congreso Nacional de Ciencias Sociales. Managua, October.

Baumeister, E. et al. 1983. *El subsistema del algodón en Nicaragua.* Managua: Second seminar, "Centroamérica y el Caribe." INIES/CRIES, February.

Belli, P. 1975. "Prolegómeno para una historia económica de Nicaragua, 1905–1966." *Revista del Pensamiento Centroamericano* 146 (January–March): 2–30.

Bendaña, A. 1978. "Crisis in Nicaragua." *NACLA Report on the Americas* 7, no. 6 (November–December).

Biderman, J. 1983. "The Development of Capitalism in Nicaragua: A Political Economic History." *Latin American Perspectives* 36 (Winter): 7–32.

Bishop, M. 1982. *Forward Ever! Three Years of Grenadian Revolution.* New York: Pathfinder Press.

Black, G. 1981. *Triumph of the People. The Sandinista Revolution.* London: Zed Press.

Bonnell, V. 1975. *The Politics of Labor in Pre-Revolutionary Russia: Moscow Workers' Organization 1905–1914.* Cambridge, MA: Harvard University Press.

Booth, J. 1982a. *The End and the Beginning: The Nicaraguan Revolution.* Boulder, CO: Westview Press.

———. 1982b. *Toward Explaining Regional Crisis in Central America: The Socioeconomic and Political Roots of Rebellion.* Prepared for delivery to the 44th International Congress of Americanists. Manchester: University of Manchester, September.

Briones Torres, I. 1980. "Los Doce en la historia." *Barricada,* October 18.

Burbach, R. and T. Draimin. 1980. "Nicaragua's Revolution." *NACLA Report on the Americas* 14, no. 3 (May–June): 1–35.

Cabestrero, T. 1983. *Ministros de Dios, ministros del pueblo.* Bilbao: - Desclée de Brouwer.

Cabezas, O. 1982. *La montaña es algo más que una inmensa estepa verde.* Managua: Editorial Nueva Nicaragua.

Cardoso, F. H. and E. Faletto. 1969. *Dependencia y desarrollo en América latina.* Mexico: Siglo XXI.

Carrión, L. 1981. *Austeridad: principio y norma de nuestro pueblo.* Managua: Departamento de Propaganda y Educación Política del FSLN.

Castilla Urbina, M. 1982a. "La educación como poder, crisis sin solución en la transición revolucionaria." In *Estado y clases sociales en Managua,* 193–252. Managua: ANICS/CIERA.

———. 1982b. *La contradicción escuela capitalista y clases populares en la fase actual de la transición revolucionaria en Nicaragua.* Document presented at the Third National Social Sciences Congress, Managua, October.

―――. 1983. *La contradicción: objetivos de la educación-producto educativo. El caso de Nicaragua.* Document presented at the Twenty-Fifth Latin American Conference on Sociology, Managua, October.

Castillo, D. 1980a. *Acumulación de capital y empresas transnacionales en Centroamérica.* Mexico: Siglo XXI.

―――. 1980b. "Nicaragua. Situación económica y aliazas políticas." *Revista Mexicana de Sociología,* 2–80, 501–21.

―――. 1983. "Una visión global del problema centroamericano: más allá de la crisis." In *Centroamérica más allá crisis,* edited by D. Castillo, pp. 13–29. Mexico: Ediciones SIAP.

Castillo, M. 1983. *La participación de los trabajadores en la gestión de las empresas.* Presented in the First Seminar of the Sandinista Administration. Managua: CONAPRO "Héroes y Mártires," September.

Castro, F. 1977. Entrevista de Simón Malley en *La Noticia* (Santo Domingo, D.R.), June 19.

―――. 1981. *La historia me absolverá.* Havana: Editorial de Ciencias Sociales.

CEPAL. 1979. *Nicaragua: Antecedentes económicos del proceso revolucionario* (doc. E/CEPAL/G 1091), August.

―――. 1981. *Nicaragua: El impacto de la mutación política.* Santiago (Chile): Naciones Unidas.

CEPAL/FAO/OIT/IICA/SIECA/OCT/OEA. 1972. *Tenencia de la tierra y desarrollo rural en Centroamérica.* San José: EDUCA.

CETRA (Centro de Estudios del Trabajo del Ministerio del Trabajo). 1982. *La productividad del trabajo en la industria manufacturera, 1977–1981.* Managua, December.

―――. 1983a. *La productividad del trabajo en la perspectiva de la política sociolaboral.* Managua, January.

―――. 1983b. *El ingreso de la población en Managua, 1981 y 1982.* Managua, March.

Chamorro, A. 1982. *Los rasgos hegemónicos del somocismo y la Revolución Sandinista.* Managua: INIES, mimeo., October.

CIERA (Centro de Investigaciones y Estudios de la Reforma Agraria). 1981. *La Mosquitia en la Revolución.* Managua: CIERA.

―――. 1983a. *La situación del abastecimiento.* Managua: CIERA.

―――. 1983b. *Distribución y consumo popular de alimentos en Managua.* Managua: CIERA.

CNI (Comisión Nacional Intersindical). 1980. *El papel de los sindicatos en la Revolucion.* Managua: CST.

Colarizi, S. 1976. *Classe operaia e cetti medi.* Venice: Marsilio Editori.

Colburn, F. D. 1983. *Rural Labor and the State in Post-Revolutionary Nicaragua.* Prepared for the Annual Meeting of the Southeastern Council on Latin American Studies, Puerto Rico, April.

Cooper, T. 1829. *Lectures on the Elements of Political Economy.* Columbia, SC: Morris & Wilson.

Córdova, A. 1979. *La ideología de la revolución mexicana.* Mexico: Ediciones ERA.

Coronel Kautz, R. 1961. "La ganadería en la economía nacional. Situación actual." *Revista Conservadora* 13 (October): 31–33.

Corten, A. 1974. "Valor de la fuerza de trabajo y formas de proletarización." *Revista Latinoamericana de Sociología* 1: 45–64.

COSEP. 1980. *Análisis sobre la estrategia del Programa de Gobierno de Reconstrucción Nacional.* COSEP, December.

Cruz, E. 1974. *Estrategias de desarrollo para los años 70 (Ideas expuestas ante la Primera Convención Nacional del Sector Privado Nicaragüense).* Managua, March 1, mimeo.

CSUCA. 1978a. *Estructura demográfica y migraciones internas en Centroamérica.* San José: EDUCA.

———. 1978b. *Estructura agraria, dinámica de población y desarrollo capitalista en Centroamerica.* San José: EDUCA.

CTM/INSSBI. 1983. *Investigación de menores en situación de riesgo.* Managua.

Dalton, R. 1972. *Miguel Mármol.* San José: EDUCA.

Deere, C. D. and P. Marchetti. 1981. "The Worker-Peasant Alliance in the First Year of the Nicaraguan Agrarian Reform." *Latin American Perspectives* 29 (Spring): 40–73.

De Franco, M. and M. Hurtado de Vigil. 1978. "Algunos aspectos del funcionamiento socioeconómico de Nicaragua." *Revista del Pensamiento Centroamericano* 159 (April–June): 38–104.

De Franco, M. and C. F. Chamorro. 1979. "Nicaragua: Crecimiento industrial y desempleo." In *El fracaso social de la integración en Centroamérica.* San José: EDUCA.

Diederich, B. 1981. *Somoza and the Legacy of U.S. Involvement in Central America.* New York: E.P. Dutton.

Donahue, J. M. 1983. *Health Policy Directions in Nicaragua.* Presented at LASA XI International Congress. Mexico, September.

DPEP (Departamento de Propaganda y Educación Política del FSLN). 1981. *Luisa Amanda Espinosa, mujer de vanguardia.* Managua: DPEP.

Dreyfus, E. 1980. *Un nuevo marco socioeconómico dentro de la revolución.* Managua: INDE.

Duncker, H. 1980. *Historia del movimiento obrero.* Mexico: Ediciones de Cultura Popular.

EGP. 1982. "Los pueblos indígenas y la revolución guatemalteca." *ALAI Servicio Especial.* Montréal, November 5.

EGP/FAR/ORPA/PGT. 1982. *Proclama unitaria al pueblo de Guatemala.* Guatemala, February.

Fernández, O. 1981. *Cuba: Reivindicaciones nacionales y revolución social.* Presented at the Fourteenth Latin American Conference on Sociology, San Juan, Puerto Rico, October.

Ferrer, A. 1981. "El monetarismo en Argentina y Chile." *Comercio Exterior* 32, no. 1 (January): 3–13; no. 2 (February): 176–92.

Fitzgerald, E.V.K. 1982a. *Acumulación planificada y distribución del ingreso en pequeñas economías socialistas periféricas.* Managua: INIES, October.

―――. 1982b. "The Economics of Revolution." In *The Nicaraguan Revolution,* edited by T. Walker, pp. 203–21. New York: Praeger.

Flora, J., J. McFadden, and R. Warner. 1983. "The growth of class struggle: The impact of the Nicaraguan Literacy Crusade on the political consciousness of young literacy workers." *Latin American Perspectives* 36 (Winter): 45–61.

Foladori, G. 1982. "Algunos resultados de las transformaciones agrarias de 1981." *Revista Centroamericana de Economía* 9 (September–December): 20–32.

Fonseca, C. 1981. *Bajo la bandera del sandinismo. Textos políticos.* Managua: Editorial Nueva Nicaragua.

FSLN (Frente Sandinista de Liberacia'on Nacional). 1980a. "Comunicado oficial de la Dirección Nacional del FSLN sobre el proceso electoral." *Barricada,* August 24.

―――. 1980b. "Comunicado oficial de la Dirección Nacional del FSLN sobre la religión." *Barricada.* October 7.

Gilbert, D. 1983. *The Bourgeoisie and the Nicaraguan Revolution.* Presented at LASA's XI International Congress, Mexico, September.

Gilly, A. 1980. *La nueva Nicaragua.* Mexico: Editorial Nueva Imagen.

Girardi, G. 1983. "Marxismo y Cristianismo en Nicaragua hoy." *Nuevo Amanecer Cultural,* 44 (March 1).

Godio, J. 1980. *Historia del movimiento obrero latinoamericano,* vol. 1. Mexico: Ed. Nueva Imagen.

―――. 1983. *Sindicalismo y política en América Latina.* Caracas: ILDIS.

Gorman, S. M. 1981. "Power and consolidation in the Nicaraguan Revolution." *Journal of Latin American Studies* 13, no. 1: 133–49.

Gramsci, A. 1977a. *Il materialismo storico e la filosofia di Benedetto Croce.* Roma: Editori Riuniti.

―――. 1977b. *Gli intelettuali e l'organizzazione della cultura.* Roma: Editori Riuniti.

Guevara, O. and C. Pérez Bermúdez. 1981. *El movimiento obrero nicaragüense.* Managua: Ediciones Dávila Bolaños.

Guido, A. J. 1981. "Sobre el movimiento guerrillero y campesino." In

CIERA, *Testimonios sobre la reforma agraria*, pp. 51–58. Managua: CIERA.

Gutiérrez Mayorga, G. 1978. "El reformismo artesanal en el movimiento obrero nicaragüense." *Revista del Pensamiento Centroamericano* 159 (April–June):2–21.

Halliday, F. and M. Molyneux. 1981. *The Ethiopian Revolution*. London: Verso.

Handal, S. J. 1982. "El poder, el carácter y la vía de la revolución y la unidad de la izquierda." *Fundamentos y perspectivas* 4:27–43.

Herdocia, O. 1982. "Análisis jurídico de la estructura actual del gobierno revolucionario." *Revista del Pensamiento Centroamericano* 176 (July–September):28–31.

Hobsbawm, E. 1962. *The Age of Revolution*. London: Weidenfeld & Nicolson.

Ho Chi Minh. 1973. *Escritos políticos*. Havana: Editorial de Ciencias Sociales.

———. 1979. *El patriotismo y el internacionalismo proletario*. Hanoi: Ediciones en Lenguas Extranjeras.

Houtart, F. and G. LeMercinier. 1981. *Sociologie d'une Commune Vietnamienne*. Louvain-la-Neuve: C.R.S.R., Université Catholique de Louvain.

Hou Yuon. 1964. "Solving Problems: A Socialist Programme to Safeguard the Nation." In *Peasants and Politics in Kampuchea, 1942–1981/1/*, edited by B. Kiernan and C. Boua, pp. 134–67. London: Zed Press.

IEPALA. 1983. *El Papa en Nicaragua. Análisis de su visita*. Madrid: IEPALA Editorial.

IES (Instituto de Estudio del Sandinismo). 1981. *El principio del fin . . . 1956. 23 años de lucha . . . El triunfo . . . 1979*. Managua: Editorial Nueva Nicaragua.

———. 1982a. *Pensamiento antiimperialista en Nicaragua*. Managua: Editorial Nueva Nicaragua.

———. 1982b. *Porque viven siempre entre nosotros*. Managua: Editorial Nueva Nicaragua.

———. 1982c. *La insurreción popular sandinista en Masaya*. Managua: Editorial Nueva Nicaragua.

INCAE (Instituto Centroamericano de Administración de Empresas). 1973. *Consecuencias económicas del terremoto de Managua*. Managua, doc. NI/PL/001.

———. 1975. *Primera encuesta sobre el empleo en las zonas urbanas de Nicaragua*. Managua, doc. NI/PL 029, June.

———. 1976. *Segunda encuesta sobre el empleo en las zonas urbanas de Nicaragua*. Managua, mimeo.

INDE (Instituto Nicaragüense de Desarrollo). 1979. *El sector privado en la insurreción*. Managua: INDE.

————. 1980. *Informe anual 1980 de INDE y sus programas FUNDE y EDUCREDITO*. Managua: INDE.

————. 1981. *Análisis económico 1981. Managua: INDE.*

————. 1982. *Informe anual 1981 de INDE y sus programas FUNDE y EDUCREDITO*. Managua: INDE.

INEC (Instituto Nicaragüense de Estadisticas y Censos). 1979. *Encuesta anual de la Industria Manufacturera 1979*. Managua: INEC.

————. 1980. *Encuesta Nacional de Hogares Urbanos 1980*. Managua: INEC.

————. 1981a. *Anuario Estadistico de Nicaragua*. Managua: INEC.

————. 1981b. *Encuesta anual de la Industria Manufacturera 1981*. Managua: INEC.

————. 1981c. *Encuesta Nacional de Hogares Urbanos 1981*. Managua: INEC.

————. 1982. *Encuesta Nacional de Hogares Urbanos 1982*. Managua: INEC.

————. 1983. *Indicadores socioeconómicos de Nicaragua, 1983*. Managua: INEC.

Jaguaribe, H. 1964. *Desarrollo económico y desarrollo político*. Buenos Aires: EUDEBA.

Jarquin, E. 1977. *Apreciaciones sobre la situación económica de Nicaragua*. Managua, s/e.

————. 1980. "Situación económica 1979." *Encuentro* 17:82–89.

JGRN (Junta de Gobierno de Reconstrucción Nacional). 1982. *Principios y políticas del Gobierno de Nicaragua*. Managua: Dirección de Divulgación y Prensa de la JGRN.

————. 1983. *Informe de la JGRN presentado al Consejo de Estado el 4 de mayo*. Managua: Dirección de Divulgación y Prensa de la JGRN

Karmowitz, D. and J. R. Thome. 1982. "Nicaragua's Agrarian Reform: The First Year, 1979–80." In *Nicaragua in Revolution*, edited by T. Walker, pp. 223–40. New York: Praeger.

Laclau, E. 1977. *Politics and Ideology in Marxist Theory*. London: New Left Books.

Lenin, N. 1905. *Socialismo pequeño burgués y socialismo proletario*. Moscow: Progress, 1978.

————. 1916a. "El derecho de las naciones a la autodeterminación." In *La lucha de los pueblos coloniales y países dependientes contra el imperialismo*. Moscow: Progreso, 1978.

————. 1916b. *El imperialismo, fase superior del capitalismo*. Moscow: Progreso, 1976.

————. 1974a. *Contenido económico del populismo*. Madrid: Siglo XXI.

————. 1974b. *Sobre el problema de los mercados*. Madrid: Siglo XXI.

————. 1981. *La alianza de la clase abrera y el compesinado.* Moscow: Progress.

Levy, P. 1976. *Notas geográficas y económicas sobre la República de Nicaragua,* 2d ed. Editorial San José.

López, J. A. 1983. "Relaciones comerciales Argentina-URSS: balance y perspectivas." *América latina* 8 (August): 55–64.

López, J. et al. 1979. *La caída del somocismo y la lucha sandinista en Nicaragua.* San José: EDUCA.

Lomnitz, L. A. de. 1975. *Cómo sobreviven los marginados.* Mexico: Siglo XXI.

Lozano, L. 1980. *Génesis y desarrollo de la situación revolucionaria en Nicaragua: enero 1978–mayo 1979.* Presented at the Fourth Central American Congress on Sociology, Managua, July.

Luxemburg, R. 1978. *Obras escogidas,* vol. 1. Mexico: Ediciones ERA.

Maier, L. 1980. *Nicaragua. La mujer en la revolución.* Mexico: Ediciones de Cultura Popular.

Makidi-Ku-Ntima. 1983. "Class Struggle and the Making of the Revolution in Angola." *Contemporary Marxism* 6:119–41.

Mariategui, J. C. 1929. "Punto de vista antiimperialista." *Obras.* Havana: Casa de las Américas, no date.

Martínez, R. J. 1980. "Los maravillosos aportes de la alfabetización." *El Nuevo Diario,* October 13.

Martínez Heredia, F. 1980. *Introducción a la sociedad nicaragüense contemporánea.* Havana: Centro de Estudios sobre América.

Marx, K. 1847. *The Poverty of Philosophy.* New York: International Publishers, 1963.

————. 1852. *The Eighteenth Brumaire of Louis Bonaparte.* In David Fernbach, ed., *Karl Marx: Surveys from Exile.* New York: Vintage, 1974.

————. 1859. *Prefacio a la contribución a la critica de la economía política.* Mexico: Editorial Quinto Sol, 1978.

————. 1971. *El Capital,* vol. 1. La Habana: Editorial de Ciencias Sociales.

Marx, K. and F. Engels. 1980. *El porvenir de la comuna rural rusa.* Mexico: Cuadernos de Pasado y Presente.

Matute Ruiz, E., no date. *Nicaragua: Impacto social de la industrialización.* San José: CSUCA, Serie Análisis económico no. 5, Programa Centroamericano de Ciencias Sociales.

Mayer, A. J. 1975. "The Lower Middle Class as Historical Problem." *Journal of Modern History* 47, no. 3 (September):409–36.

Mayorga, S. 1981. "La experiencia agraria de la Revolución Nicaragüense." In *Reforma agraria y revolución popular en América latina,* pp. 89–117. Managua: CIERA.

MED (Ministerio de Educación). 1981. *Consulta Nacional para obtener criterios que ayuden a definir los fines y objetivos de la educación nicaragüense. Informe preliminar.* Managua: MED.

———. 1983a. *La educación en cuatro años de revolución.* Managua: MED.

———. 1983b. *Fines, objetivos y principios de la nueva educación.* Managua: MED.

MED/DEI. 1981. *Nicaragua triunfa en la alfabetización.* San José: DEI.

Medal, J. L. 1982. "Política económica y revolutión." Managua, Third National Congress on the Social Sciences, October 29–31, mimeo.

MICOIN (Ministerio de Comercio Interior). 1983. *Estudio de sistemas de comercialización de productos básicos.* Managua, March.

MIDINRA (Ministerio de Desarrollo Agropecuario y Reforma Agraria). 1982a. *Marco jurídico de la reforma agraria nicaragüense.* Managua: CIERA.

———. 1982b. *3 años de reforma agraria.* Managua: MIDINRA.

———. 1982c. *Estrategia de desarrollo cooperativo.* Managua: December.

———. 1983. *Informe de Nicaragua a la FAO.* Managua: CIERA.

Miliband, R. 1970. *El Estado de la sociedad capitalista.* Mexico: Siglo XXI.

Miller, V. 1982 "The Nicaraguan Literacy Crusade. In *Nicaragua in Revolution,* edited by T. Walker. New York: Praeger.

Ministerio de Bienestar Social. 1981. *Colectivos estatales de producción.* Managua, March, mimeo.

Ministerio de Industria. 1980. *La pequeña industria en Nicaragua.* Managua: Ministerio de Justicia.

MINSA (Ministerio de Salud). 1982. *El Servicio Nacional Único de Salud: Tres años de revolución, 1979–1982.* Managua:MINSA.

MIPLAN (Minsterio de Planificación). 1980. *Programa de reactivación y emergiencia en beneficio del pueblo.* Managua: MIPLAN.

———. 1981. *Programa económico de austeridad y eficiencia.* Managua: MIPLAN.

Miro, C. and D. Rodriguez. 1982. "Capitalismo y población en el agro latinoamericano. Tendencias y problemas recientes." *Revista de la CEPAL* (April):53–74.

MLD (Movimiento de Liberación Dominicana). 1959. *Programa mínimo de la revolución dominicana.* s/e, June.

Molina, U. 1981. "El sentido de una experiencia." *Nicaráuac 5* (April-June): 17–37.

Moore, B. 1966. *Social Origins of Dictatorship and Democracy.* Boston, MA: Beacon Press.

———. 1978. *Injustice. The Social Bases of Obedience and Revolt.* White Plains, NY: M.E. Sharpe.

Morales, M. 1981. "Sobre la reforma agraria en Nueva Segovia, Madriz, Estelí." In CIERA: *Testimonios sobre la reforma agraria,* pp. 22–39. Managua: CIERA.

Navas Mendoza et al. 1983. *Algunos elementos para un análisis de los perídos críticos del algodón en Nicaragua.* Presented at the Fifteenth

Latin American Congress on Sociology. Managua, October.

Nolff, M. 1982. "La vía crusis de la Revolución Sandinista." *Nueva Sociedad* 63 (November-December):33–46.

Nun, J. 1967. "The Middle-Class Military Coup." In *The Politics of Conformity in Latin America,* edited by C. Véliz. London: Oxford University Press.

Núñez, C. 1980a. "La Revolución y la organización de los trabajadores." In *La Revolución a través de nuestra Dirección Nacional.* Managua: Secretaría del FSLN.

———. 1980b. *Un pueblo en armas.* Managua: Secretaría Nacional de Propaganda y Educación Política del FSLN.

———. 1980c. *El papel de las organizaciones de masas en el proceso revolucionario.* Managua: Secretaría Nacional de Propaganda y Educación Política del FSLN.

———. 1983. "Democracia: El camino que nos señala el pueblo." In *El reto democrático en Centroamérica,* edited by R. Sol, pp. 157–88. San José: DEI.

Núñez, O. 1980a. *El Somocismo: Desarrollo y contradicciones del modelo capitalista agroexportador en Nicaragua (1950–1975).* Havana: Centro de Estudios sobre América.

———. 1980b. "La tercera fuerza social en los movimientos de liberación nacional. *Estudios Sociales Centroamericanos* 27 (September-December): 141–57.

———. 1982a. "La ideología como fuerza material y la juventud como fuerza ideológica." In *Estado y clases sociales en Nicaragua,* 125–47. Managua: ANICS/CIERA.

———. 1982b. *La revolución social y la transicion en América Central. El caso de Nicaragua.* Presented at the Fifth Central American Congress on Sociology, San José, November.

O'Connor, J. 1973. *The Fiscal Crisis of State.* New York: St. Martin's Press.

OEDEC (Oficina Ejecutora de Estadísticas y Censos). 1975. *Encuesta de situación del empleo urbano 1975.* Managua: OEDEC.

———. 1976. *Encuesta de situacion del empleo urbano 1976.* Managua: OEDEC.

Oliveira, F. 1972. "A economía brasileira: Crítica á razao dualista." *Estudos Cebrap* 2 (October): 3–82.

ORPA. 1982. "Acerca del racismo." *ALAI, Servicio especial* (Montréal), November 5, pp. 1–7.

Ortega, H. 1980. "La insurrección nacional victoriosa." *Nicaráuac* 1 (May-June): 26–57.

———. 1981. "Un sólo ejército." In *Habla la Dirección de la Vanguardia.* Managua: Departamento de Prensa, Educación y Propaganda del FSLN.

Ortega, M. 1983. *La participación obrera en la gestión de las empresas agropecuarias del APP.* Presented at the Fifteenth Latin American Congress on Sociology, Managua, October.

Ortega Hegg, M. 1982. "El conflicto etnia-nación en Nicaragua." In *Estado y clases sociales en Nicaragua,* pp. 167–91. Managua: ANICS/CIERA.

Padover, S. 1973. *Karl Marx on the First International.* New York: McGraw-Hill.

Pasos, M. 1977. *Grado de desarrollo de conciencia de clase sindical de un grupo de obreros de Managua.* Managua: Universidad Centroamericana, Escuela de Sociología, mimeo.

PCS (Partido Comunista de El Salvador). 1980. *Fundamentos y tesis de la línea general del PCS.* San Salvador, June.

Percy, J. 1982. "Introduction." In Bishop, *Forward Ever!* New York: Pathfinder.

Pérez-Stable, M. 1982. "The Working Class in the Nicaraguan Revolution." In *Nicaragua in Revolution,* edited by T. Walker. New York: Praeger.

Petras, J. 1981. "Nicaragua: The Transition to a New Society." *Latin American Perspectives* 29 (Spring): 74–94.

PGT (Partido Guatemalteco del Trabajo). 1982. "La cuestión indígena." *ALAI, Servicio especial* (Montréal), November 5, pp. 14–16.

Piñeiro Losada, M. 1982. "La crisis actual del imperialismo y los procesos revolucionarios en América latina." *Cuba Socialista* 4 (September-November): 15–63.

Poulantzas, N. 1977. "El problema del Estado capitalista." In *Ideología y ciencias sociales,* edited by R. Blackburn. Barcelona: Grijalbo.

PREALC/OIT. 1981. *Balance de la fuerza de trabajo agropecuaria, 1981–82.* Managua.

Ramírez, S. 1980. Conferencia de clausura del IV Congreso Centroamericano de Sociología "Blas Real Espinales." *Barricada* July 8.

———. 1981. *El pensamiento vivo de Sandino.* Managua: Editorial Nueva Nicaragua.

———. 1982. "Los sobrevivientes del naufragio." In *Estado y clases sociales en Nicaragua,* pp. 63–87. Managua: ANICS/CIERA.

———. 1983a. "Nicaragua, la primera frontera." *Barricada,* July 3.

———. 1983b. "Una revolución propia y un modelo soberano." *Barricada,* July 18.

Randall, M. 1980. *Todas estamos despiertas. Testimonios de la mujer nicaragüense de hoy.* Mexico: Siglo XXI.

Rivas, C. 1983. *El movimiento obrero y las luchas populares en Nicaragua (1956–1979).* Presented at the Fifteenth Latin American Congress on Sociology, Managua, October.

Roberts, B. 1980. *Ciudades de campesinos.* Mexico: Siglo XXI.

Rodríguez, C. R. 1979. *Cuba en el tránsito al socialismo, 1959–1963.* Havana: Editora Política.

Rodríguez García, J. L. 1979. "Política económica de la Revolución Cubana (1959–1960)." *Economía y Desarrollo* 54 (July-October).

Rosenthal, G. 1982. "Pricipales rasgos de la evolución de las economías centroamericanas desde la postguerra." In *Centroamerica: Crisis y politica internacional,* pp. 19–38. Mexico: Siglo XXI.

Ruben, R. 1983. *Desarrollo popular dentro del marco de una economía mixta. El caso de la comercialización de alimentos básicos en Nicaragua.* Presented at the Fifteenth Latin American Congress on Sociology, Managua, October.

Ruiz, H. 1980a. "La montaña era como un inmenso crisol donde se forjaban los majores cuadros." *Nicaráuac* 1 (May–June): 8–24.

———. 1980b. *El papel poliico del APP en la nueva economía sandinista.* Managua: Secretaría Nacional de Propaganda y Educación Política del FSLN.

Samandu, L. and R. Jansen. 1982. "Nicaragua: dictadura somocista, movimiento popular e Iglesia, 1968–1979." *Estudios Sociales Centroamericanos* 33 (September–December): 189–219.

Sandino, A. 1979. *Pensamientos.* Managua: Ministerio de Educación.

Seligson, M. A. 1980. *El campesino y el capitalismo agrario de Costa Rica.* San José: Editorial Costa Rica.

Selser, G. 1966. *Sandino, general de hombres libres,* 4th ed, Buenos Aires: Iguazú.

Serra, L. 1982. *Las instituciones religiosas y la ideolgía burguesa en la Revolución Sandinista.* Presented at the Third National Congress on the Social Sciences, Managua, October.

Serra, L. et al. 1981. *La lucha ideológica en el campo religioso y su significado político.* Presented at the Second National Congress on the Social Sciences, Managua, August.

Silva, O. 1982. "Imagen del hombre, imagen de Dios." *Barricada,* July 27.

Sizonenko, A. 1981. "URSS-países latinoamericanos: resultados y perspectivas de las relaciones interestatales." *América latina* 1–2:5–20.

Smith, A. 1776. *An Inquiry into the Nature and Causes of the Wealth of Nations.* Chicago: University of Chicago Press, 1976.

Smutko, G. 1980. *Los Héroes y Mártires de Bluefields.* Bluefields: CEBIC.

Spalding, H. 1977 *Organized Labor in Latin America.* New York: New York University Press.

Stone, S. 1975. *La dinastía de los conquistadores.* San José: EDUCA.

Strachan, H. W. 1976. *Family and other Business Groups in Economic Development. The Case of Nicaragua.* New York: Praeger.

Talavera, J. L. 1978. *El desarrollo económico y el nuevo carácter del Estado, Nicaragua 1950–1967.* Presented at the Third Central American Congress on Sociology, Tegucigalpa, April.

———. 1979. "Nicaragua: Crisis de la dictadura militar (1967–1978)." *Estudios Sociales Centroamericanos* 23 (May–August): 213–44.

Tefel, R. A. 1978. *El infierno de los pobres*. Managua: El Pez y la Serpiente.

Therborn, G. 1977. "The Rule of Capital and the Rise of Democracy." *New Left Review* 103 (May–June): 3–41.

———. 1979. "The Travail of Latin American Democracy." *New Left Review* 113–114 (January–April): 71–109.

Thomas, C. 1974. *Dependence and Transformation. The Economics of the Transition to Socialism*. New York: Monthly Review Press.

Thompson, E. P. 1963. *The Making of the English Working Class*. New York: Vintage Books.

———. 1979. *Tradición, revuelta y conciencia de clase*. Barcelona: Editorial Crítica.

Torres Rivas, E. 1980. "El Estado contra la sociedad: Las raíces de la revolución nicaragüense." *Estudios Sociales Centroamericanos* 27 (September–December): 79–95.

———. 1982. "Notas para comprender la crisis política centroamericana." In *Centroamérica: Crisis y Política internacional*, pp. 39–69. Mexico: Siglo XXI.

UNAG Unión Nacional de Agricultores y Ganaderos. 1982. *Asamblea Nacional Constitutiva. Pequenos y Medianos Productores Agropecuarios de Nicaragua. Plan de Lucha*. Managua, April 25–26, mimeo.

UNAG/ATC/CIERA. 1982. *Producción y organizacion en el agro nicaragüense*. Managua: CIERA.

UPAFEC (Unión de Padres de Familia por la Educación Cristiana). 1981. "Respuesta a la Consulta Nacional de Educación." *Revista del Pensamiento Centroamericano* 172–173 (July–December): 124–34.

Valdes Paz, J. 1980. "Notas sobre la socialización de la propiedad en Cuba." *Estudios Sociales Centroamericanos* 27 (September–December): 251–75.

Vanden, H. 1982 "Marxism and the Peasants in Latin America: Marginalization or Mobilization?" *Latin American Perspectives* 35 (Fall): 74–98.

Van Eeuwen, D. 1982. "Nicaragua: L'an II de la revolution. Hégemonie sandiniste et montée des périls." *Problems d'Amerique Latine* 63: 9–66.

Vargas, O. R. 1978. "La crisis del somocismo y el movimiento obrero nicaragüense." *Coyoacán* 2 (January–March): 61–78.

———. 1979. "Notas sobre el nuevo eje de acumulación en Centroamérica. El caso de Nicaragua." *Estudios Sociales Centroamericanos* 22 (January–April): 251–77.

———. 1981. *Economía y revolución*. Presented at the Second National Congress on the Social Sciences, Managua, August.

Vega Carballo, J. L. 1979. *Las bases sociales de la democracia en Costa Rica*. Instituto de Investigaciones Sociales de la Universidad de Costa Rica, mimeo.

Velázquez, J. L. 1977. "La incidencia de la formación de la economía agroexportadora en el intento de formación del Estado nacional en Nicaragua, 1860–1930." *Revista del Pensamiento Centroamericano* 157 (October–December): 11–31.

Vilas, C. M. 1973. "Pouvoir politique et domination sociale en République Dominicaine." *Nouvelle Optique* 9: 33–88.

———. 1974. *La dominación imperialista en Argentina.* Buenos Aires: EUDEBA.

———. 1979a. "Notas sobre la formación del Estado en el Caribe: La República Dominicana." *Estudios Sociales Centroamericanos* 24 (September–December): 117–77.

———. 1979b. "El populismo como estrategia de acumulación." *Revista Centroamericana de Economía* 1 (September–December): 54–87.

———. 1980a. "Hipótesis sobre liberación nacional y liberación social en la etapa actual del imperialismo." *Estudios Sociales Centroamericanos* 27 (September-December): 99–127.

———. 1980b. "Clases sociales, Estado y acumulación periférica en la República Dominicana." *Caribe Contemporaneo* 1 (March): 66–69.

———. 1981. "Campesinos y plantaciones en la agricultura del Caribe." *Estudios Sociales Centroamericanos* 29 (May–August): 79–90.

———. 1982a. "Las contradicciones de la transición. Clases, nación y Estado en Nicaragua." In *Estado y clases sociales en Nicaragua,* pp. 95–114. Managua: ANICS/CIERA.

———. 1982b. *Nicaragua: Una transición diferente.* Presented at the Third National Congress on the Social Sciences, Managua, October.

———. 1982c. "The Legacy of Dictatorship: Nicaragua." *Caribbean Review* 9: 3.

———. 1983. *Democracia popular y participación obrera en la Revolución Sandinista.* Presented at LASA's XI International Congress, Mexico, September.

Villagra, W. 1980. "Las posiciones políticas de las corrientes sindicales nicaragüenses." *Anuario de Estudios Centroamericanos* 6: 83–94.

von Werdhoff, C. and H. P. Neuhoff. 1982. "The Combination of Different Production Relations on the Basis of Non-Proletarianization: Agrarian Production in Yaracuy, Venezuela." *Latin American Perspectives* 34 (Summer): 79–100.

Weber, H. 1981. *Nicaragua: The Sandinista Revolution.* London: Verso.

Weber, M. 1947. *The Theory of Social and Economic Organization.* New York: The Free Press.

Weeks, J. 1981. *Análisis preliminar del desarrollo manufacturero, 1960–1979.* Managua: FINAPRI.

Wheelock, J. 1976. *Imperialismo y dictadura.* Mexico: Siglo XXI.

———. 1979. *Frente Sandinista. Diciembre victorioso.* Managua: Secretaría Nacional de Propaganda y Educación Política del FSLN.

———. 1981. "Logros y perpsectivas de la economía sandinista." In *La*

Dirección Nacional en el Primer Encuentro Internacional de Solidaridad con Nicaragua, pp. 53–87. Managua: Departamento de Prensa y Educación Política del FSLN.

―――. 1983. *El gran desafío.* Managua: Editorial Nueva Nicaragua.

Williamson, C. 1960. *American Suffrage from Property to Democracy, 1760–1860.* Princeton, NJ: Princeton University Press.

Witmer, H. E. 1943. *The Property Qualifications of Members of Parliament.* New York: Columbia University Press.

Wolf, E. 1969. *Peasant Wars of the Twentieth Century.* New York: Harper & Row.

World Bank. 1981. *Nicaragua: The Challenge of Reconstruction.* Washington, D.C.: The World Bank.

Zavala Cuadra, X. 1982. "El sentido cristiano de la educación." *Revista del Pensamiento Centroamericano* 175 (April–June): 86–91.

Index

Carlos M. Vilas has taught at universities in Argentina, the Dominican Republic, Honduras, and Nicaragua. From 1980 to 1984 he worked at the Ministry of Planning in Nicaragua and now works at CIDCA, a research center concerned with the indigenous populations of Nicaragua's Atlantic coast.